AF473827

CHRISTINA TUNG WAI

BREATH OF THE UNIVERSE

–

A FEATHER'S TALE

100 FEATURED ARTISTIC CREATIONS

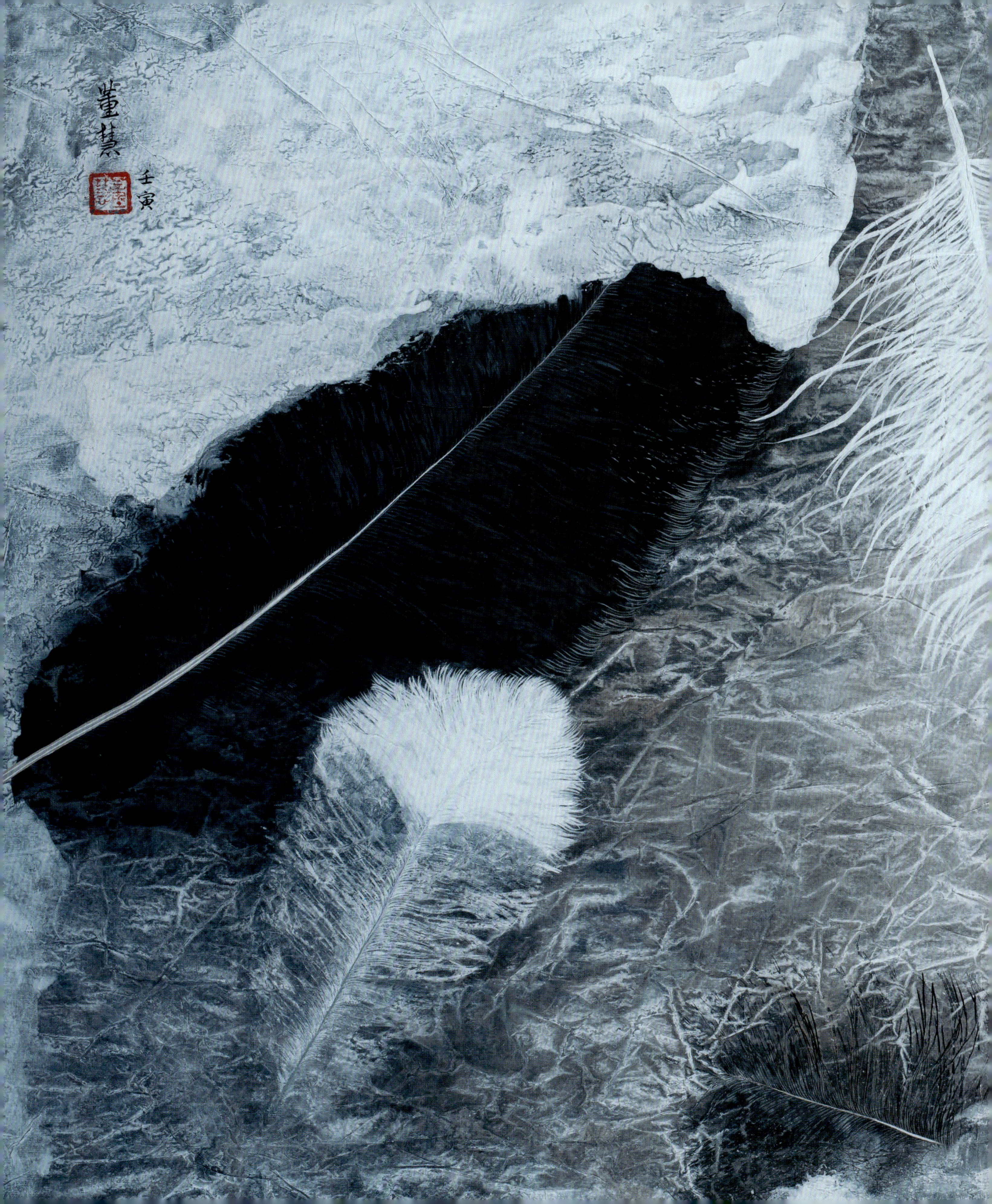
董慧
壬寅

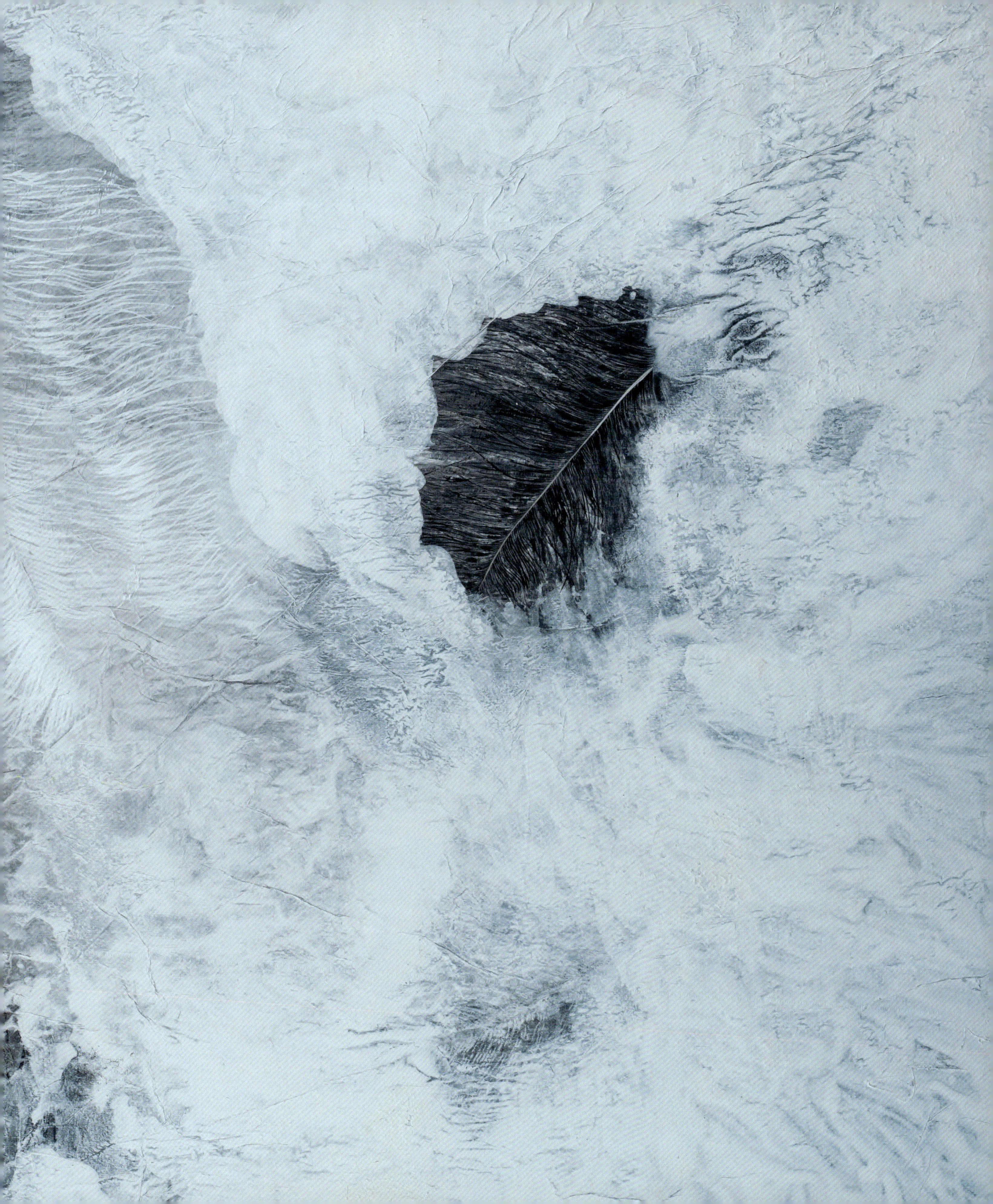

Frozen Echoes (Cover artwork)
2022
Mixed Media on Paper
73 cm x 102 cm

CHRISTINA TUNG WAI
BREATH OF THE UNIVERSE

A FEATHER'S TALE
100 FEATURED ARTISTIC CREATIONS

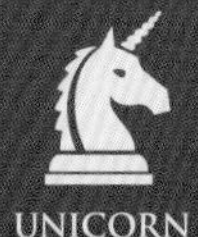

UNICORN

Published in 2025 by Unicorn,
an imprint of Unicorn Publishing Group
Charleston Studio
Meadow Business Centre
Lewes BN8 5RW
www.unicornpublishing.org

ISBN 978-1-916846-46-3

10 9 8 7 6 5 4 3 2 1

Designed by XYCO.UK
Printed in Turkiye by FineTone Ltd

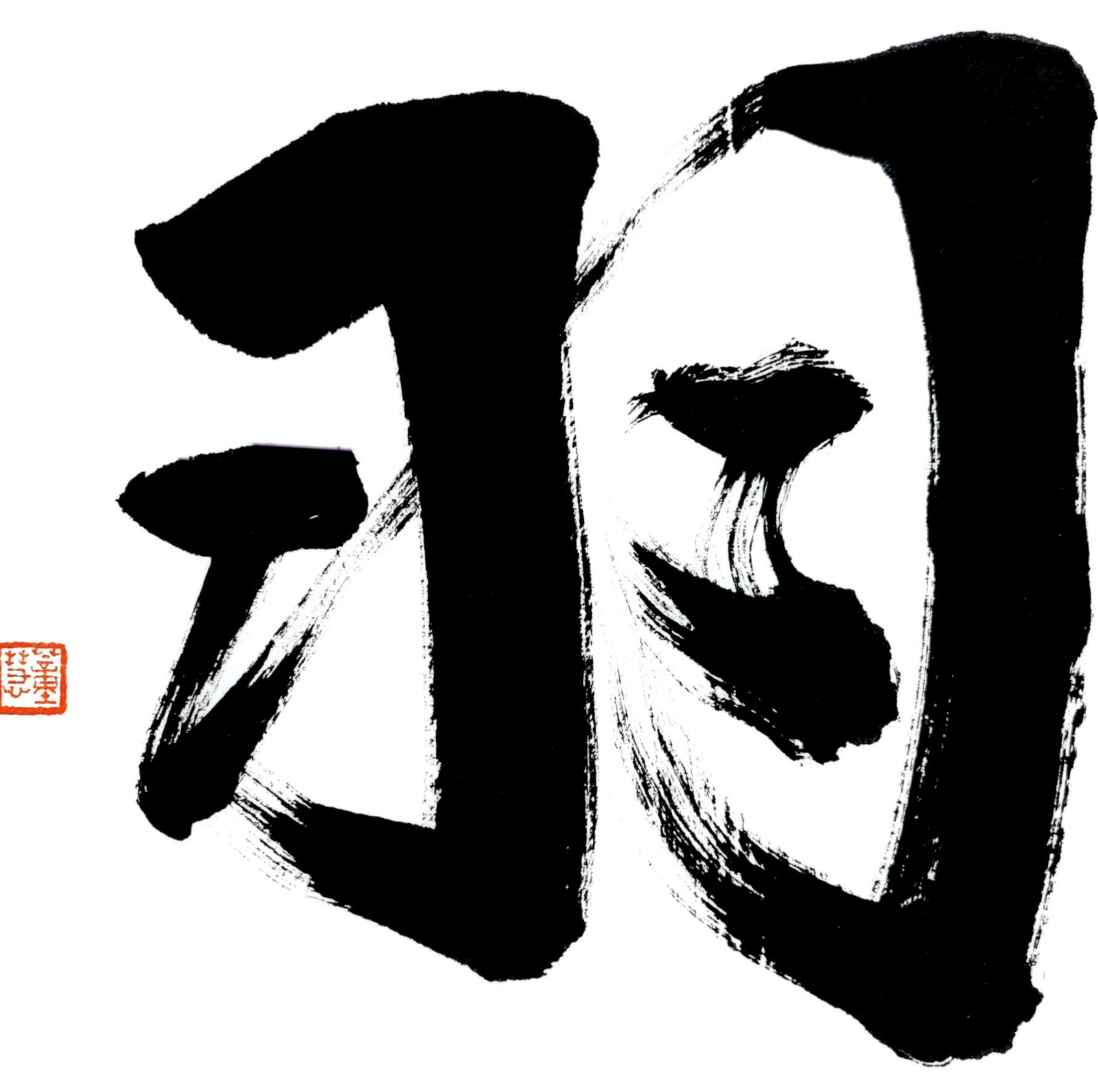

Feather
2024
Ink and Colour on Rice Paper
35 cm x 44 cm

A calligraphy of the word 'Feather'
by Christina Tung Wai

Contents

Foreword

Christina Tung's Feather Art: Breath of the Universe – A Feather's Tale

When I agreed to write the foreword for this art book, I pondered over what to write about. Should I write about Christina's artistic trajectory or her feather art? I decided on the latter, which should reflect my opinion towards the importance of this book, and my sincerity and admiration for Christina. In this sense, this could represent my respect for the readers and my eager anticipation.

So, what am I anticipating? I anticipate for us to find resonance and surprises in the series of feather art, to find what we already knew, to explore what is unknown and to discover critical moments and turning points. It is said that art originates from daily life and surpasses it. The part that surpasses life is how beauty and legend of art came to be. However, if there are no roots nor vehicles to speak of in art, dreams will not come true and those who dream big are only wasting their time. Then there would be no amazing success and fruitful results from their dreams to show. Likewise, this commemorative art book, into which Christina has poured her blood, sweat and tears for ten years, would not exist at all.

Why paint feathers? This question is much the same as asking, 'Why paint flowers?' or 'Why paint people?' It is not particularly easier to paint feathers compared to others. Contrary to what one might think, it is more challenging to present the layers and texture in feathers. Omens have always borne great cultural significance among the Chinese community. Feathers to life is of paramount importance just as yin to yang and sun to moon. A line in one of the poems I wrote reads 'Rooted in life yet detached from life, this is a kind of weight named light'. An eagle without feathers would not be able to soar in the sky. It would not be able to reach the faraway places it wants to go. It would not be able to lead its freedom-loving companions to embark on journeys and return safely time and time again. Now let's imagine a duck without feathers – it would not be able to float in water and kick its webbed feet to swim across the lake. It would not be able to flutter its wings comfortably in the river, letting winds and seasons howl over its neck and back. And let's imagine a flock of sparrows without their feathers – would they not be harmed by pests and vermin? All of these have proven the importance of feathers to life, and having feathers as necessary conditions for survival. As such, the signification of feathers to life is so much greater than we could ever imagine. Feathers, more specifically in the form of wings, are often seen in Chinese idioms like '*dàzhǎn-hóngtú*' (meaning to carry out one's great plan), '*péngchéng-wànlǐ*' (meaning to have brilliant prospects and a bright future) and '*rúhǔ-tiānyì*' (meaning to make a strong individual even stronger). They imply our aspirations for the future and its possibilities. In this sense, feathers are principally redefined and reinterpreted from common sense to a wider context. It gives people philosophical thoughts about being relieved from a heavy burden. When a feather is set apart from the body of life that it bestows on birds, it gives people a sense of nostalgia and cherishment. Yet when the feather is drifting, we feel the existence of life in another form. These characters explain how feathers are realised to the fullest under the brush of the artist Christina Tung Wai. It is indeed surreal and out of this world!

As Christina chooses feathers, feathers choose Christina too, so to speak. The affinity is mutual, and each has an energy field that interacts with the other. This connection creates a vision of faith between their choices. As a successful woman in the international financial city, Christina has experienced the glamorous phase of life. At the age of forty-eight, she has chosen feathers as a pivotal means of expression in her artistic journey. To this day, I believe that she is wise, that she is fortunate. Her perseverance and dedication on this lonely path of accumulation and creation have led her to where she is today. This journey is a long one, from process as basic as the study of the anatomy of a feather, to the selection of materials, colour-mixing, brushworks, and drying technique. Each stroke is more astounding than the last, painted lighter and more carefully than what has come before. Whether from half a foot to ten feet, or from smaller frames to larger frames, you can picture a proud and ambitious woman indulged in her world of feathers day and night. Perhaps time did take the sharp edge off, keeping her grounded and bringing her closer to the feathers under her brush – splendorous yet gentle, candid yet delicate. I see these precious qualities emerging from and shimmering on her. Ten years have fleeted by, flowing through the top of her head, through the tip of her brushes and every nerve fibre without a sound, without a trace. During this period of time, she has presented to us astonishing paintings one after another. Subsequently, I have written poems for many of her paintings and given some of her new works poetic names, such as 'Everlasting Love', 'Acquaintances', 'Close to You' and 'Playing Around'. All of these stem from Christina's many talents, her demeanour and the way she carries herself, which I am so inspired and moved by. As I said, poems are not simply written words; they either leap out or they cascade out with feelings. Words of pretence don't deserve to be associated with the soul of paintings. If it weren't for God opening up the door to my inspiration, I could not have written any vivid words for Christina. The same goes for how she is able to make the fine shaft and the vane of the feather come alive on any kind of medium. In every exhibition of hers, each and every piece of feather that she paints is like a replica of the Creator's creation. It seems that even the slightest hint of flaw or imperfection would desecrate the divine will. It is magnificent and noble, highlighting the lifelike intricacy of each stroke calmly and honourably. How many hours, minutes and seconds of hard work, perseverance and dedication must it take to be able to perfectly capture the vigour of an inanimate object or figure? It must take an impeccable mix of craftsmanship spirit and natural artistic talent to create breath-taking and earth-shattering works as she did.

Once there was this thought, why didn't Christina choose peonies? I imagine that if she did, I may not be able to squeeze out a single line of poetry that is decent enough, let alone the epic verse 'Breath of the Universe – A Feather's Tale'. In hindsight, I am honestly quite thankful to her for inspiring some of the best works and famous lines I have ever written. On the path of life, some encounters complement and complete one another, like rain and spring, flowers and greenery, literati fulfilling the elegance of the times and, last but not least, artists fulfilling the continuous iteration and improvement of people's aesthetic instincts.

Christina is a versatile artist and, as she herself says, is obsessed with feathers to the extent that everything looks like a feather to her. Although it is a joke, it encapsulates her focused attention on and deep affection for feathers. If feathers could understand Christina's confession, they must be saying the same in return – 'In my eyes, everything looks like Christina.' Mutual affection such as this is also evidenced in Li Bai's poetry, especially in the line that reads, 'Gazing on Mount Jingting, nor I, am Tired of him, nor he of me'.

Zhang Xuan, a Chinese painter in the Tang dynasty specialising in painting court ladies, is known for his use of rich colours as well as detailed and smooth brush strokes. More importantly, he dared to expand and break through the subject matter of classical female figures at that time. Rather than painting the commonly seen subjects such as imperial concubines and heroic and filial women, he painted court ladies in intriguing scenes such as on spring outings, tea making, butterfly chasing and playing hide-and-seek. It requires careful observation of daily life and the courage to make bold attempts so as to lead the cultural and aesthetic trends and zeitgeists of that time. Take his well-known work 'Lady Guoguo's Spring Outing' as an example. The flourishing social landscape of the Tang dynasty is depicted through Zhang's delicate outlines and vibrant colours of the composition. Another artist who made their way to establishing a distinctive artistic style that matured over time and still holds significant influence on future generations is Pan Yuliang. As a female artist in the Republican China, Pan had created colourful and vibrant artworks despite being in the times of feudal oppression and social turbulence. Looking through the history of art on female figures and by female artists, Christina's study and development of feather art is deemed to be one of a kind in the Hong Kong art scene. When it comes to the conception and innovation of 'New Woman' in the contemporary art scene, people would naturally think of Christina and her feather art. An artist must present herself before people by means of her intellect and mind-blowing mise-en-scène. I believe her popularity in the world will then grow in the blink of an eye and spread to those enthralled by beauty.

He Jialin
January 2024

He Jialin, also known by the pen name Dumuluofei, is a poet and writer. She is now a member of the China Writers Association, the president of the Hong Kong Women Writers Association and the chairperson of Hong Kong International Association of Creativity. She began writing literature in 1984 and has won numerous awards, including the sixteenth International Writers' Club's Contemporary Poetry Outstanding Contribution Gold Award, China's Top Ten Female Poets Award (New Era) and Global Top Ten Chinese Ecological Chinese Poets Award. Her works are selected as reading materials for many Hong Kong primary and middle schools, compiled into and published as a number of poetry collections. She serves as a film critic-columnist at Hong Kong Wen Wei Po, as well as the Editor in Chief of journals *Nǚ Ye Literary* and *Hong Kong Literary Circles*.

Preface

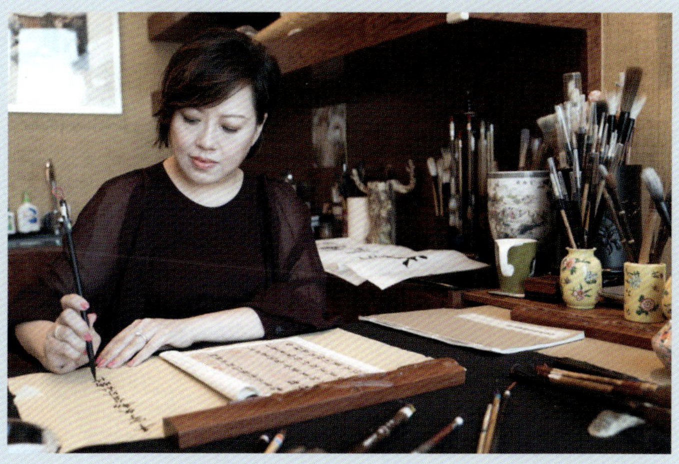

My Voyage to Arts

Christina Tung Wai

As the year 2011 drew to a close, I immersed myself into the mesmerising world of ink painting and have been captivated by it ever since. Making art has become an integral part of my second life, pulling at my heart and soul constantly.

I often find myself daydreaming, longing for a colossal feather to carry me up into the skies. I envision myself resting on the fluffy, billowy clouds, sprinkling handfuls of feathers gracefully as pixie dust like a fairy. The sense of freedom and purity is truly incomparable. Some of the feathers drift away swiftly with the trickling stream; others dance joyfully with the wind, and some find their way into the laughter of children... As I join in their merriment, my feathers warmed the world around me. Now, here I am basking in bliss and offering my fondest prayers and dreams in my weightless utopia.

Coincidentally, this special reverie echoes a remarkable poem written for me by the esteemed female poet He Jialin: 'Breath of the Universe – A Feather's Tale'.

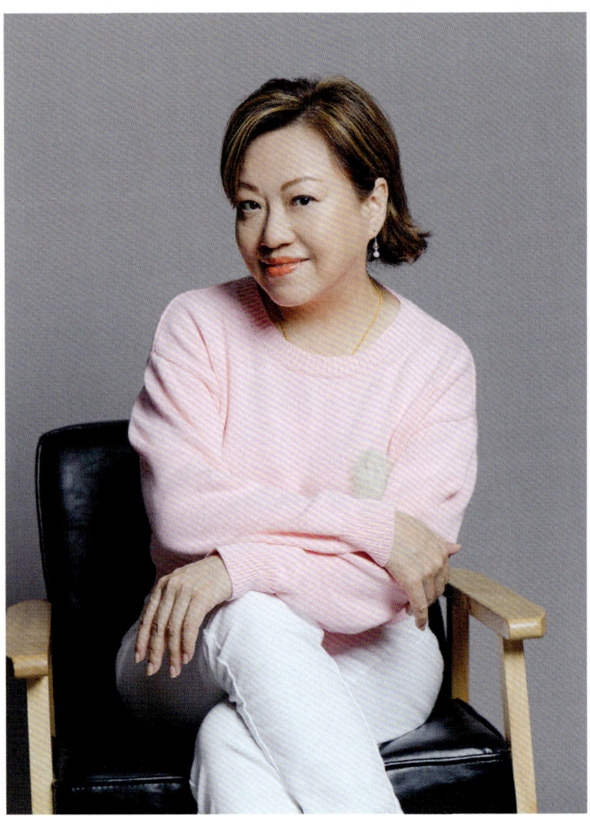

Christina Tung Wai

Artist Biography

Christina Tung Wai is a Hong Kong based contemporary ink feather artist and a curator. She is known for incorporating feathers and Taoist philosophy into her creations that represent the revelations in her life and her longing for freedom. To Christina, the beauty of the feather lies in its lifelessness but that which bestows upon the bird a blissful life surfing the boundless sky. Enlivened with different forms under Christina's brushstroke, the feather is the epitome of softness and strength combined, a life philosophy of resilience: it is at once carefree, at the whims of the winds, and at other times audacious, undaunted by limitations.

She started her endeavour in art by studying ceramic art under Ms Janet Tso in 2010, and later, Chinese ink art under contemporary ink colour Master Lam Tian Xing and Lingnan School ink painting Master Lam Wu Fui, and Chinese calligraphy under Chinese calligraphers Cheung Sing Kwo and Bai He. In 2019, she completed the Contemporary Ink Artists Summit Program at the Shanghai Institute of Visual Arts, and is now studying Chinese ink art under the tutelage of Master Liu Kuo-sung, Father of Modern Ink Painting.

In 2018, she made her debut and second solo exhibition at the Russian Academy of Fine Arts Museum and Molbert art gallery, respectively, in St Petersburg, Russia. She was then invited by the Consulate General of the Russian Federation in Hong Kong and Russian Club Hong Kong to hold her third solo exhibition '*Inspirations*' in late 2018, where her work titled 'Noble Aspiration' became a collection of the Russian Consulate. In 2020, Christina became one of the selected artists of 'Chinese Contemporary Art Document'. In 2021, her fourth solo exhibition, '*Birds of a Feather*', was held at Cheer Bell Gallery. In 2022, her fifth and sixth solo exhibitions, '*Odyssey of Feather*', were held at Hong Kong City Hall and Fine Art Asia, respectively. In 2023, her seventh solo exhibition, '*Odyssey of Feather*', was held at the AsiaWorld-Expo, Hong Kong. In 2024, her eighth solo exhibition was held at the 24th International Art Expo Beijing 2024 at Beijing Exhibition Center, China.

Throughout her career as an artist, Christina has taken part in various international and overseas joint expositions and exhibitions, such as '*Salon du Dessin et de la Peinture à l'Eau*' 2020 of Paris, Art Taipei, Affordable Art Fair Hong Kong and '*Thailand-Malaysia International Women Artists Art Exhibition*'. Collectors of her works include the Consulate General of the Russian Federation in Hong Kong.

The year 2020 was a significant one for Christina's art path. Her work 'Anti-coronavirus' was featured in '*Beijing International Art Biennale'Fighting with Love' Anti-coronavirus Series (Hong Kong)*'. Moreover, her work 'Propitious Portent' was selected as 1 of the 500 ink masterpieces worldwide in '*Ink Global*'. Other than that, she was the award winner of the Salvatore Ferragamo shoe design collaboration between Hong Kong Art Gallery Association (HKAGA) and prestige Italian brand Salvatore Ferragamo. The pair of Viva ballet flats, hand-painted by Christina, was then showcased at '*Phillips' 20th Century and Contemporary Art, Famous Paintings, Design, Jewels and Watches*' auctions, and was collected by Salvatore Ferragamo then.

In 2024, Christina Tung Wai receives the Fellowship of Creative Arts from the Asian Institute of Creative Education. She is now the Standing Committee Member of the Hong Kong Modern Ink Painting Society and the Committee Member of The 4-D Art Club of Hong Kong. She is also a member of The Hong Kong Artists Association, HongKong Guangzhou Arts Association, Contemporary Innovative Ink Painting Association, Shine Art Association and Woodland Art Association.

Cheer Bell Gallery's website:
www.cheerbell.com

Contact Christina Tung Wai
Tel: +852 9725 8019
Email: ctung0327@gmail.com
Instagram: feather_artist_christina_tung
Facebook: beautyofarthk

Introduction

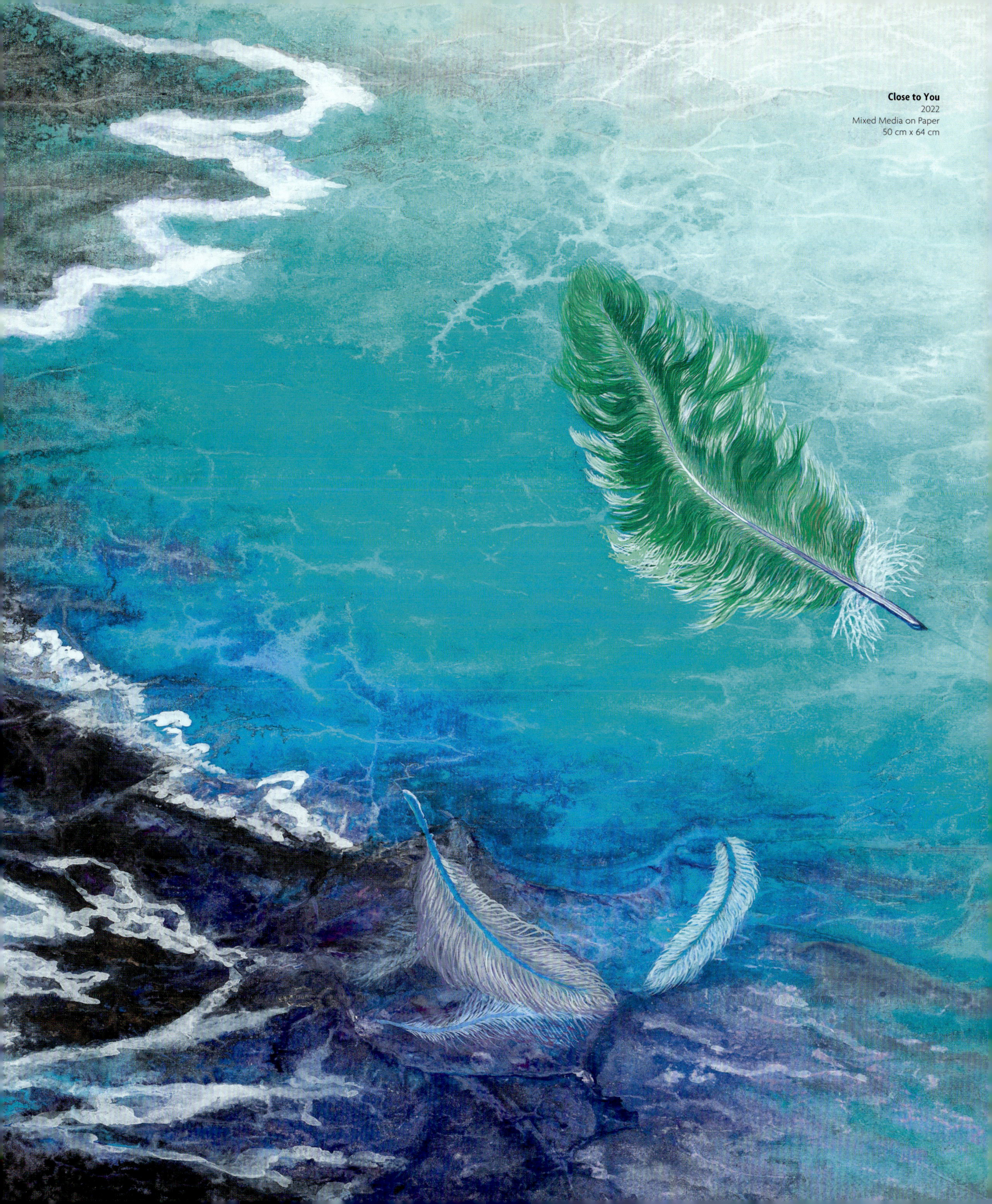

Close to You
2022
Mixed Media on Paper
50 cm x 64 cm

Christina Tung Wai: Breath of the UNIVERSE – A Feather's Tale

Harry Liu
Editor in Chief of ART.ZIP

August 2024

Beautiful pictures.
Beautiful phrases.
But what she wished to
get hold of was that
very jar on the nerves,
the thing itself
before it has been made anything.

Virginia Woolf

To the Lighthouse[1]

Virginia Woolf's description in *To the Lighthouse* seeking to capture the raw, unfiltered essence of life resonates deeply with Christina Tung Wai's artistic vision. Like Woolf, Christina Tung Wai aims to grasp the intangible emotions before they are shaped into something familiar, and this pursuit defines her work. Hong Kong feather artist Christina Tung Wai encapsulates a personal longing for freedom and a thirst for artistic innovation in her *Feather* collection. This body of work profoundly explores themes of liberation, joy and humanity, capturing both the local identity of Hong Kong and its expanding global artistic influence. At the intersection of local identity and global artistic trends, Tung's work showcases her deep understanding of contemporary art, emphasising the values of diversity, inclusivity, and emotional power.

Leaving behind the rigid world of finance, Christina Tung Wai embraced art as a liberating force. This shift, much like the feathers she paints, reflects a delicate harmony between vulnerability and strength, symbolising her personal journey towards a liberating world. Since beginning her artistic journey in 2010, she has demonstrated a unique and evolving vision. Her

1. Woolf, V., 2013. *To the Lighthouse*. Kindle edition. Oxford University Press, Loc. 2625.

ability to experiment continually with traditional ink painting has transformed the medium into an expressive, contemporary art form imbued with emotional depth and quiet elegance. From the very beginning of her artistic exploration, she has shown an affinity for feathers – symbols bursting with the energy of liberty, rendered with a distinctive visual style that resonates deeply.

Through her study and experimentation with feathers, Christina Tung Wai has developed her own distinctive artistic language – a feather-like approach. Amidst the rich hues of ink, the feather of life takes centre stage, expanding and evolving into various forms. Flowers and birds, long-standing themes in traditional Chinese painting, reflect the aristocracy's and literati's fascination with rare and exotic creatures as well as revealing the common people's yearning for nature. Yet, Tung reinterprets these motifs through the lens of the feather, bridging nature's beauty with the complexity of human experience. Her work translates these traditional Chinese elements into contemporary explorations of independence and self-discovery, embodying a fresh and modern artistic perspective.

Christina Tung Wai's innovative use of materials sets her work apart. By seamlessly blending traditional Chinese ink with unconventional materials like flimsy paper, leather and acrylics, she creates a layered texture that not only captivates the eye but invites the viewer to physically sense the tenderness and durability within each brushstroke. Flimsy paper, with its delicate and semi-transparent appearance, enhances the sense of vulnerability in her works. In contrast, her application of inks and acrylics adds depth, bringing out the strength and fortitude inherent in the feather. This interplay of materials offers a layered visual experience that allows viewers to see and feel the symbolism and meaning embedded in her work.

Christina Tung Wai's paintings delve deeply into the myriad forms of feathers, exploring their interaction within natural landscapes and their anthropomorphic representations within cultural contexts. Through this, Tung revitalises traditional ink painting by integrating modern techniques and emotional resonance, mirroring the fluidity of life itself in each feather – a carefully crafted expression of balance, fragility and the inevitable passage of time. Her brushwork captures this rhythm of time, making each feather a metaphor for the triumphs, challenges and emotions that define human existence on personal and universal levels.

Through her extraordinary talent, a simple feather reflects the infinite tapestry of existence.

Take the work *Infinity* as an example in which Christina Tung Wai explores the intersection of time and space. She came to understand that humanity's greatest joy doesn't come from wealth but from the freedom of thought. In this work, clocks and feathers overlap, with Roman and Arabic numerals interwoven, representing that, despite adversity, the idealised feather can still transcend the constraints of time and space to reach its ultimate liberation. Here, the feather embodies not only liberation but also an unyielding spirit, fearless in the face of the future and unbounded by the limitations of time.

In another profound series, *A Wintry Ballet*, Christina Tung Wai combines a mix of ink, acrylic, cowhide leather and wool – to craft a theatrical monologue portrayed on a visual stage. The ballet's ethereal grace, personified by feathers, takes centre stage against a dark backdrop, where bursts of golden light symbolise life's most dramatic and poignant moments.

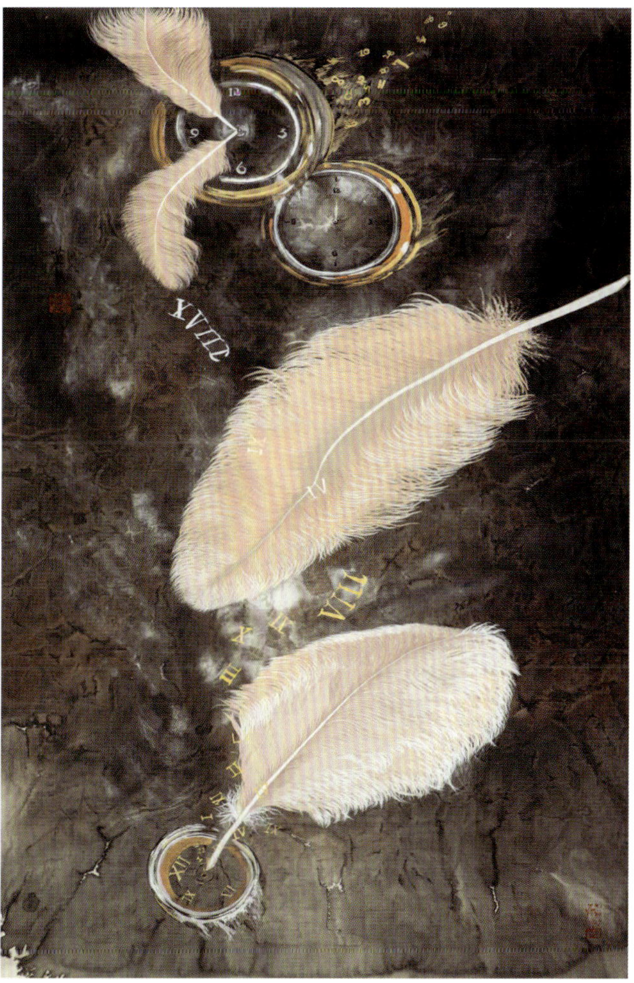

Infinity
2019
Ink and Colour on Rice Paper
125 cm x 70 cm
Her artistry transforms the elegant feather into a vessel of time and space.

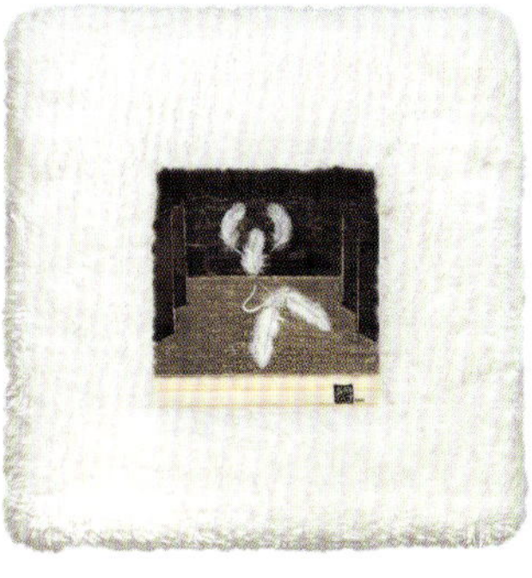
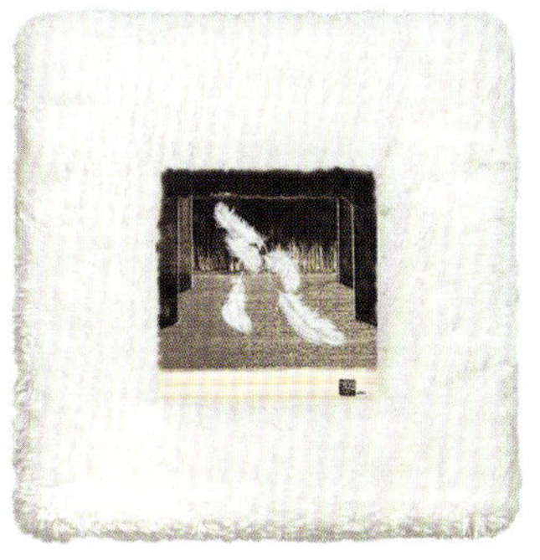
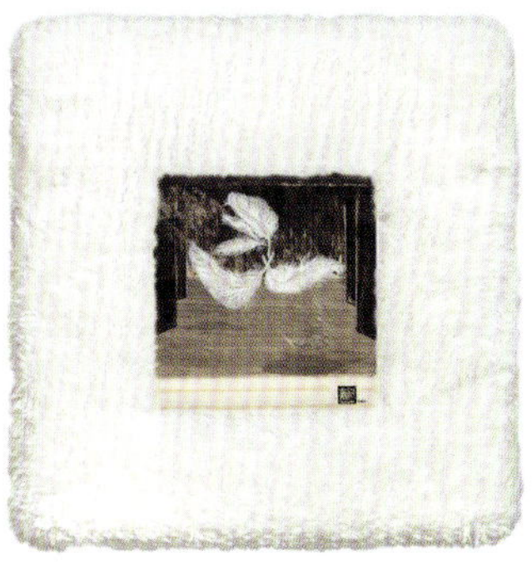
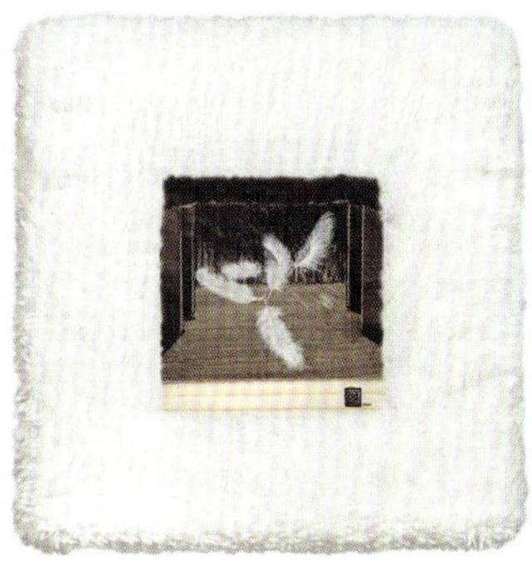

A Wintry Ballet (1)(2)(4)(3) (clockwise)
2021
Ink and Acrylic on Cowhide Leather
31.5 cm x 31.5 cm
In her hands, a feather becomes a compass guiding us through the realm of imagination.

Christina Tung Wai's art not only embodies her personal journey but also offers viewers a space for reflection, hope, memory and emotional release. For Tung, art is both a product of history and a creative outlet through which humanity can truly thrive. In her own words, 'People cannot live without emotional autonomy, and I hope my creativity can inspire people and my paintings can breathe alongside the public, offering not just beauty but a way to express and process the complex emotions of life – strength, vulnerability, hope and loss.' Her work reflects the richness of human experience and serves as a powerful meditation on the complexity and fluidity of life. Through the metaphor of the feather, Christina Tung Wai's art captures both the fragility and resilience of the human spirit.

Journey of a Feather

Like many other esteemed cultural pioneers in Hong Kong, Christina Tung Wai's parents emigrated from mainland China. This influx of migration from the mainland brought a surge of fresh energy to Hong Kong. Tung's father came from Tianjin, a key northern port and a gateway to Beijing. Tianjin spearheaded the modernisation of Chinese art during the late Qing dynasty and early Republican period through its community of scholars and artists. Tung's mother came from Shandong, a cradle of rich traditional culture and the homeland of the revered Confucian philosophers Confucius and Mencius. Tung also has a brother who resides in the USA. This diverse cultural inheritance informs Tung's work. Her family's deep roots in Chinese tradition, combined with a modern, international outlook, shaped her cross-cultural vision. This fusion of tradition and contemporary elements defines her art, where Eastern philosophy and Western techniques converge to form her unique artistic language.

Christina Tung Wai's early years were shaped by her parents' values. Her parents taught her the importance of perseverance and self-reliance, instilling the motto, 'Where there's a will, there's a way'. They encouraged her to push on regardless of fortune or hardship and to stay true to herself. At the age of twelve, Tung began managing her own finances, opened her first bank account and developed a strong sense of financial planning. During holidays, her mother encouraged her to take summer jobs to experience the myriad facets of life in Hong Kong, understand the struggles of the common people and cherish the value of hard-won happiness.

Although locals may jest that Hong Kong is a cultural desert, its economic surge, as one of the Four Asian Tigers, has been paralleled by the burgeoning global influence of its unique culture. Hong Kong's modern novels, film industry and arts economy have significantly shaped contemporary trends, and exerted a substantial cultural pull on mainland China. As Hong Kong's economy underwent a transition during the 1980s to the 1990s, so too did Christina Tung Wai's journey. When the level of industrialisation increased on the mainland, Hong Kong's manufacturing base shifted there, thus making room for finance, real estate and port operations to become the city's economic mainstays. The workforce in these sectors grew as a result, and Tung worked for more than two decades in finance. For most of the time, Tung travelled extensively all over the world for business. Before 2008, she was swamped with work and it was only during long flights at thirty thousand feet that she could truly enjoy moments of seclusion and solitude – an experience that planted the seeds for her eventual move into the world of art.

The year 2008 proved to be a landmark year for both China and Christina Tung Wai. Stamped by the global success of the Beijing Olympics, China's international influence grew. Likewise, global investors' interest in contemporary Chinese art developed rapidly. Hedge funds and private collectors alike began seeking out opportunities in this burgeoning field, driving the value of Chinese contemporary art.

Yet, as Tung was swept up in the fast-paced world of finance, she was also facing the stresses of the 2008-9 global financial crisis, which would ultimately prompt her to seek new avenues of creative and personal fulfilment. At the same time, a revival of traditional Chinese arts and culture was taking place. Many contemporary artists began rejecting the earlier trend of appeasing Western modernist ideals and instead turned back to Chinese traditions, embracing cultural identity with renewed pride. However, this return to tradition was often constrained by outdated education and limited perspectives, leaving much room for true innovation.

It was during this time that Christina Tung Wai realised she needed to seek out new creative pathways to express her inner truth. Encouraged by a relative, Tung began her studies in the studio of the ceramic Master, Janet Tso King. Master Janet Tso King's ceramics, intimately tied to everyday life and bursting with colour and interest, differed distinctly from traditional ceramics in style and taste. The material and techniques of pottery allowed Tung to experience the pleasures of art through tactile shaping and moulding. This hands-on creative approach proved more conducive to expressing emotions and exploring personal values than the rigid frameworks of finance and management.

The concept of creating bird-themed art emerged while Christina Tung Wai was studying pottery. When Master Tso asked her what form she wished to sculpt, Tung immediately decided on a bird since she recalled that when she was twelve, a parrot once flew into her house. Her mother adopted it, giving Tung the opportunity for close contact with a bird. Through daily interactions, she grew to appreciate the parrot's intelligence and agility. Each day after school, she would have conversations with the parrot, and it entertained her by performing somersaults. In her youthful innocence, she felt the power present in birds.

To provide Tung with visual references for inspiration, Master Tso gave her a catalogue from a Japanese museum with many ceramic pieces inspired by birds. While the genesis of an idea might seem straightforward, the execution requires substantial effort. Three weeks after stating her intention to model a small bird, Tung finally crafted one with which she was reasonably satisfied.

Master Janet Tso King found Tung a passionate and bold student, as Master Tso shared her thoughts on Tung, 'A seed of creativity, dormant for years within Christina, longs for the light of day. The seed soon grows into a tree of vision, with artworks that are vibrant with life, energy and individuality, free from boundaries and rules set by tradition. Her visionary ideas infuse her creations with meanings that are both pure and thought-provoking.'

Unwilling to stop her artistic journey, Christina Tung Wai had an opportunity to learn painting from Master Lam Tian Xing in 2011. She tried her best to fit ceramics and painting courses in between her fully packed agenda.

Master Lam Tian Xing is a distinguished heavy coloured ink artist and the chairman of The Hong Kong Artists Association. He is committed to the ethos of Lin Fengmian, a trailblazer in Chinese modernist painting and education: 'Introduce Western art, organise Chinese art; harmonise Eastern and Western art, and create art for the era.'[2] In his work, Master Lam blends the fluidity of ink painting with the vibrant colours of Western art. In his style and technique, he brings fresh perspectives, vividly capturing the dynamic essence of Hong Kong's urban life. Importantly, he adopts the lotus from traditional literati paintings as a symbolic motif, focusing on the purity of art and the sincerity of human nature in his work.

This innovative approach has significantly influenced Christina Tung Wai's art. Under the mentorship of Master Lam, Tung has not only solidified her foundation in ink painting but also turned her creative inspiration inward, exploring the deep emotional resonance of her art.

In one of Master Lam's classes, he presented a challenge to his students: on a four-foot (138 cm) sheet of rice paper, each was to find their unique way of depicting a lotus. This task contrasted sharply with pottery, where the concept of creating functional objects is prevalent. Whether moulding a cup or a vase, the form is always achievable with clay; however, translating a three-dimensional lotus on to a two-dimensional paper tests the artist's skills. At that time, Christina Tung Wai, still contemplating the essence of the lotus, had yet to master the techniques of brush and ink. After watching the students reflect for a while, Master Lam began to demonstrate his approach. He began by splashing the background with ink, colouring the lotus leaves and flower and finally outlining the roots. All students were encouraged to follow his method. However, witnessing Master Lam's demonstration sparked inspiration in Tung, and she found a way that the lotus could be interpreted in her unique style. Seizing her brush, she chose not to mimic Master Lam's technique; rather, she let her intuition guide her hand, thus capturing the lotus as she envisaged it.

Master Lam was pleased to see Tung's deviation. He recognised in his student a depth of substantial independent thought. He approached her, patted her

---

2. Lin Fengmian's words cited in Gong, J., 2023. *Chinese Art Today: From 20th Century Tradition to Contemporary Practice*. Unicorn Publishing Group, p. 28.

shoulder and said, 'I know you're a finance expert, a formidable woman with strong opinions. That's admirable. Creativity is essential for innovation in art.' After this encouragement, Master Lam added emphatically, 'However, while you study here, mastering the basics of ink techniques will be crucial; even if you were to acquire only 90 per cent mastery, that would still significantly aid your development.'

Master Lam explained that painting, like any discipline, requires a foundational grasp of form, achieved through technique training that allows the artist to unify intention and execution, thereby enabling personalised visual effects. After mastering a mature system, one should employ critical thinking to innovate with these techniques, thus ensuring a stable demonstration of one's artistic skills. With this stable foundation and the addition of inspired strokes, an artist truly reaches a level of maturity and professionalism.

Christina Tung Wai was naturally gifted and she immediately understood Master Lam's teachings, diligently and humbly learning from him. Within a year, she had advanced significantly. Her artistic style began to be closely mirroring that of Master Lam, who recognised her progress and courage. He proposed an exhibition to celebrate the advancements of his students. By this time, Tung's ink painting skills had significantly improved. Her strong fundamentals – managing the dryness, wetness and intensity of ink, subtle shifts in colour and nuanced composition adjustments – deepened her understanding of contemporary heavy-colour ink painting and would support her future innovations in artistic language.

Christina Tung Wai holds deep respect and gratitude for Master Lam Tian Xing's mentorship. Having roughly mastered Master Lam's methods for floral art, Tung began to explore the theme she was most passionate about – the depiction of birds. Since she did not possess the skill nor knowledge to paint a bird, at that moment she already recognised feathers as an icon for freedom. Then, the first pair of feather paintings were created in 2013 out of her passion for birds. This pair of works surprisingly established itself as a representative work for the future development of Tung's feather art.

To Christina Tung Wai, birds and feathers represent both a reservoir of life and a path to artistic liberty. Feathers, unique biological derivatives, cover almost all of a bird's body. They are not merely lightweight and flexible – essential for flight, they are also elastic and insulating, protecting the bird. Moreover, feathers are vividly colourful, and their oily composition gives them their distinctive sheen. Therefore, feathers are profoundly

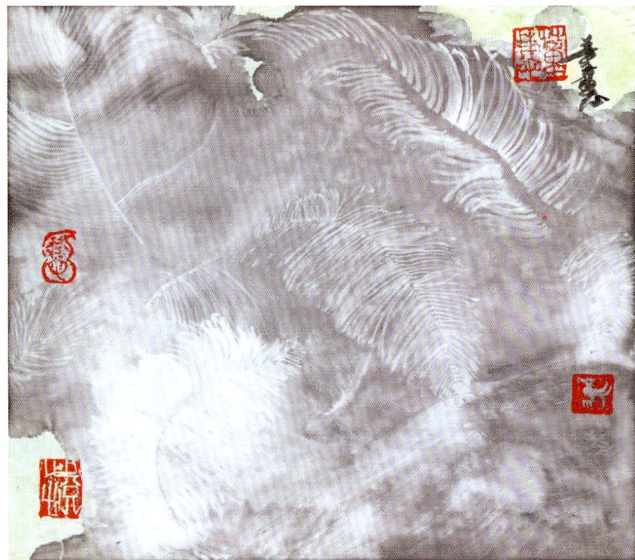

See You Again
2013
Ink and Colour on Rice Paper
24 cm x 27 cm

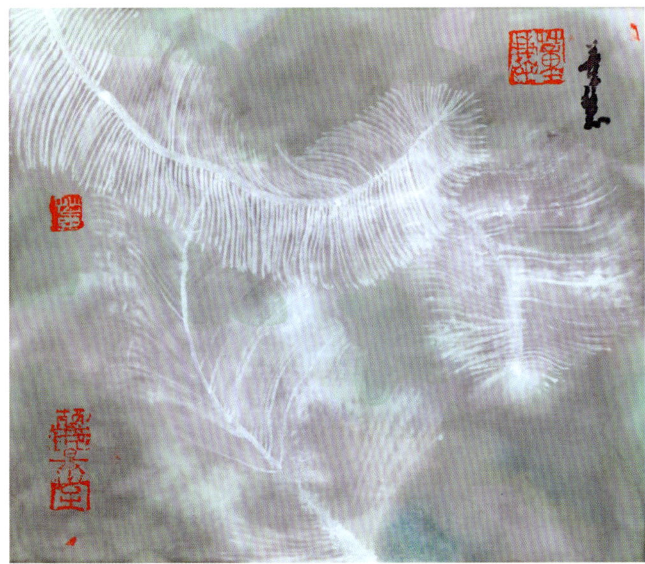

Still Loving
2013
Ink and Colour on Rice Paper
24 cm x 27 cm

significant. They affirm a bird's identity, underpin its ability of flight and are the fountainhead of their aesthetic appeal.

In 2015, she sought guidance from Master Lam Wu Fui, known for his expertise in bird-themed paintings. Master Lam Wu Fui's style is derived from the Lingnan School of painting; he studied under Masters Liang Boyu and Zhao Shao'ang. The Lingnan School is one of the most pivotal modern art movements in contemporary Chinese art history. Its founders, Gao Jianfu, Gao Qifeng and Chen Shuren, were committed to revolutionising national painting by enhancing the expressiveness of Chinese ink. They pioneered innovative techniques like 'water collision' and 'colour collision', which involved the dynamic interaction of water and white pigment to create striking visual effects. Master Lam Wu Fui's depictions of cranes are elegantly coloured, dynamically shaped and dreamily lit. Christina Tung Wai found these qualities and techniques to be profoundly influential.

After vigorous instruction from Master Lam Wu Fui and continual practice on the Lingnan School's bird techniques, Christina Tung Wai gradually established her own signature symbolic expression: feathers. This motif crystallised during her exploration of avian forms. To strengthen the intention and expressiveness of her work, and to break away from traditional representational art, Tung intentionally simplified her depictions of birds and explored the deeper symbolism embedded in their feathers.

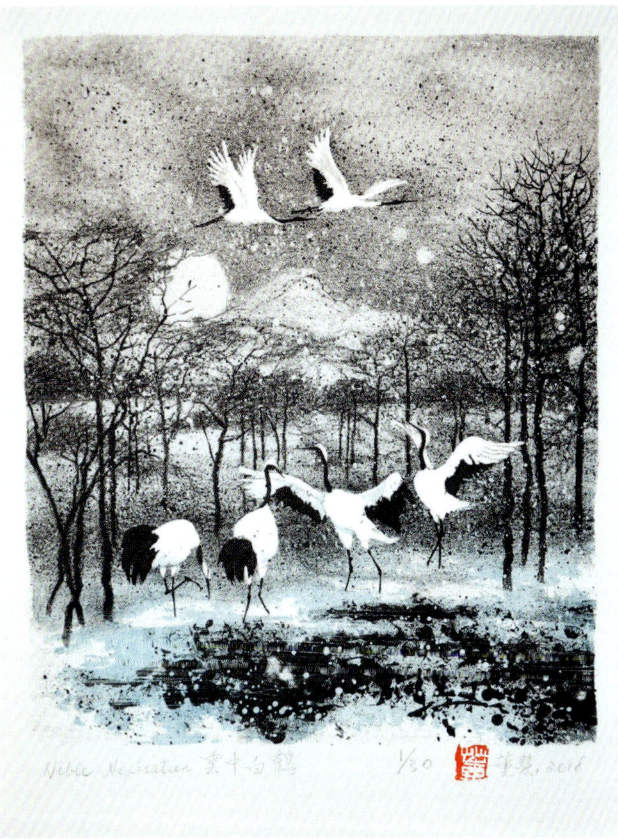

Noble Aspiration
2018
Colour Lithograph
39.5 cm x 26.5 cm

Year 2018 – Feather of Liberation and Joy

For someone who has not received formal artistic training, 2018 seemed to be an incredibly important and fortunate year for Christina Tung Wai. Her inaugural solo exhibition was held in 2018 at the Russian Academy of Fine Arts Museum, St Petersburg, Russia. A Russian professor from the Academy, who had admired Tung's art during his teaching stint in China, invited her to host her solo exhibition at the museum. The exhibition was a triumph. Tung not only showcased her new experimental ink paintings but also enriched the space with her ceramic works, thereby intensifying the unique style of her artistic expression. Moved by the Academy exhibition, the owner of Molbert art gallery in St Petersburg promptly invited Tung to host her second solo exhibition at his gallery space.

The year 2018 proved to be one of both academic recognition and market success for Christina Tung Wai. She also became increasingly prominent in the art scene. At her third solo exhibition the same year, her lithograph *Noble Aspiration* was acquired by the Consulate General of the Russian Federation in Hong Kong.

The story behind *Noble Aspiration* is particularly fascinating. On the final day of her solo exhibition at the Russian Academy of Fine Arts Museum, the professor who had invited her suggested she experiment with lithography in the academy's printmaking studio. In the studio, Tung chose a piece of more than 100-year-old lithography stone from Munich, Germany and started drafting her design. She dedicated twenty hours over two days to this effort, during which she engaged in deep discussions and even debated with the professor about printmaking techniques. The session was extraordinarily gratifying, yielding thirty printed works. The creation of *Noble Aspiration* was rather fortuitous, demonstrating that art often arises from unexpected cultural interactions and collisions.

In addition to having three solo exhibitions in 2018, Christina Tung Wai was privileged to be accepted into the Contemporary Ink Artists Summit Program at the Shanghai Institute of Visual Arts (SIVA), becoming one of only fifteen artists from Southeast Asia to join. Fortuitously, her mentor was Master Liu Kuo-sung, the dean of the Academy of Contemporary Ink Art at the SIVA and a trailblazer in contemporary Chinese art. Upon reviewing five of Tung's artworks, Master Liu recognised that her techniques were refreshingly unburdened by academic conventions. Her pieces expressed a distinctive personal stance, aligning well with his own creative philosophy. Thus, Tung was admitted into his class. Then she travelled to Shanghai to study under Master Liu, Shi Mo, the dean of School of Fine Arts at SIVA, and Professor Lin Mingjie for a week every month.

Dubbed the Father of Modern Ink Painting, Master Liu Kuo-sung is one of the pioneers who embraced modernist reforms in China following the Second World War. In 1956, he was instrumental in founding the May Painting Society, which advocated for a modernisation of Chinese art that was rooted in tradition rather than merely mimicking Western styles. He declared, 'Imitating the new should not displace imitating the old; and copying Western styles should not supersede emulating Chinese ones.'[3]

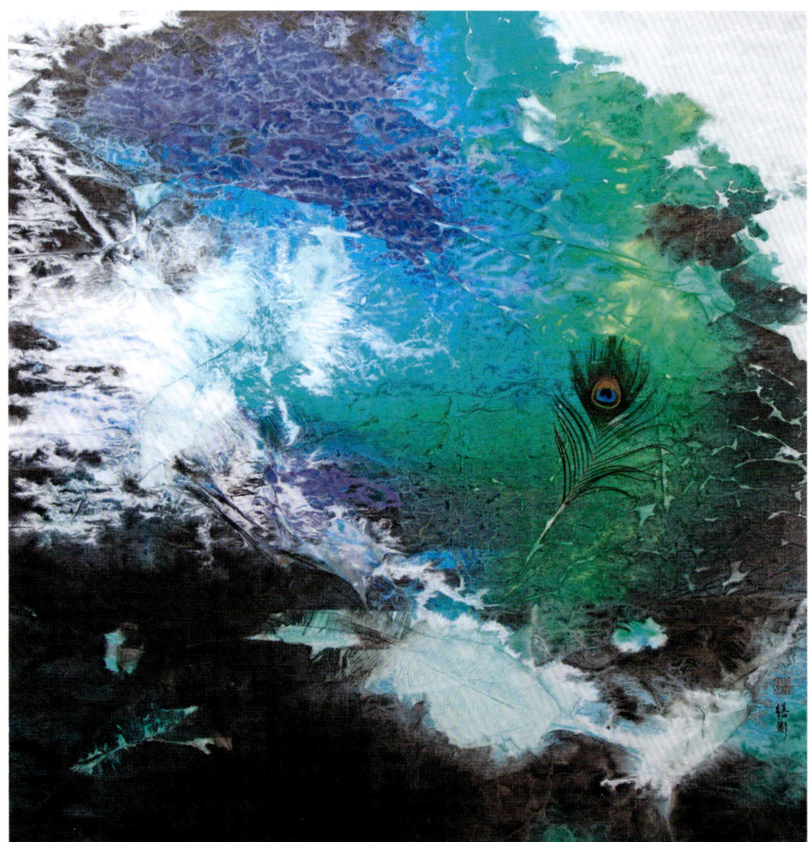

Propitious Portent
2019
Ink, Colour and Feather on Paper
98 cm x 98 cm
The feather's delicate lightness mirrors humanity's endless quest for liberation.

3. Liu, K., 'Self-statement'. Available at: https://www.liukuosung.org/about.php?lang=cn (Accessed: 18 June 2024).

Master Liu's philosophy of 'first seeking uniqueness, then seeking excellence' greatly influenced Tung's creative approach, encouraging her to fearlessly explore new artistic expressions before refining her technique. He also emphasised that art must be distinct from others, that its greatness lies in its divergence from the mainstream. He advocated for a principle of innovation, urging an approach of 'seeking diversity', similar to that of a scientist experimenting with new possibilities. This gave Tung the confidence to push the boundaries of materials and methods, and further expand her artistic expression.

Consequently, Christina Tung Wai turned her attention to the possibilities of materials and textures. Upon mastering ink painting techniques, she realised that varying types of paper could enhance the effects of her ink paintings. While the Lingnan School traditionally used rice paper and Japanese *washi*, Tung chose flimsy paper (also known as *Xueli* paper in Chinese, a packaging paper commonly used to wrap pears, from which it derives its name). Flimsy paper is available in various types, characterised by its semi-transparent appearance and delicate texture. It is frequently used as a filler in packaging for items such as shoes and clothing.

Christina Tung Wai found that different flimsy papers possessed distinct absorbencies and thus produced unique artistic effects. Wetting the paper also revealed varying creases and textures, adding another dimension to her work. Having discovered this intriguing paper, she experimented with how different coloured inks interacted with it.

Since then, Christina Tung Wai's artistic hallmark, the feather-like approach, has increasingly resonated within the contemporary art world. During the preparations for an exhibition, Christina Tung Wai met the founder of Ink House, the exclusive agent of German brand LAMY in China and Hong Kong regions. Tung was direct in her approach, telling him, 'I'm an artist and I'm interested in using your inks for creative experimentation.' The founder was only too happy to help and supplied her with a hundred bottles of ink with which to experiment.

Back in her studio, Christina Tung Wai mixed Western inks, Chinese pigments, and acrylics in various proportions, testing them on flimsy paper, rice paper and even cowhide leather. Through these experiments, Tung achieved the visual effects she had been seeking. Tung's ink experiments had led to new artistic breakthroughs, earning praise from Master Liu. One of her pieces from this new batch of experimental works, titled *Propitious Portent*, was selected for the prestigious '*Ink Global*' 2020 as an exemplary ink painting.

The two years of learning at SIVA where Tung came under the guidance of Master Liu Kuo-sung allowed her to enlighten her mind, charging forward without fear. It marked a decisive juncture for her, as Master Liu's illuminating teachings have since inspired Tung to venture out and pursue fresh, imaginative ways to realise her feather-like approach and create unprecedented artistic works that are truly striking.

Christina Tung Wai's journey has proved to us that she is a deeply passionate and resolute artist, distinguished by her unwavering creativity and unique individuality. Her approach to art is marked by a profound sense of reverence and an unrelenting drive for artistic exploration and innovation. For Tung, the feather is not simply a symbol; it is the core of her artistic identity. Deeply rooted in Eastern philosophy, particularly the concepts of non-action and natural harmony, Tung's work is infused with both contemporaneity and timeless poetry that reveal her cultural duality. Each feather carries layers of personal, cultural and philosophical meaning, embodying the evolution of her way of feather.

Feather of Wisdom: Feather-like Approach

In pursuit of this artistic theme, Christina Tung Wai immersed herself in an extensive study of the biology of feathers, laying the groundwork for her innovative breakthroughs. The journey to perfecting her feather motif was not without challenges. 'No one taught me how to paint feathers,' Tung admits, reflecting on the many instances where she felt lost or wanted to give up. Some paintings took months to complete, as she often struggled with composition, colour balance and knowing when a work was finished. She recalls one particular piece that took her eight months to finish. 'There were times when I had to step away, forget about the piece and then return to it with fresh eyes,' she explains, showing her perseverance and commitment to excellence. A significant work that affirms feathers as an icon of Christina Tung Wai and her feather-like approach is *Courteously*.

With maturity, her understanding of feathers deepened and intertwined with philosophical reflections on life. The act of reflecting on the journey of a feather – how it glides effortlessly on the wind – can lead to deeper insights into our own paths and the knowledge we gather along the way.

Feathers, though inanimate, contain potent organic elements and use their inherent qualities to foster life. Following that Christina Tung Wai draws parallels to ancient Chinese Taoist philosophy, which posits, 'By never seeking its own greatness, it ultimately attains true greatness.'

Furthermore, Christina Tung Wai is of the same mind as Laozi on the wisdom in embracing softness and gentleness, 'The highest good is like water', as water nourishes all beings selflessly without striving against them and finds its place in the humblest of spots. It just so happens that water flows downwards in nature while a feather moves upwards, making it an intriguing contrast. The feathers under Tung's brushstrokes always fly gracefully in the air, unfettered by mundane restrictions, reminding us not to be weighed down by burdens or rigid beliefs.

Other times the feathers are filled with ideals that transcend the boundaries of time and space, reaching true freedom. Embracing a more fluid approach allows us to navigate life's complexities with greater ease, leading to a richer understanding of ourselves and the world around us. In that way, feathers become a powerful metaphor for the wisdom we cultivate throughout our own journeys.

Christina Tung Wai's feather-like approach symbolises lightness, adaptability and the ability to navigate various challenges with grace. It refers to a gentle, light and flexible method of handling a situation or task, suggesting a way of engaging that is soft and unobtrusive, much like the delicate nature of a feather. This type of approach can be applied in various settings such as leadership, communication and problem-solving where sensitivity and tact are important.

For Christina Tung Wai, the feather serves as a metaphor for life's complexity. It embodies the balance between sensitivity and strength, and the constant flux between transience and perpetuity. Each brushstroke reflects her meditation on the ebb and flow of existence, capturing both life's triumphs and struggles. Her artistic creations have nurtured a comforting and rewarding force that would continue to inspire her.

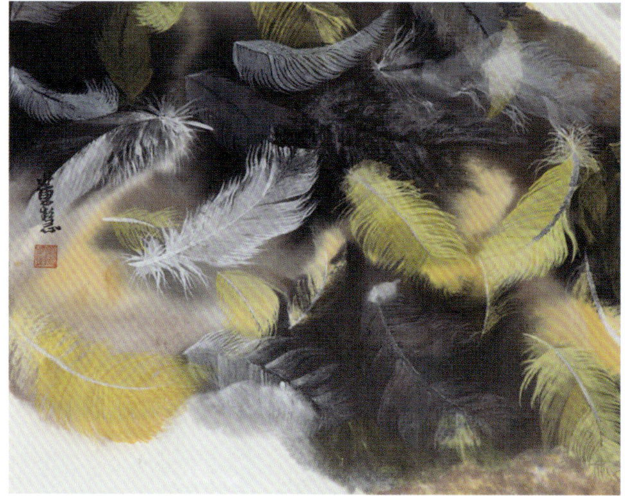

Courteously
2018
Ink and Colour on Rice Paper
33 cm x 42 cm

Song of the Soul

In recent years, with the backing of the Central People's and the Hong Kong Special Administrative Region governments, Hong Kong has significantly revamped its arts and cultural framework. The establishments of the M+ art museum, Art Basel in Hong Kong and the Hong Kong Palace Museum have reaffirmed Hong Kong's support in contemporary art and traditional culture.

Christina Tung Wai's art, whether in theme, medium or intent, stems from her inner vision and originality, garnering increasing acclaim for her artistic achievements from the global art community. From 2018 to 2024, Tung held eight solo exhibitions.

While feathers in Western art often symbolise purity, lightness or spiritual ascension, Christina Tung Wai's interpretation adds layers of complexity. Her work explores the duality of frailty and unwavering strength, emphasising personal and collective transformation, particularly in response to contemporary challenges like the internal personal contemplation and the pandemic.

A personal dilemma in 2019 had led Tung to delve deeply into the past, leading to the creation of her *Liberation* series. In this series, Tung revisited things once tightly held, realising that even the most precious possessions and memories cannot escape the passage of time. Only by letting go, she realised, can one achieve rebirth, as seen from *Liberation (1)*; whereas in *Liberation (2)*, the flames symbolically burn away the past, representing the courage to say goodbye and embrace the future. As she noted, only through releasing these attachments can true inherent bliss and renewal be achieved.

Beyond personal reflection, Christina Tung Wai's creations draw on the shifting cultural and social landscape. In terms of cultural landscape, Christina Tung Wai's feather icon has attracted attention from the fashion industry. In June 2020, the Hong Kong Art Gallery Association, in collaboration with the Italian luxury brand Salvatore Ferragamo, hosted a footwear design competition. Tung saw the potential for the light and airy essence of feathers to convey significant emotional value to Ferragamo's target demographic: professional women. She created a bespoke design and hand-painted

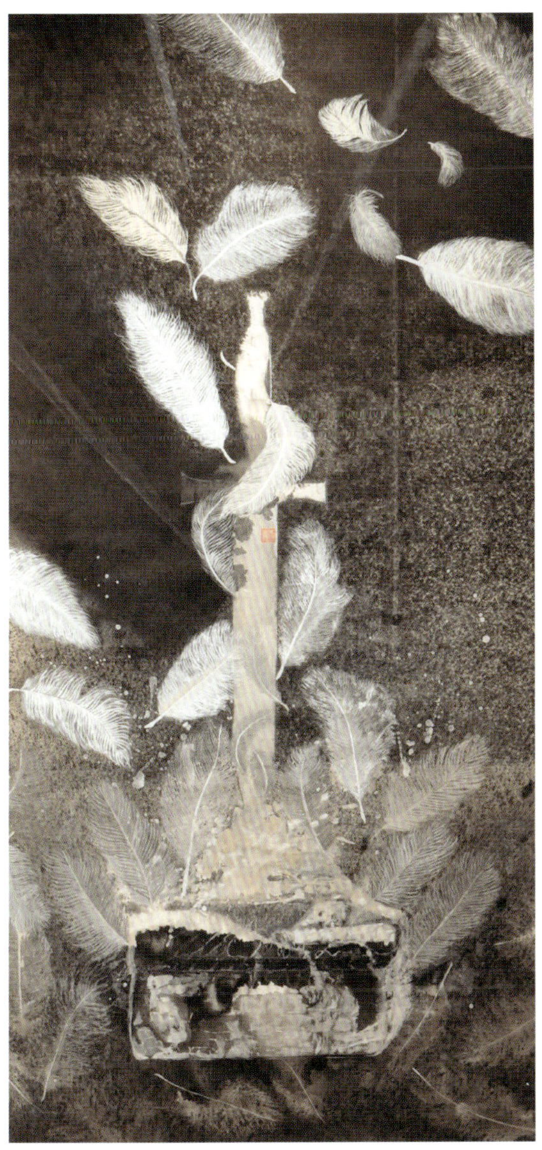

Liberation (1)
2019
Mixed Media on Rice Paper
123 cm x 65 cm

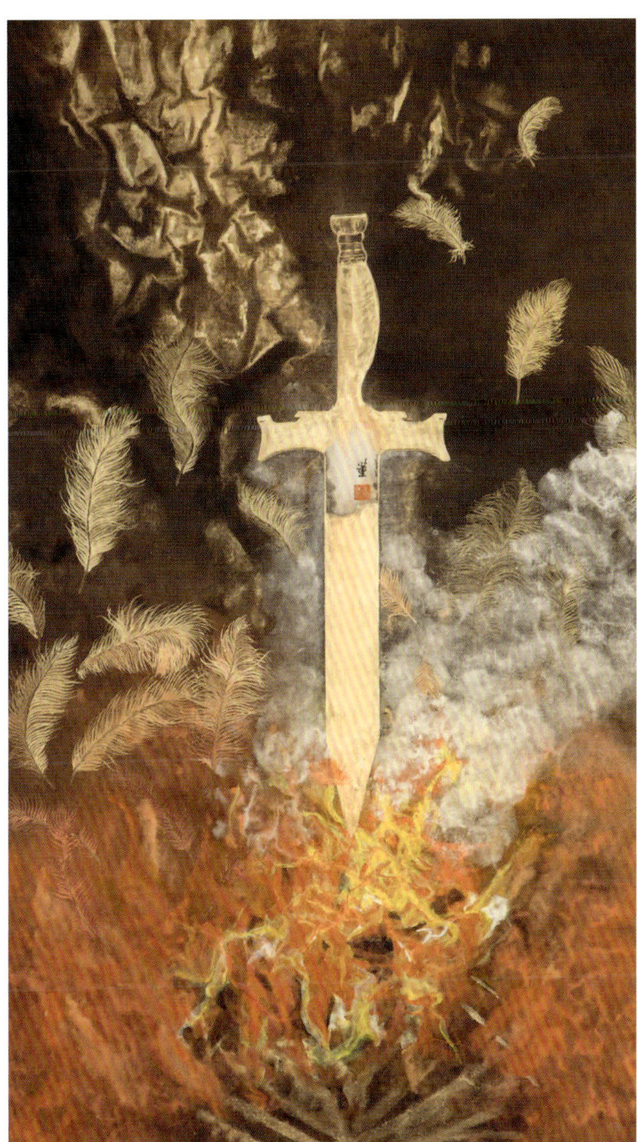

Liberation (2)
2019
Mixed Media on Rice Paper
109 cm x 69 cm

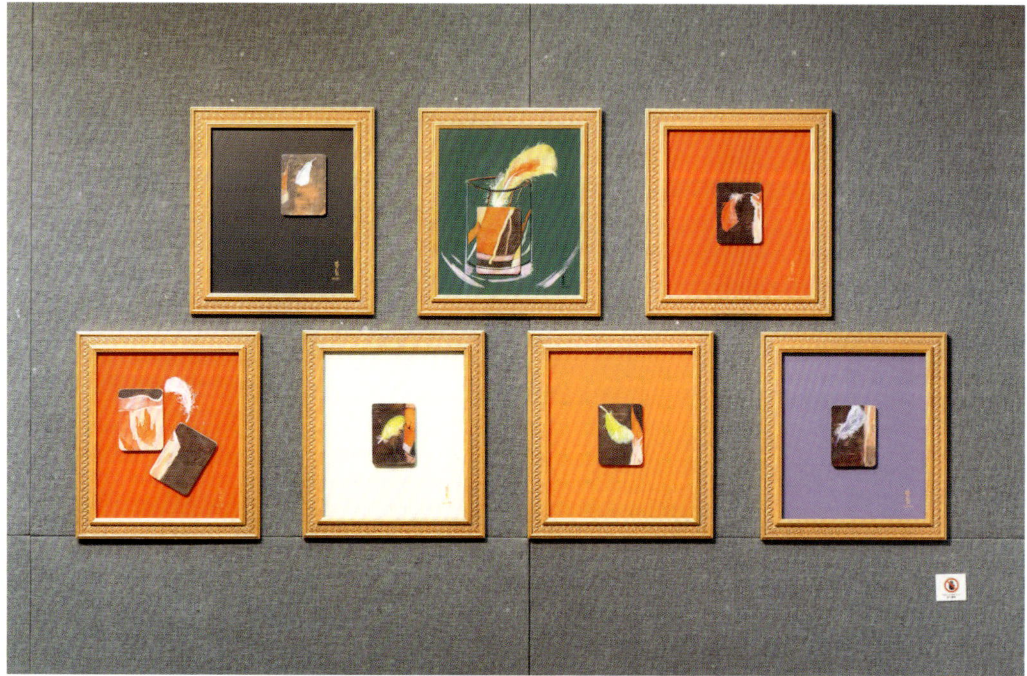

Unchained Melody Series
2021
Ink and Acrylic on Cowhide Leather
41 cm x 34.5 cm each

the footwear. Tung's design philosophy and visual impact earned accolades from the organising committee, and she won the competition's top design award. This blending of art and fashion allowed Tung's feather philosophy to be explored in even broader realms.

During the global pandemic, the world was enveloped in sudden uncertainty, pain and isolation. For Christina Tung Wai, this crisis became both personal challenge and a pivotal turning point in her artistic career. Confronted with the collective suffering of humanity and her own inner turmoil, she chose not to remain still. Instead, she used her art as a medium for healing and connection. Her works during this period reflect not only her personal recovery but also shared perseverance. In these delicate feathers, she captures the strength found from vulnerability and the hope that can emerge from despair. For Tung, the feather symbolises something more than simple conception of emotional independence – the deep-seated emotions of human suffering and hope.

A representative example would be the *Unchained Melody* series inspired by the pandemic, in which Christina Tung Wai cut up her intact leather works into segregated pieces and created new works from them, giving them a second life. The process of cutting up leather pieces symbolised the isolation and frustration felt by people during the pandemic, but once assembled and presented as unique artworks with meanings of their own, they were exalted as the vessels of hope – a hope that even if life separates us, we can still shine and perhaps reunite someday.

In another work, *Love of My Life,* Christina Tung Wai continued her artistic pursuit of beauty and emotion under the pandemic. This art piece in Chinese aesthetic appeal carries on the bright colours and blending

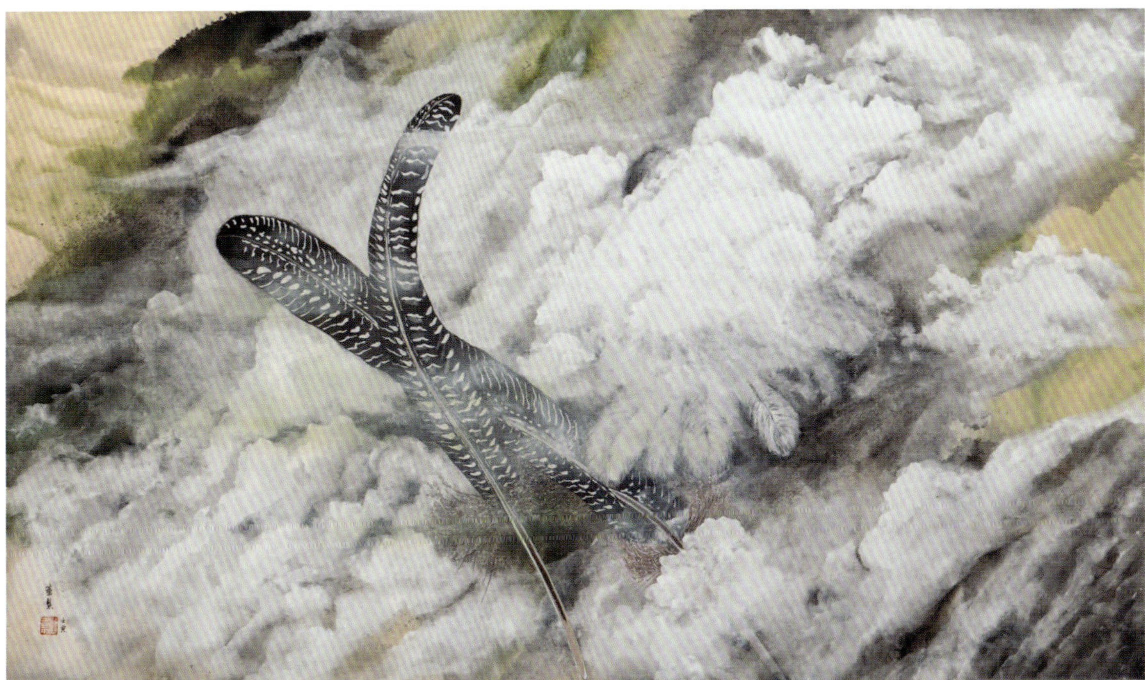

Love of My Life
2022
Mixed Media on Rice Paper
96.5 cm x 188 cm

techniques of the Lingnan School but steps outside the traditional frameworks. She illustrated the spirits of two lovers transforming into pheasant feathers, gently drifting through misty mountains, representing their eternal love and devotion to each other during the forced separations of the pandemic. It reflects the unyielding desire for companionship – the universal human need for love and closeness, even in the face of death.

It goes without saying that physical connections between people were abruptly severed during the pandemic, as if the world was trapped in an invisible cage. Christina Tung Wai's feather-themed artworks became a visual metaphor for release from this isolation. Created in response to the global crisis, her *Blessing* series is too a remarkable one. Using 1,800 brightly coloured leather pieces, she assembled three massive pairs of wings, each more than three meters in length. These wings symbolise powerful potency, hope and freedom, representing the tenacity of Hong Kong and the world's potential for post-pandemic recovery. Her works convey warmth and strength, encouraging viewers to overcome their present challenges, transcend their limitations and embrace the future.

Through these works, Christina Tung Wai's feather motif reaches new philosophical heights. Drawing on the teachings of Laozi, she explores the delicate balance between fragility and strength, lightness and weight. Her feather embodies ancient wisdom while expressing modern artistic sensibilities. As light as a feather is, it carries the dream of flight and the power of transformation. This exploration of the tension between vulnerability and resilience gives her art profound philosophical meaning, creating layers of emotional and intellectual depth.

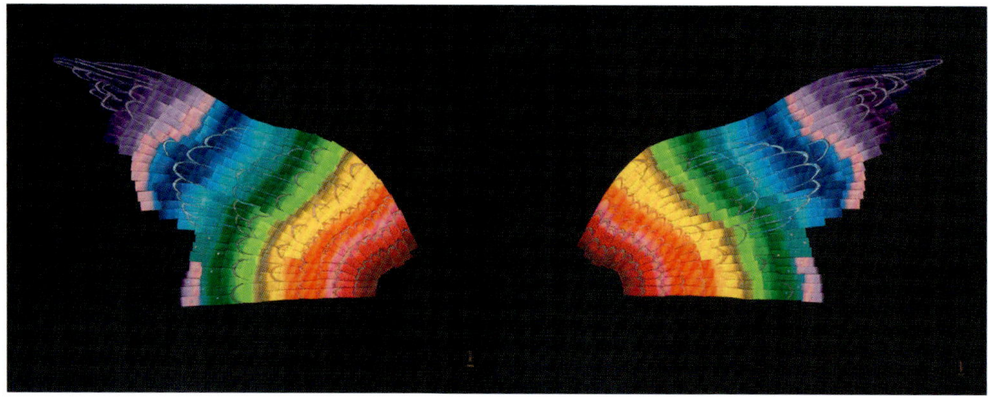

Blessing of the Night Sky
2022
Acrylic on Cowhide Leather
Set of two: 123 cm x 306 cm

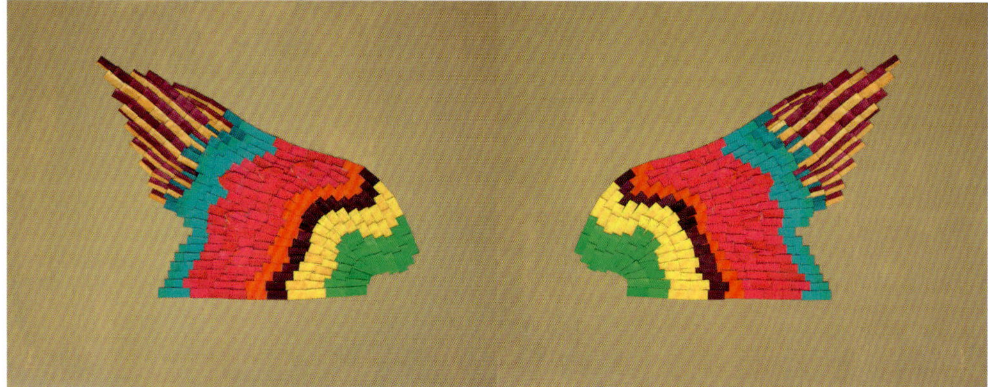

Blessing of the Earth
2022
Acrylic on Cowhide Leather
Set of two: 123 cm x 306 cm

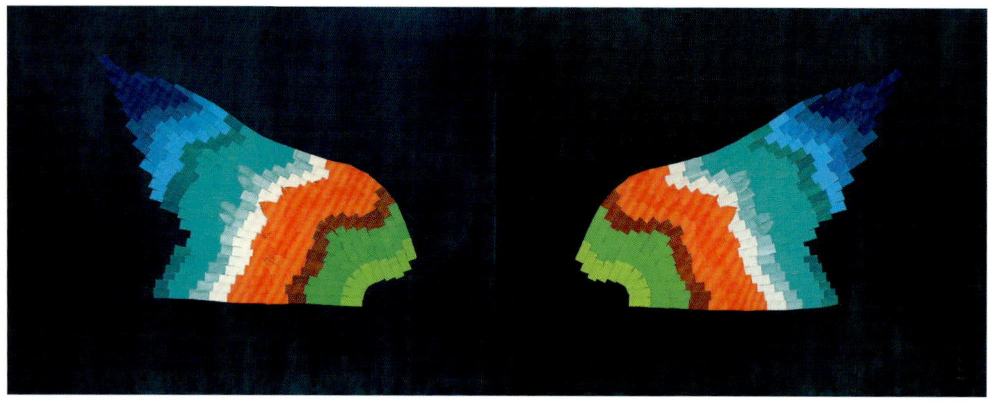

Blessing of the Ocean
2022
Acrylic on Cowhide Leather
Set of two: 123 cm x 306 cm

As Emily Dickinson wrote in her famous poem[4]:

'Hope' is the thing with feathers–
That perches in the soul–
And sings the tune without the words–
And never stops–at all–
And sweetest–in the gale–is heard–
And fierce must be the storm–
That could abash the little bird
That kept so many warm–
I've heard it in the chilliest land–
And on the strangest sea–
Yet–never–in extremity,
It asked a crumb–of me.

Dickinson's poem highlights the enduring hope that feathers symbolise – a hope that Christina Tung Wai masterfully weaves into her art. Her work is not just a visual expression, but a light-hearted song of the soul, guarding humanity's eternal hope. In times of turmoil and uncertainty, Tung's feathers drift gently through the darkness, bringing with them a quiet, yet steadfast strength and the promise of renewal.

Resonating with universal themes of resilience, metamorphosis and the passage of time, one will surely find Christina Tung Wai's transformation of her personal journey into her own unique artistic language striking a chord with them. Through the graceful flight of her feathers, Tung invites us to appreciate the feather-like approach and a meditation on the human spirit – its enduring quest of throwing off one's shackles, its versatility in the face of impermanence and its ability to bridge the gap between tradition and modernity. Each feather, light yet malleable, encourages us to soar alongside her, embracing both life's transient beauty and its boundless possibilities.

When asked about her wish for the future, Christina Tung Wai asserted, 'In the new era of the twenty-first century, I have transitioned from a business career to artistic creation. Being able to produce a unique series of feather artworks makes me extremely happy and proud of myself! I wholeheartedly support and encourage the inspiration of youth in the field of art, as it not only motivates them to express themselves and explore uniqueness, but also enhances their spiritual and aesthetic abilities. I hope the government and educational institutions could foster an open artistic environment, enrich young people's creative experiences and encourage innovative ideas, which also enhance their sense of social responsibility and improve their communication skills and touch others through art! In the days to come, I will dedicate my time to promoting art and continuing my own creative endeavours.'

4. Dickinson, E., 2020. *Collected Poems*. Amazon Classics, p. 21.

Artworks

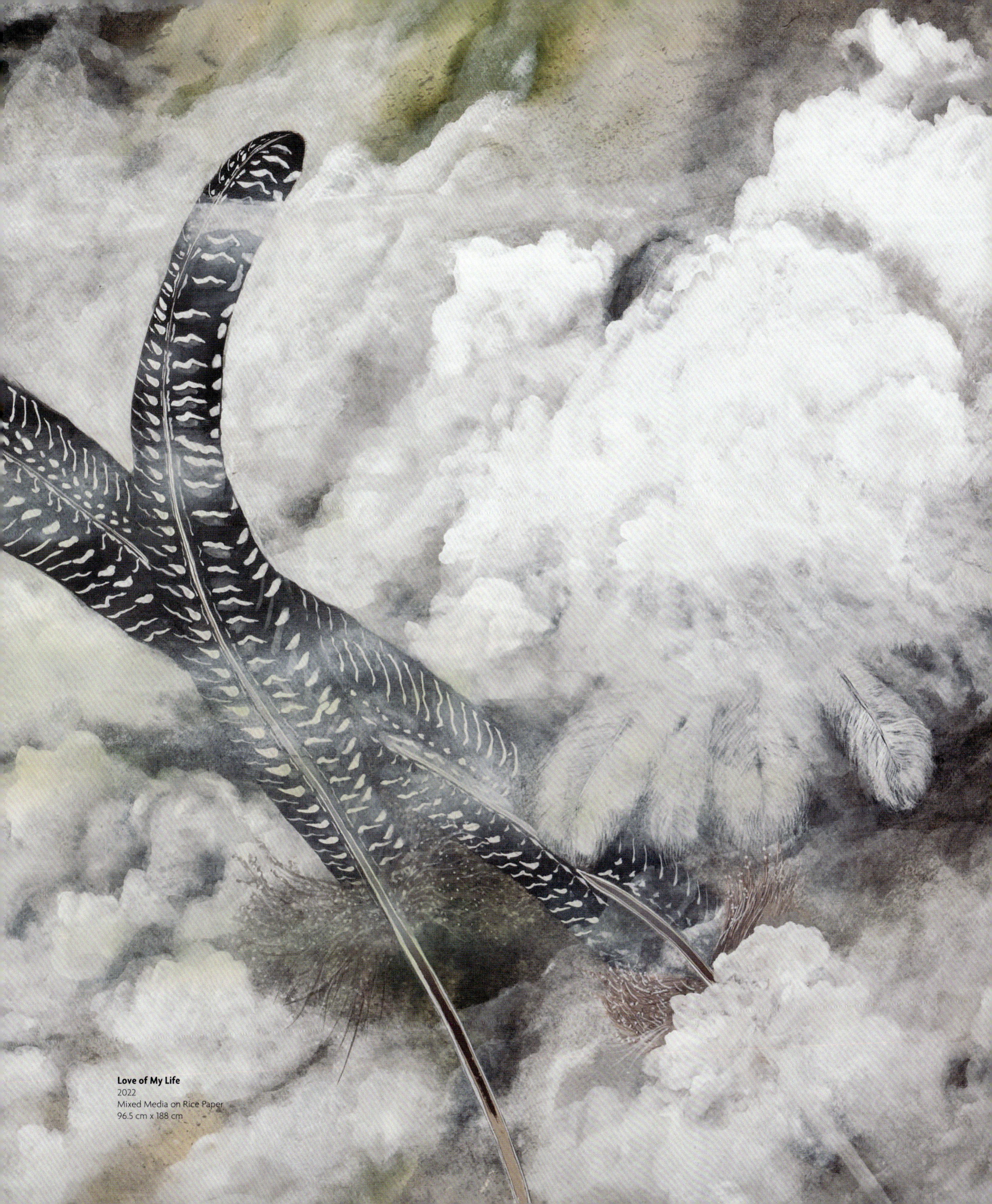

Love of My Life
2022
Mixed Media on Rice Paper
96.5 cm x 188 cm

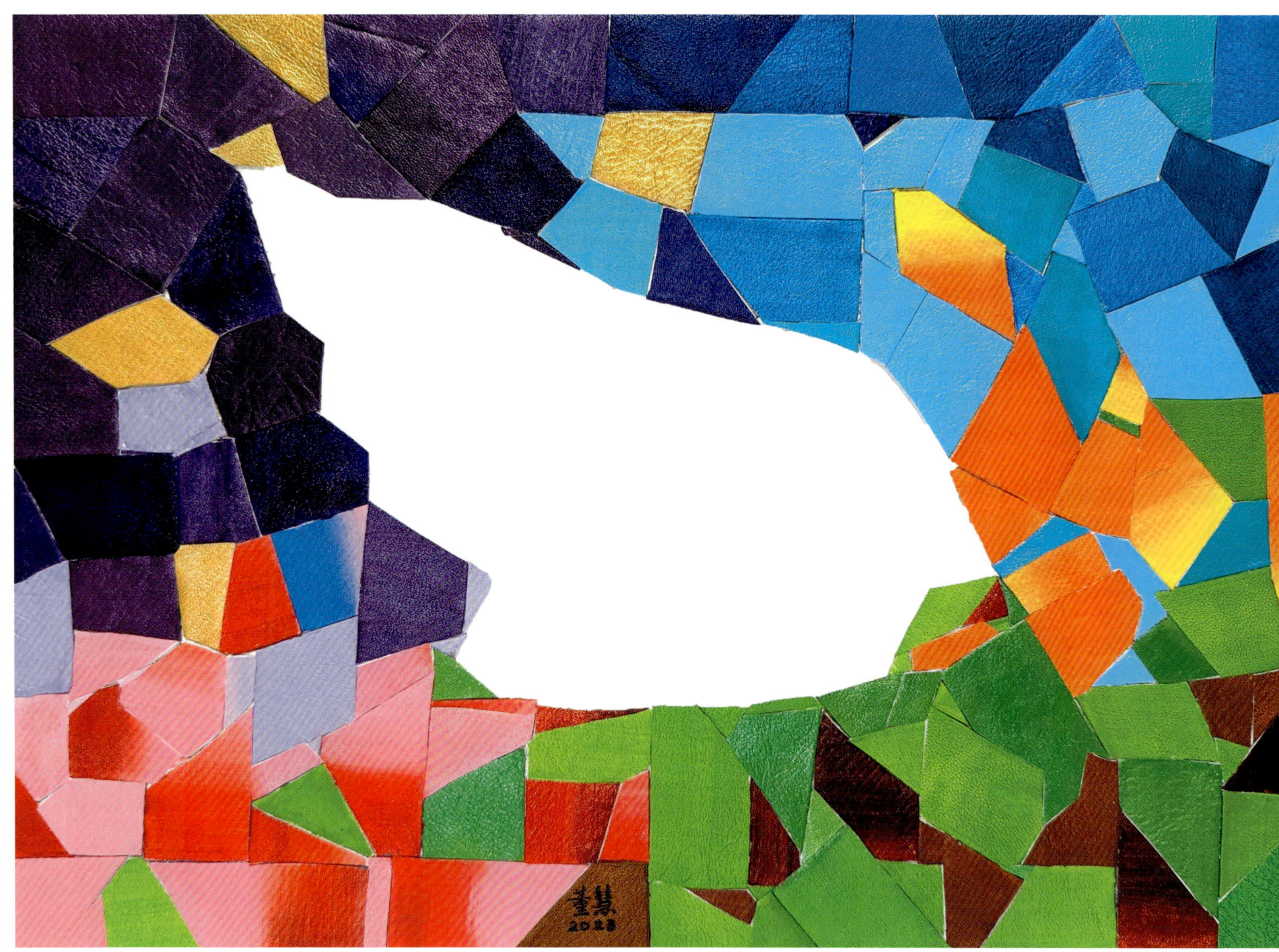

Blessing
2023
Acrylic on Cowhide Leather
Set of two: 28 cm x 76 cm

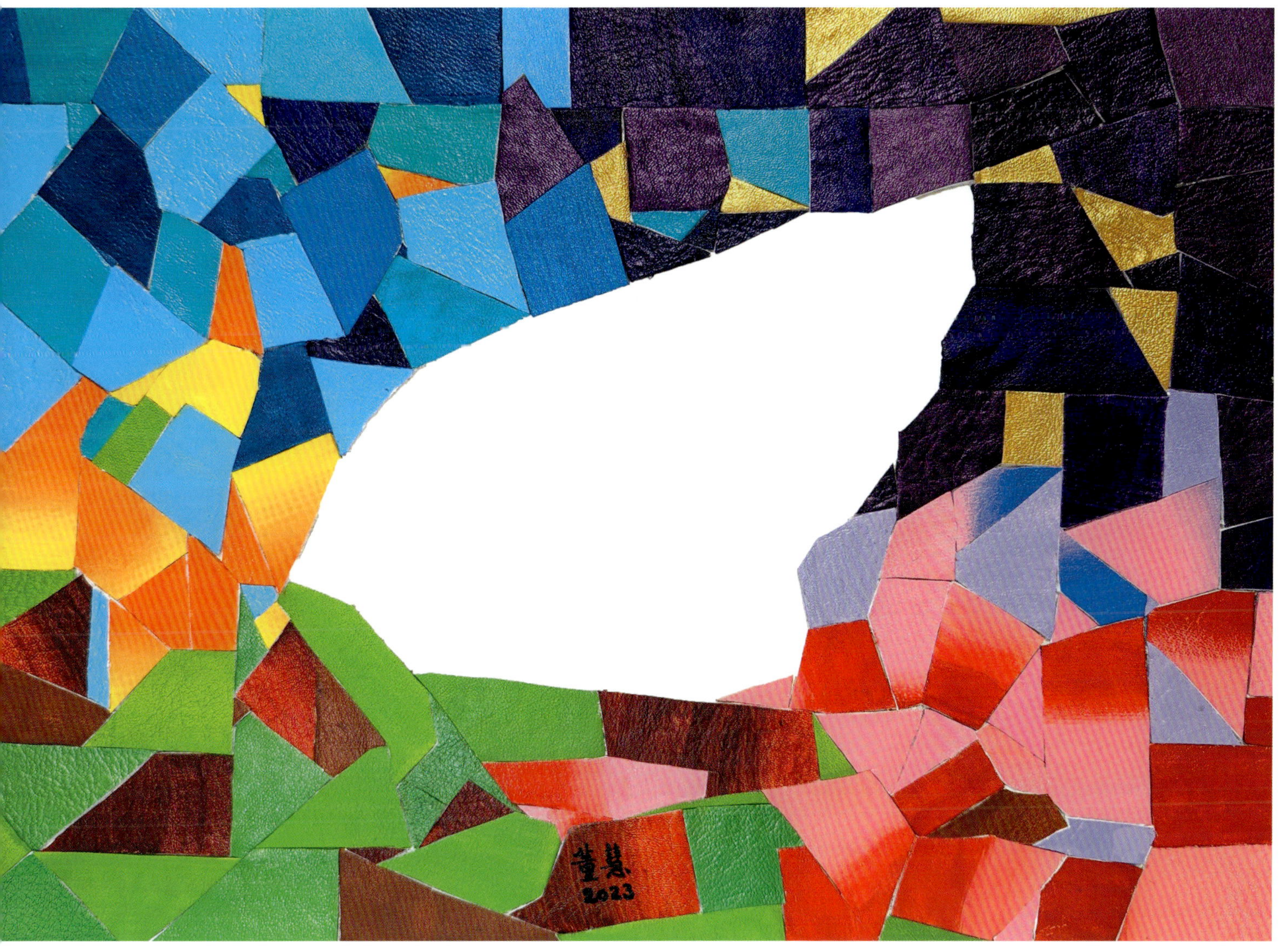
2023

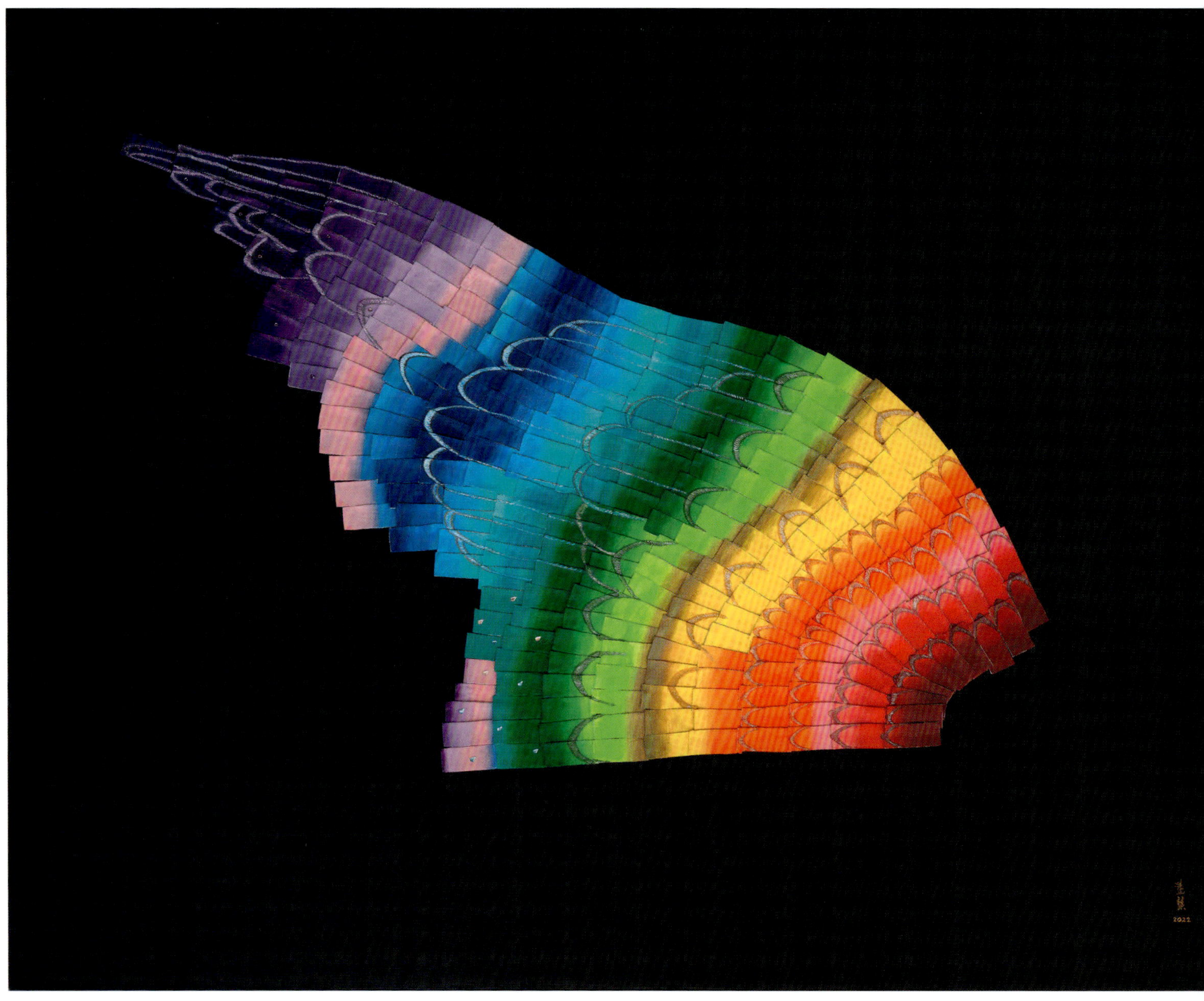

Blessing of the Night Sky
2022
Acrylic on Cowhide Leather
Set of two: 123 cm x 306 cm

Xiu Shi is a prolific Hong Kong writer and poet. He is currently the president of the Association of Hong Kong Poetry and the Editor in Chief of *The Roundtable: A Journal of Poetry and Poetics*. Among his many publications are the poetry collections *Snow Leopard* and *Seagull* and the critical essays 'The Pupa and the Butterfly' and 'Liu Ban Nong and His Poetry'.

Artworks: Leather Series

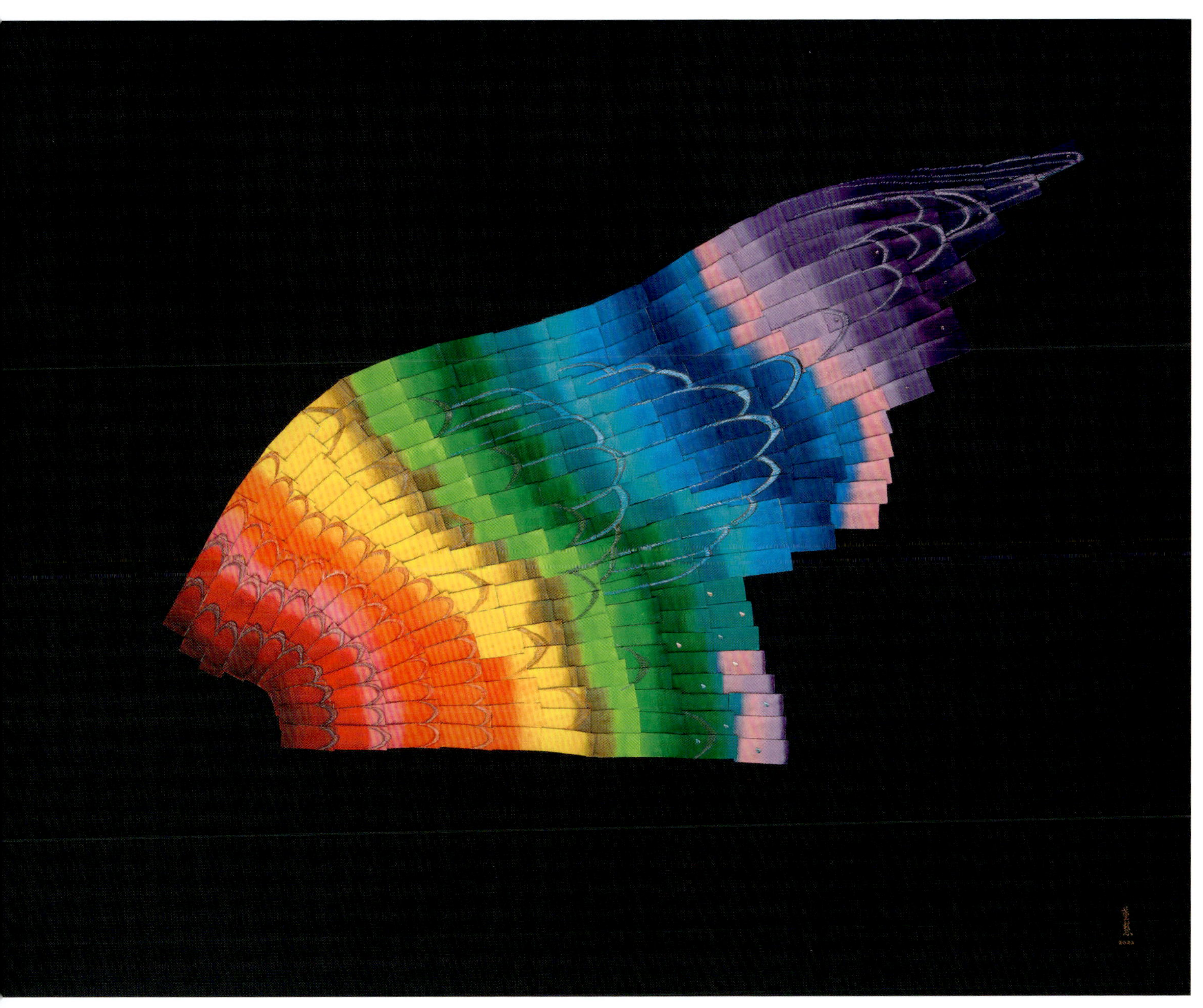

With hues precede,
taking flight in the form of wings,
Yet, such is the static source of light,
That veils the unseen flesh.

Xiu Shi

(Translated by Allen Zhuang)

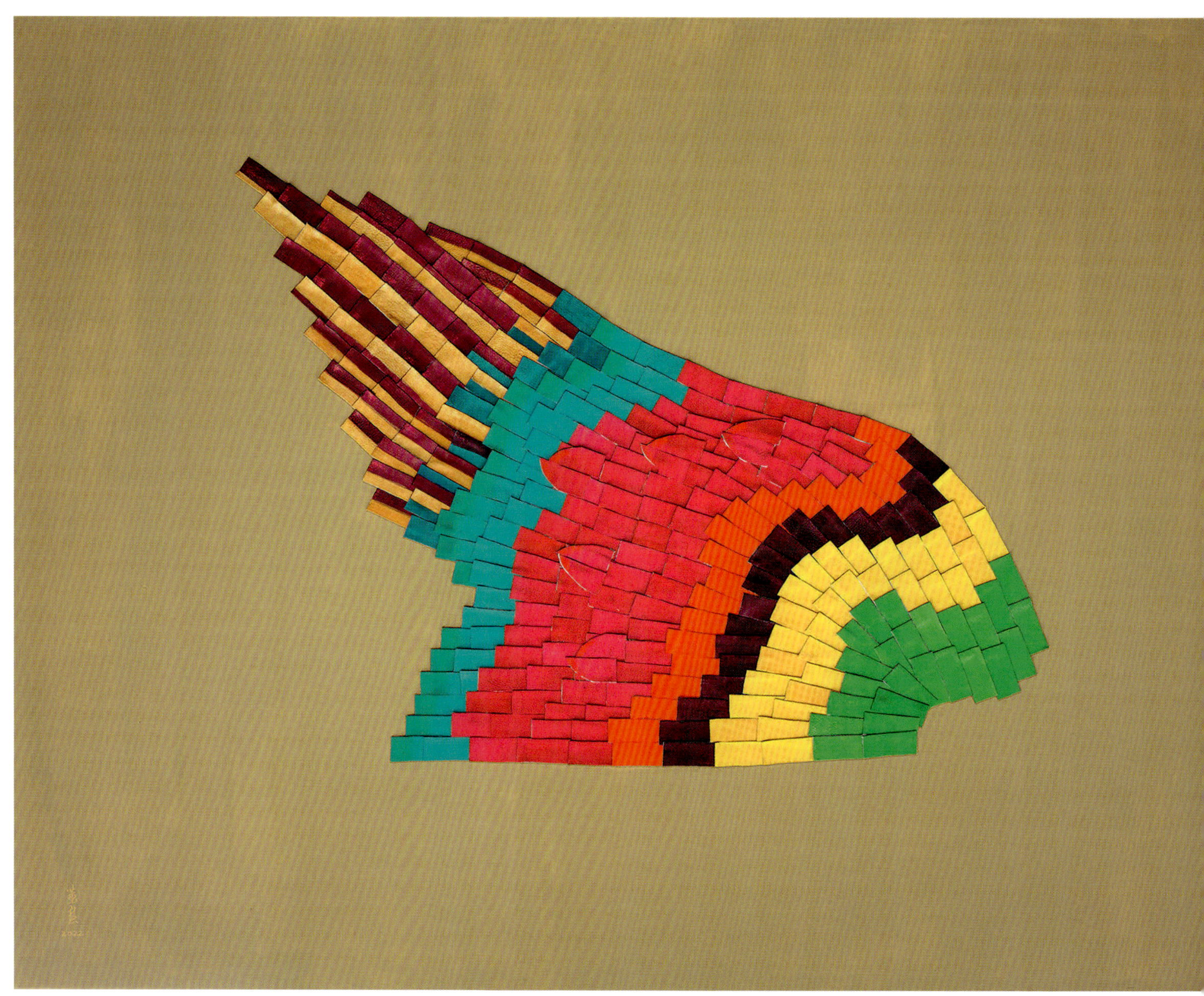

Blessing of the Earth
2022
Acrylic on Cowhide Leather
Set of two: 123 cm x 306 cm

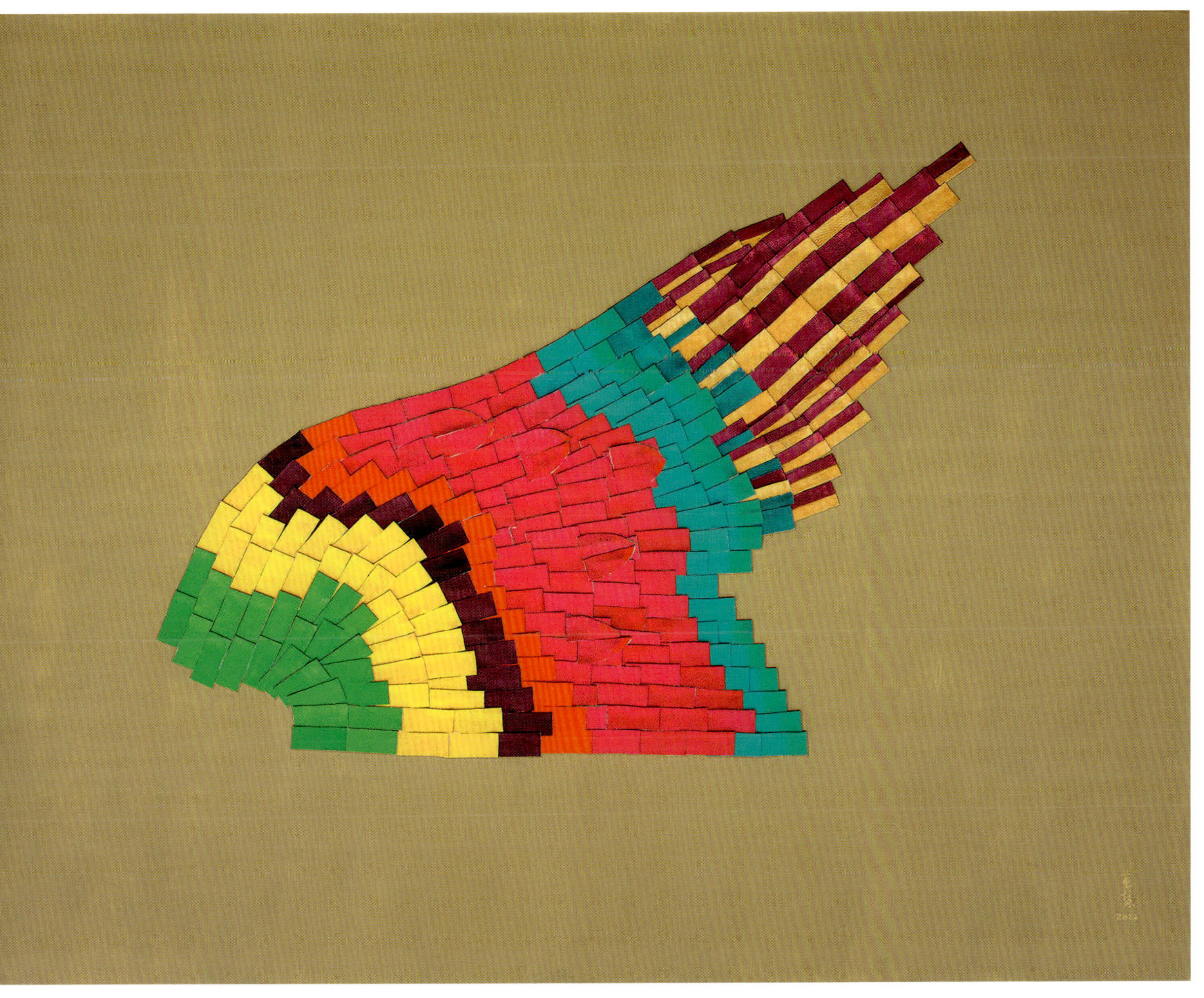

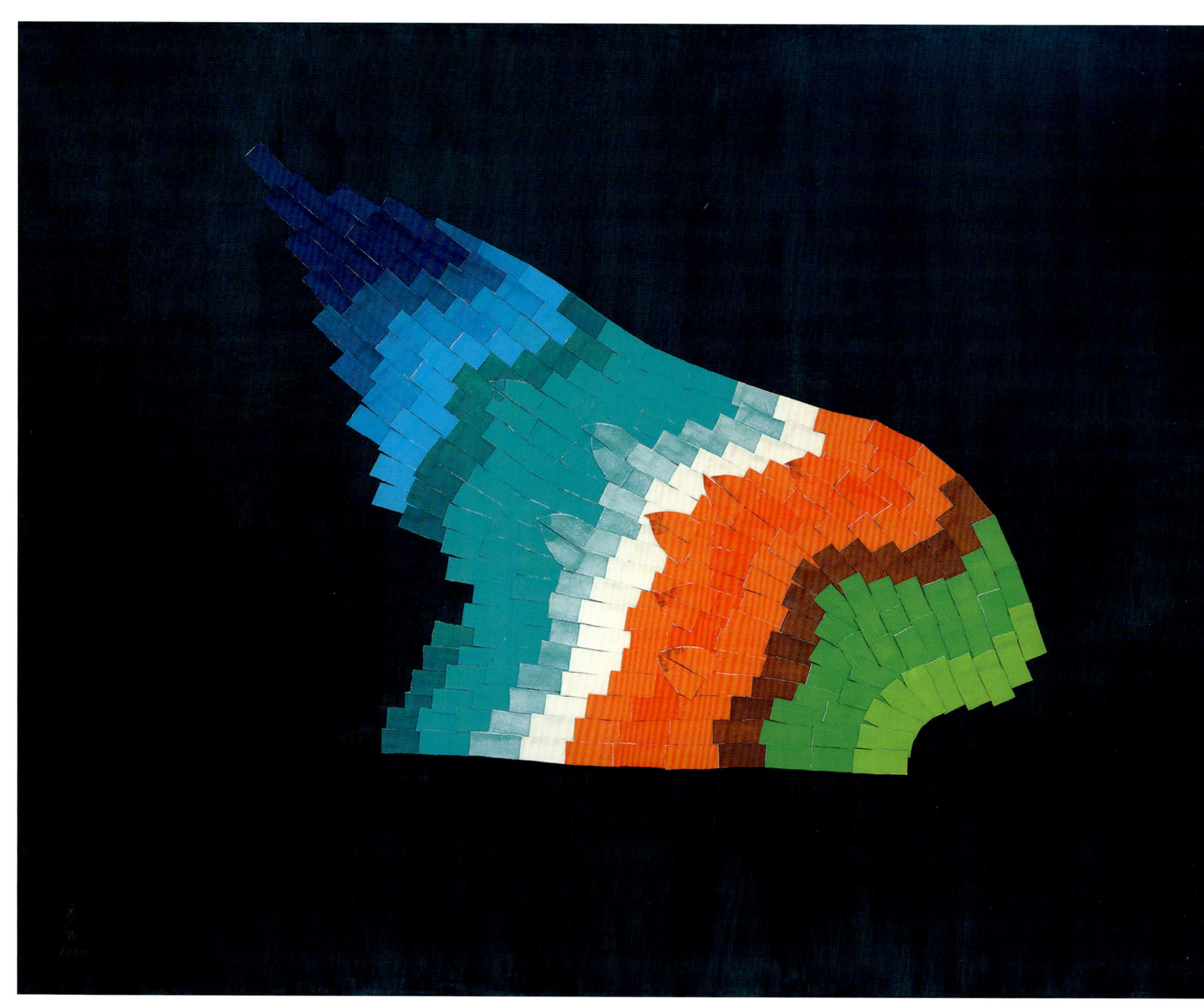

Blessing of the Ocean
2022
Acrylic on Cowhide Leather
Set of two: 123 cm x 306 cm

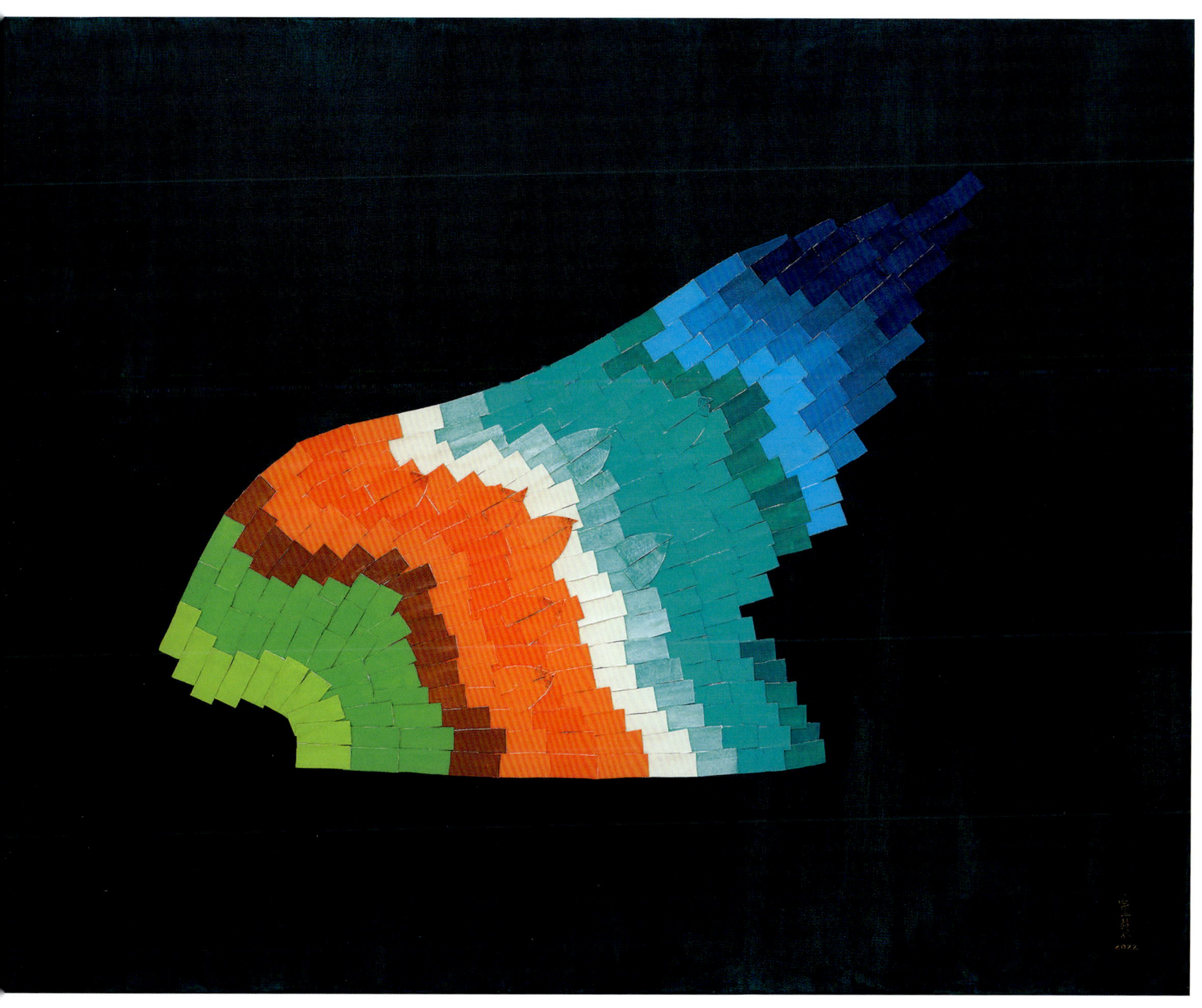

MADE IN HEAVEN

With winds and rains hiding away,
Vinaceous scene emanates words of God.
Familiar root words are getting e'er fainter.
A lucid soul has been brought to light.
A heavenly union!
You're here,
where I am meant to be.

He Jialin

(Translated by Allen Zhuang)

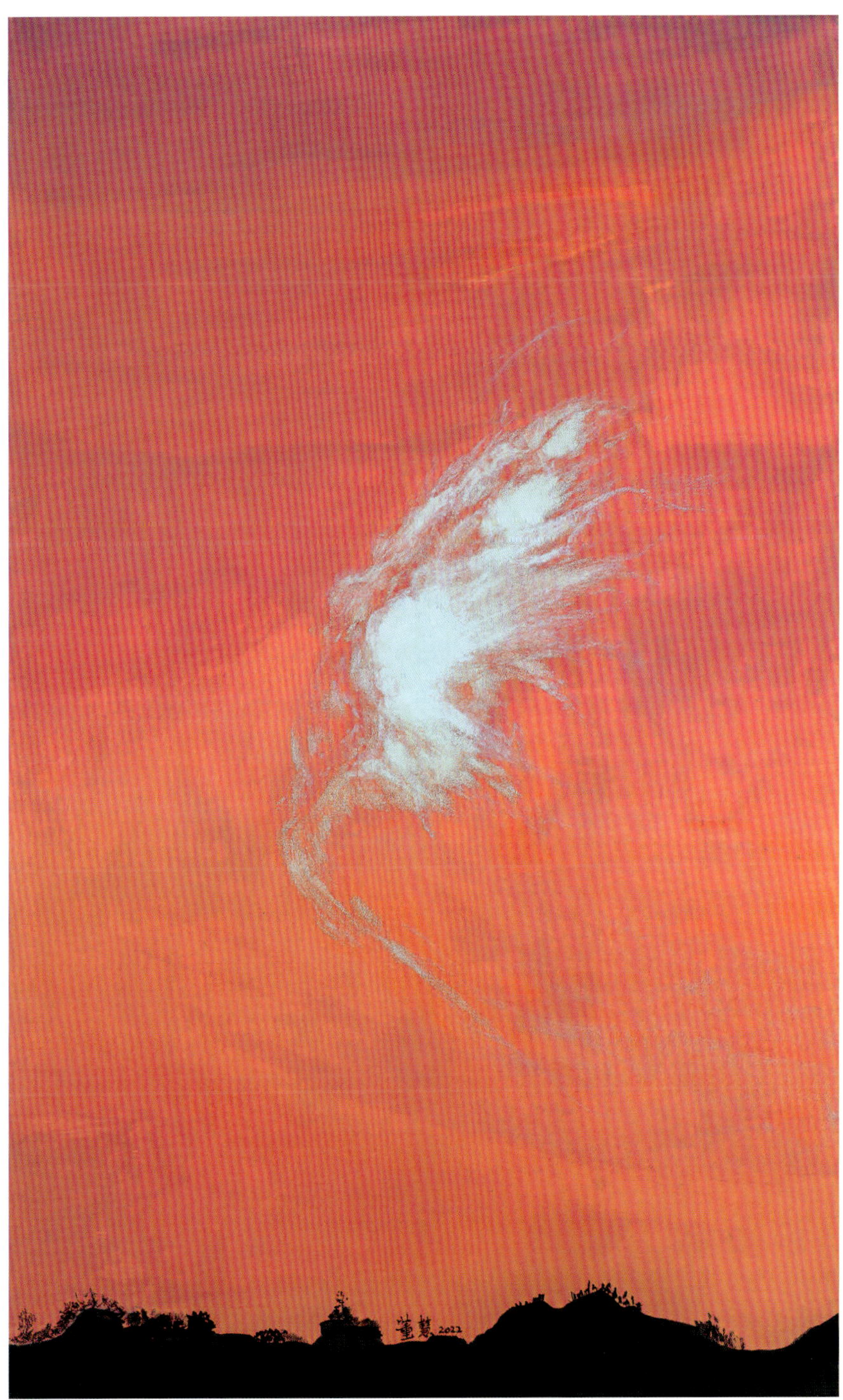

Made in Heaven
2022
Acrylic on Cowhide Leather
73.5 cm x 43.5 cm

Poetry celebrating objects takes single-minded gaze.
Faith in Violet, adrift above,
All the upward-looking points of view.

Xiu Shi

(Translated by Allen Zhuang)

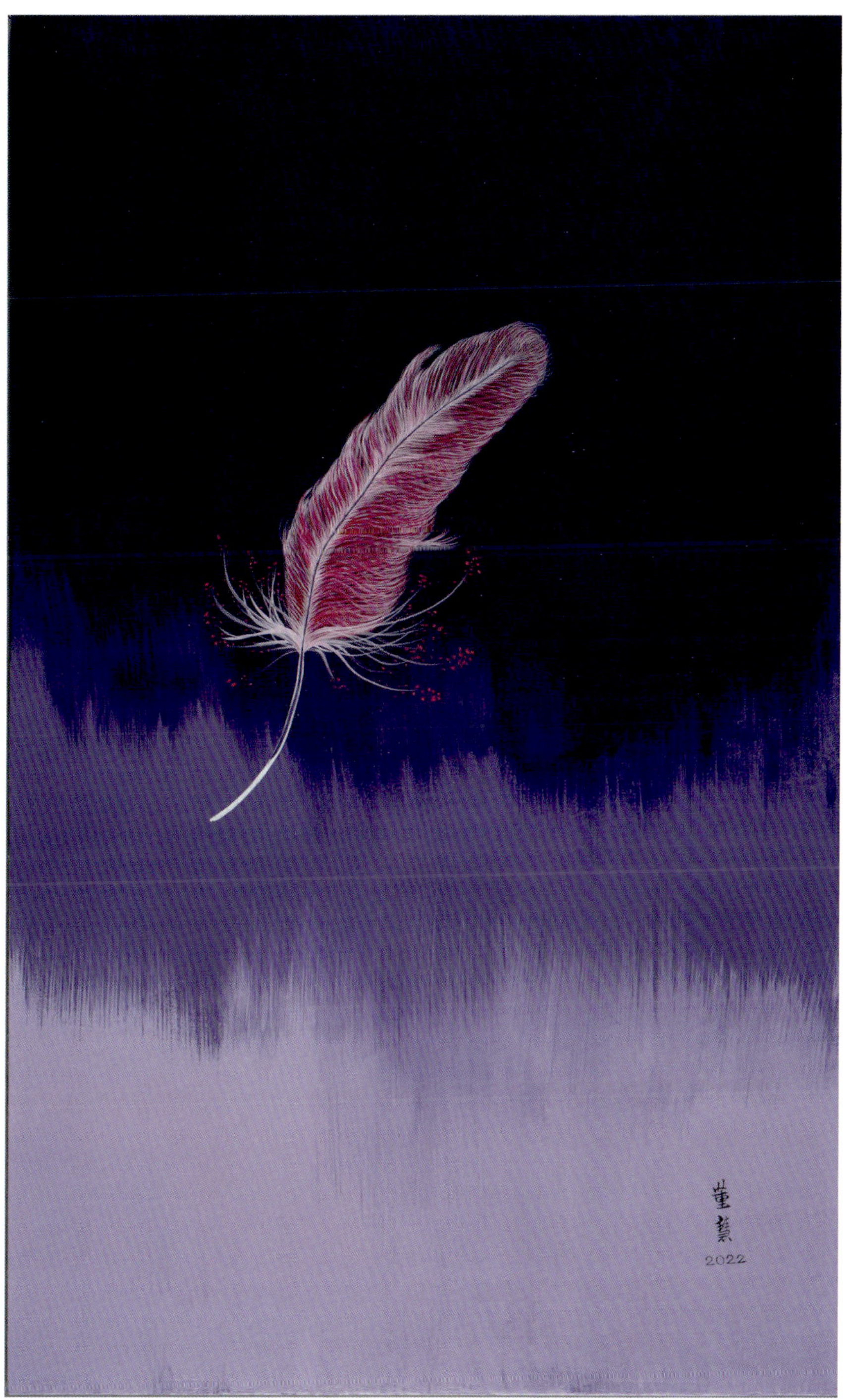

Sweet Memory (9)
2022
Acrylic on Cowhide Leather
73.5 cm x 43.5 cm

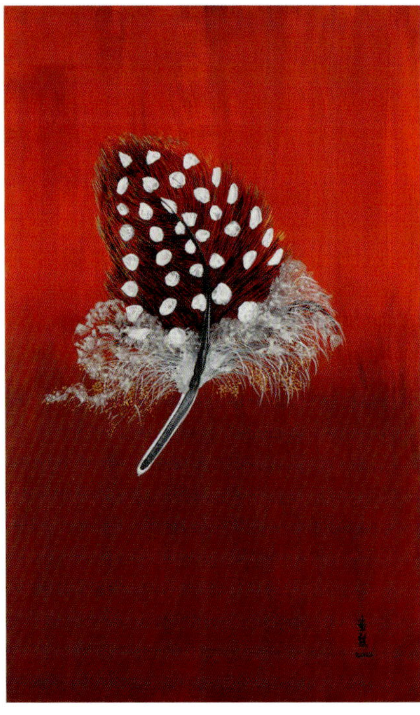

Sweet Memory (1)
2022
Acrylic on Cowhide Leather
73.5 cm x 43.5 cm

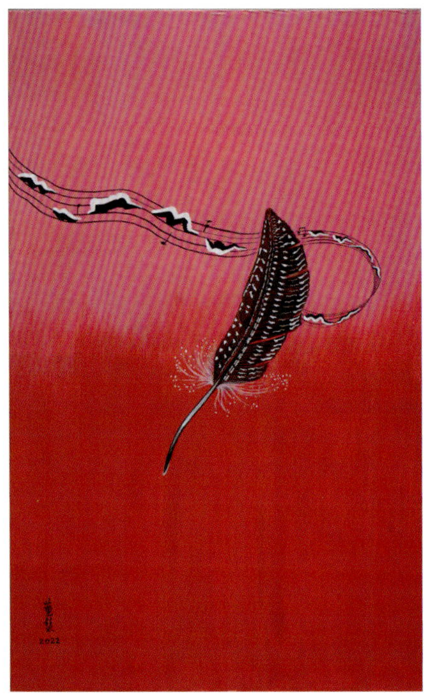

Sweet Memory (2)
2022
Acrylic on Cowhide Leather
73.5 cm x 43.5 cm

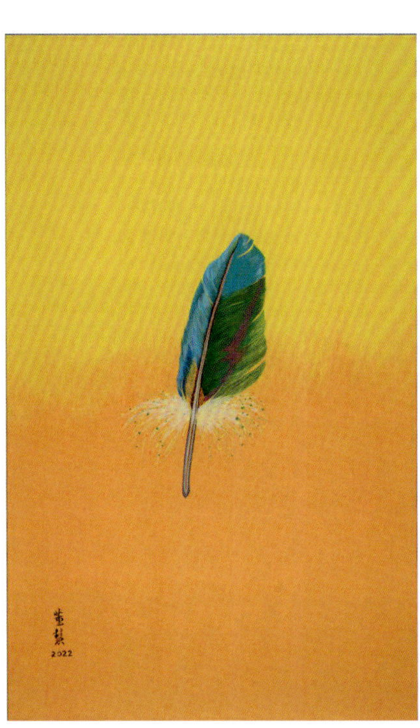

Sweet Memory (3)
2022
Acrylic on Cowhide Leather
73.5 cm x 43.5 cm

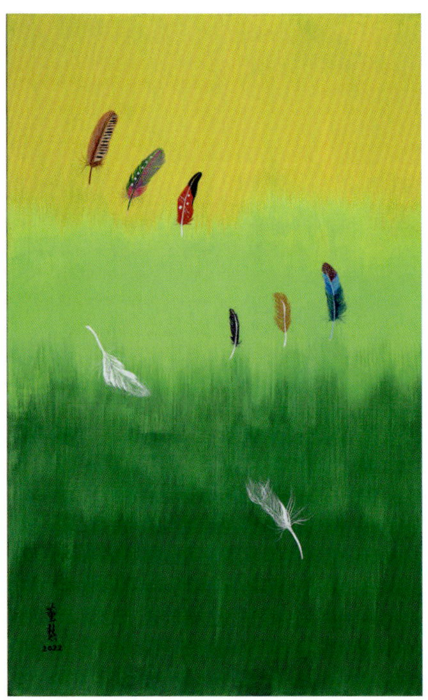

Sweet Memory (4)
2022
Acrylic on Cowhide Leather
73.5 cm x 43.5 cm

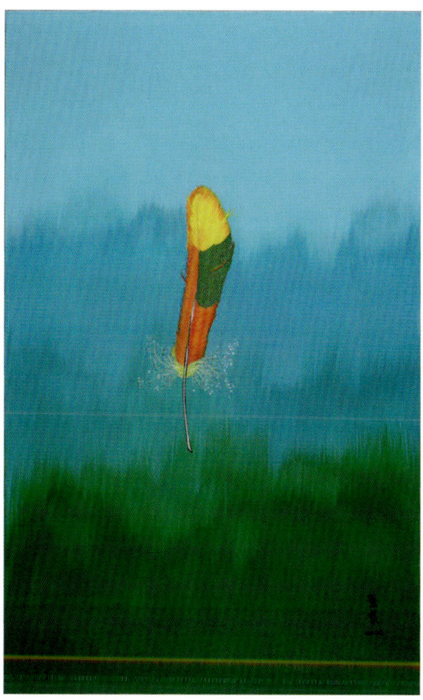

Sweet Memory (5)
2022
Acrylic on Cowhide Leather
73.5 cm x 43.5 cm

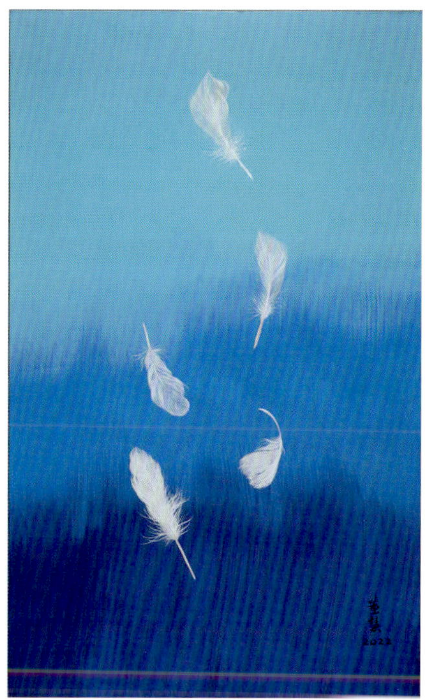

Sweet Memory (6)
2022
Acrylic on Cowhide Leather
73.5 cm x 43.5 cm

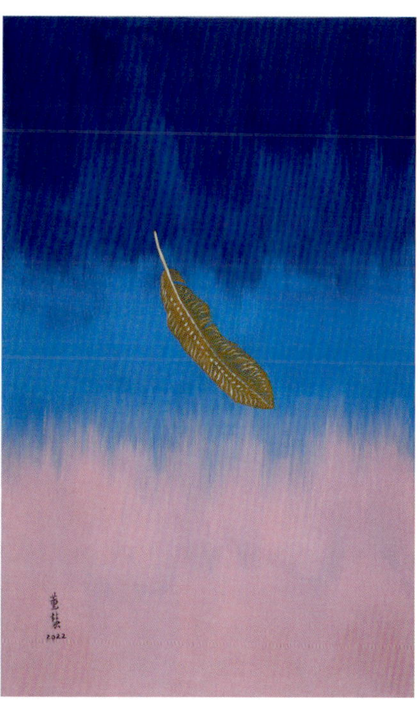

Sweet Memory (7)
2022
Acrylic on Cowhide Leather
73.5 cm x 43.5 cm

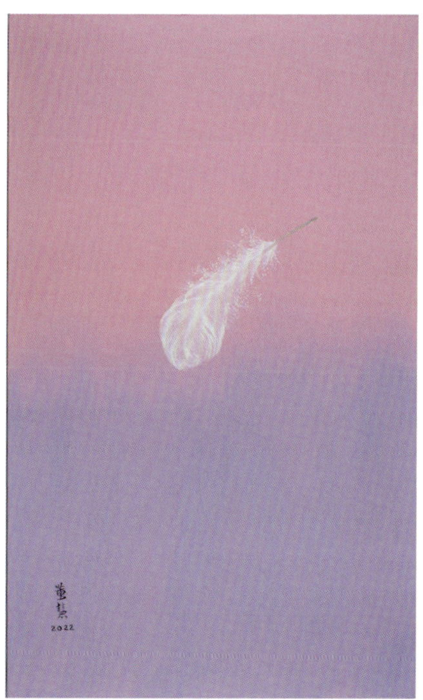

Sweet Memory (8)
2022
Acrylic on Cowhide Leather
73.5 cm x 43.5 cm

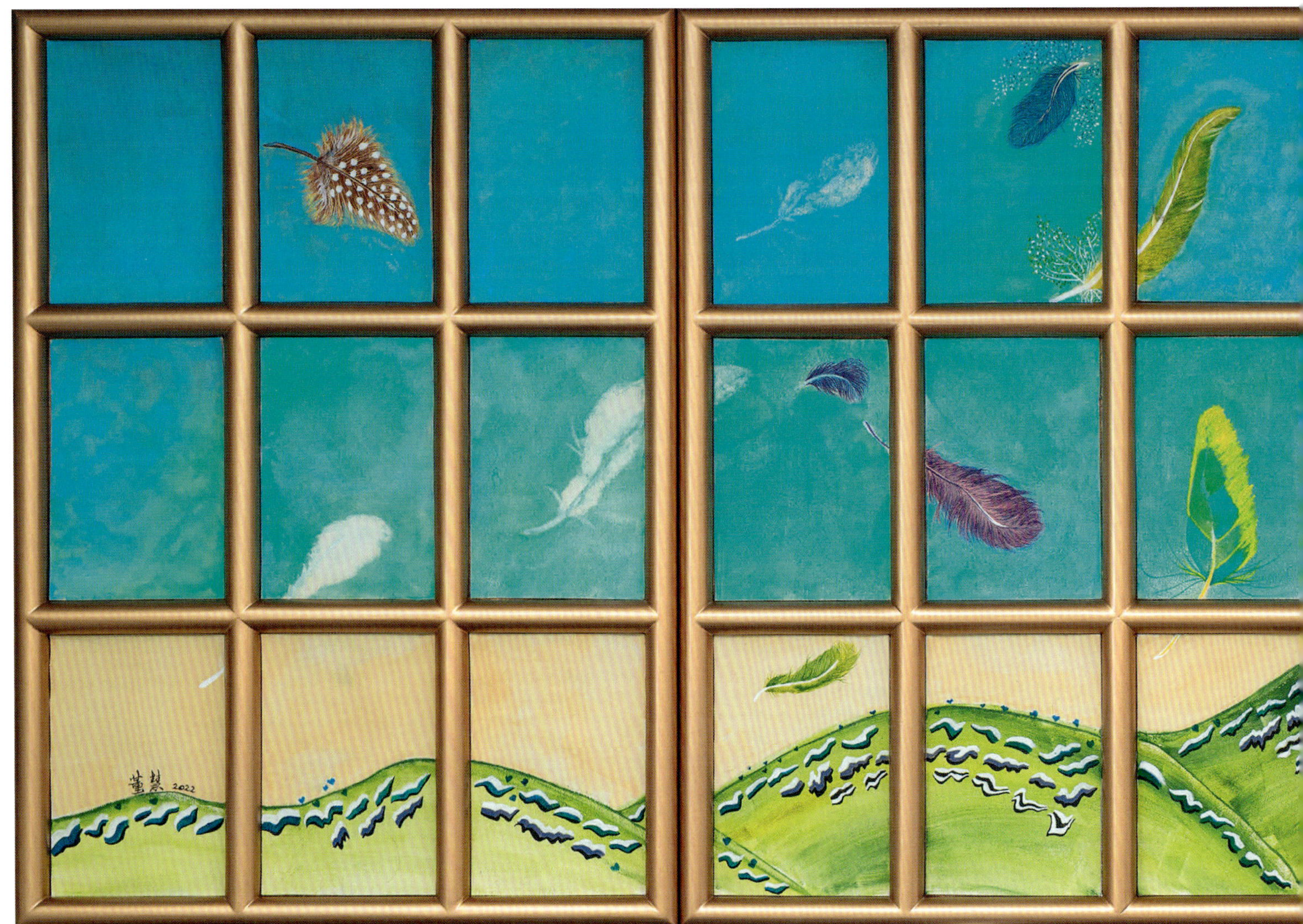

Playing Around
2022
Acrylic on Cowhide Leather
Quadriptych: 56 cm x 160 cm

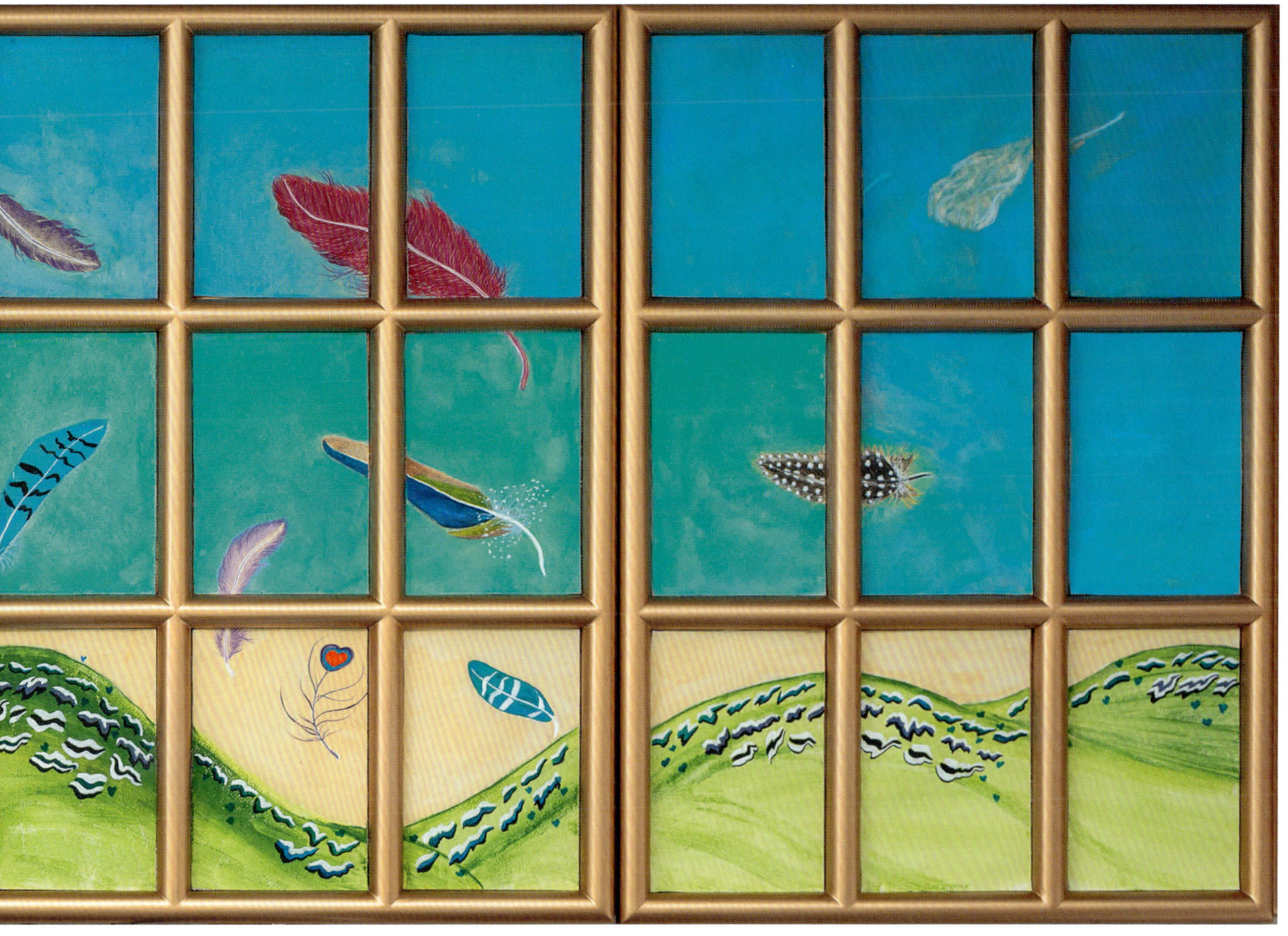

EXPLORING

Another three metres in the cold and it'll be Spring;
Verdant vines and branches climbed right o'er the wall.
Hope seems not far off.
How should I look for you?
Amid a concealed fate,
We continue to explore each other,
nearing each other.

He Jialin

(Translated by Allen Zhuang)

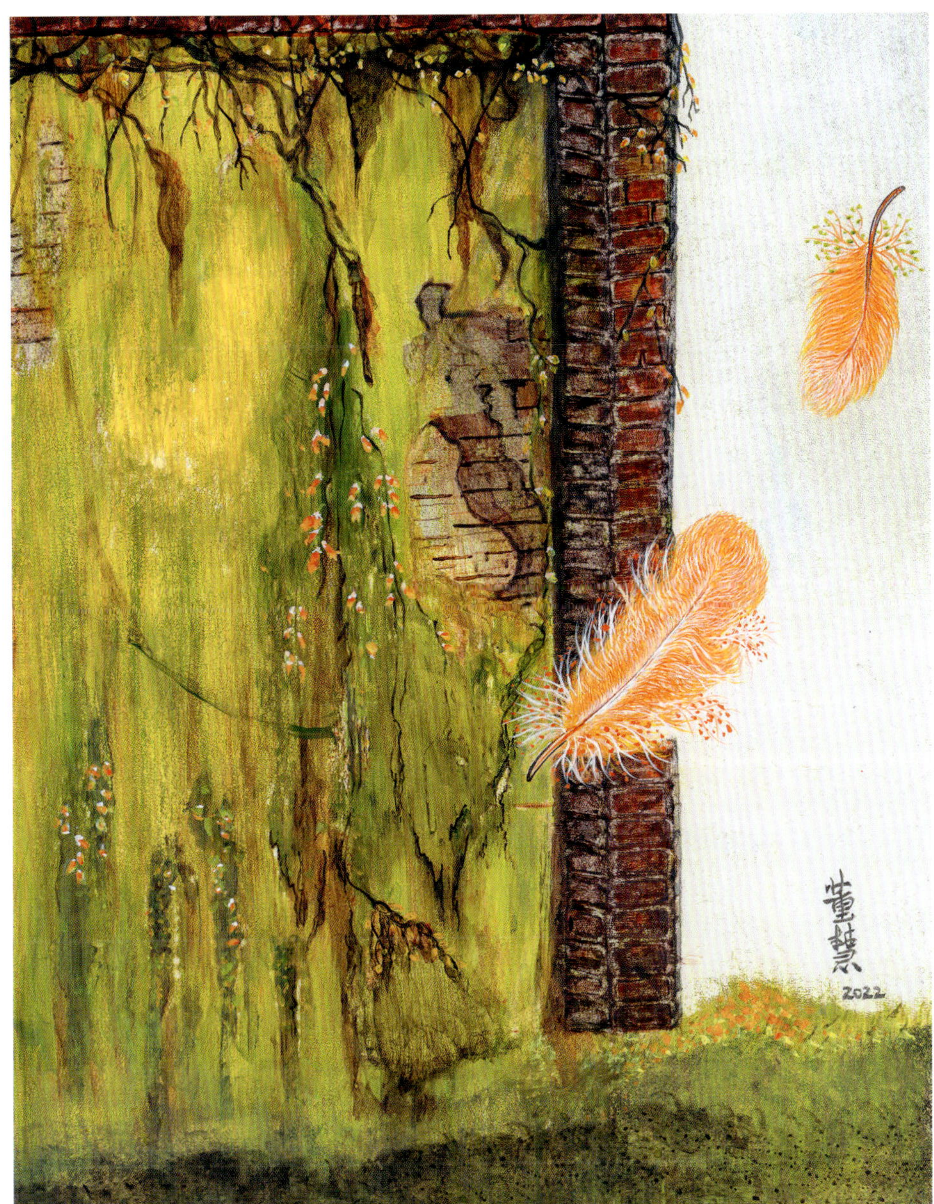

Exploration
2022
Acrylic on Cowhide Leather
38 cm x 28 cm

Unchained Melody
2021
Ink and Acrylic on Cowhide Leather
56 cm x 40 cm

In this series 'Unchained Melody', Christina Tung Wai cut up her intact leather works into segregated pieces and created new works from them, giving them a second life. The process of cutting up leather pieces symbolised the isolation and frustration felt by people during the pandemic, but once assembled and presented as unique artworks with meanings of their own, they were exalted as the vessels of hope – a hope that even if life separates us, we can still shine and perhaps reunite someday.

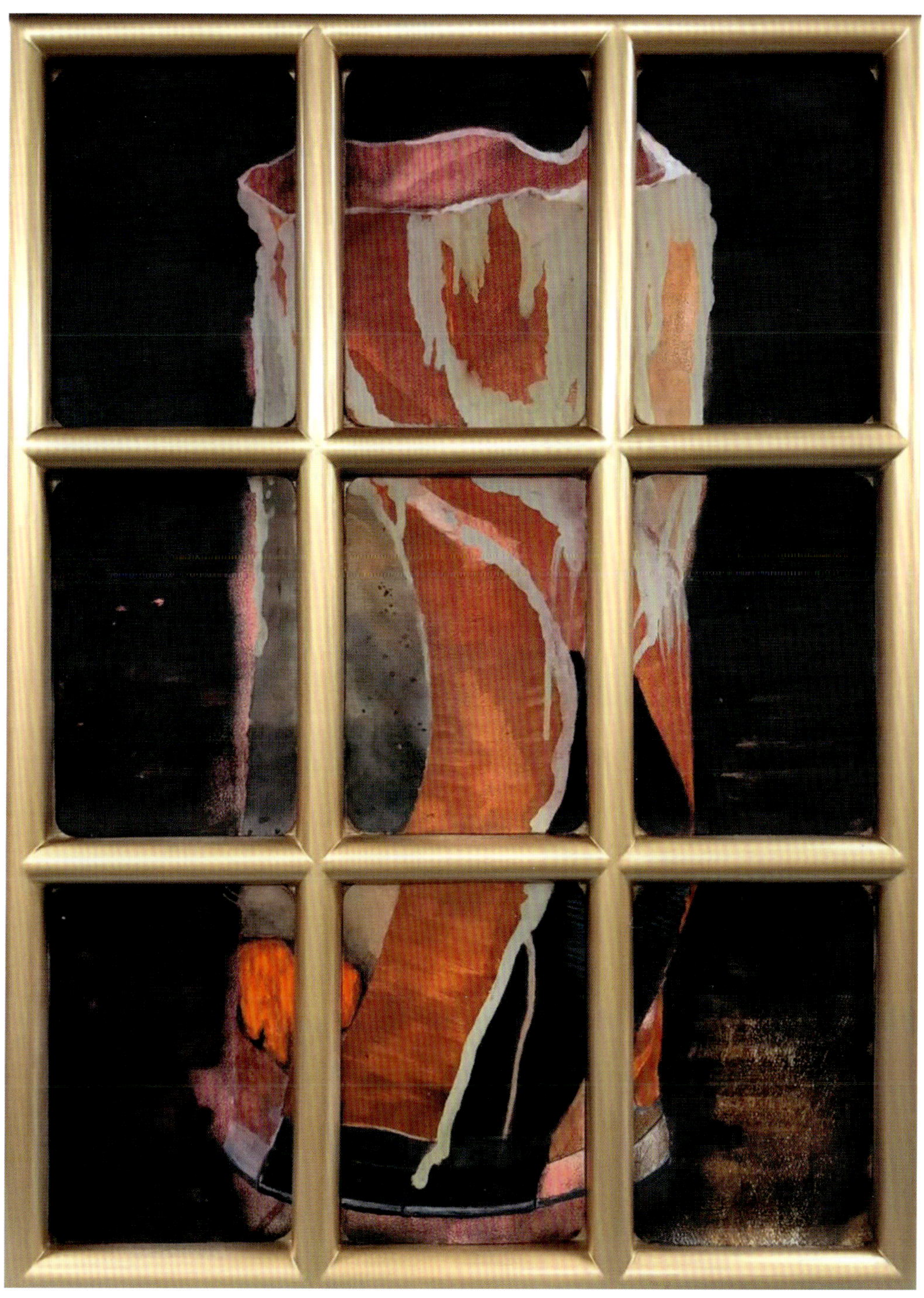

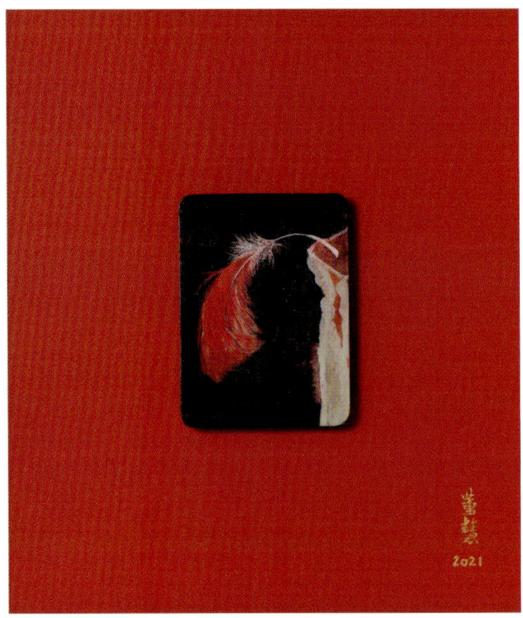

Unchained Melody (1)
2021
Ink and Acrylic on Cowhide Leather
41 cm x 34.5 cm

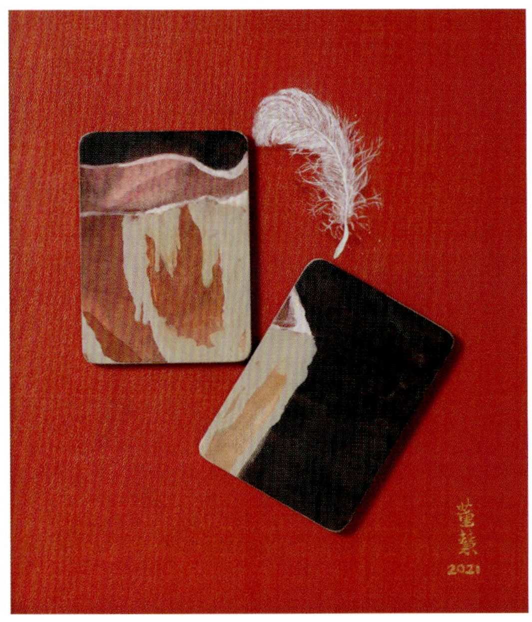

Unchained Melody (2)
2021
Ink and Acrylic on Cowhide Leather
41 cm x 34.5 cm

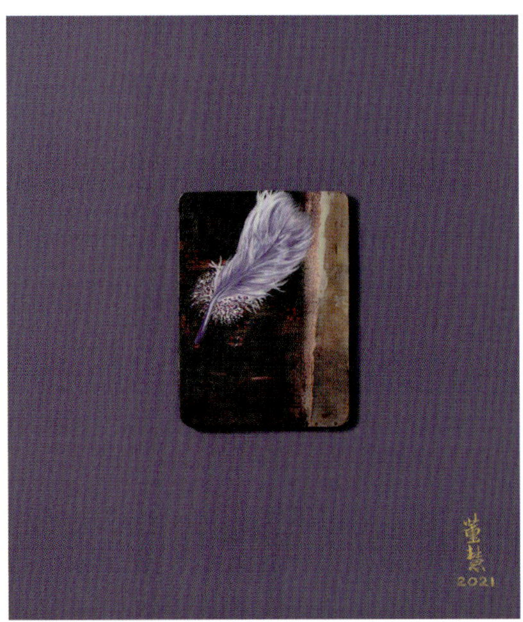

Unchained Melody (3)
2021
Ink and Acrylic on Cowhide Leather
41 cm x 34.5 cm

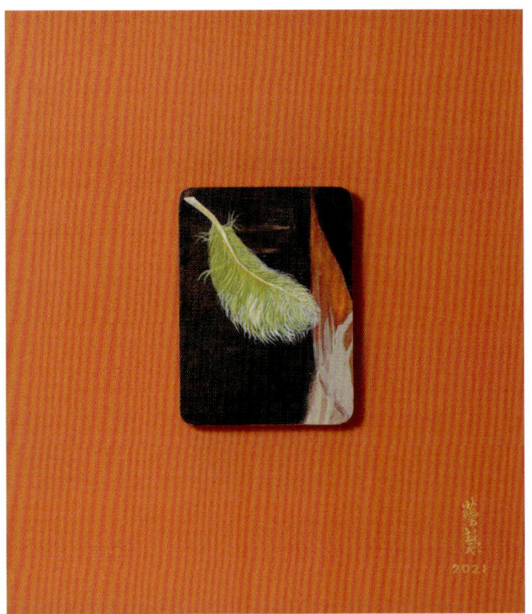

Unchained Melody (5)
2021
Ink and Acrylic on Cowhide Leather
41 cm x 34.5 cm

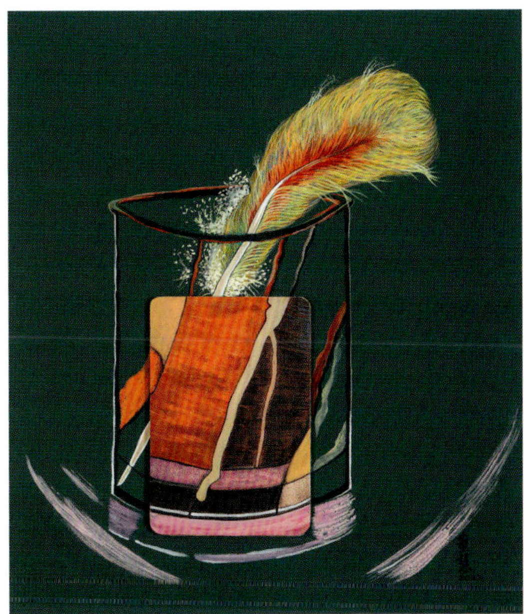

Unchained Melody (7)
2022
Acrylic on Cowhide Leather
41 cm x 34.5 cm

Unchained Melody (6)
2021
Ink and Acrylic on Cowhide Leather
41 cm x 34.5 cm

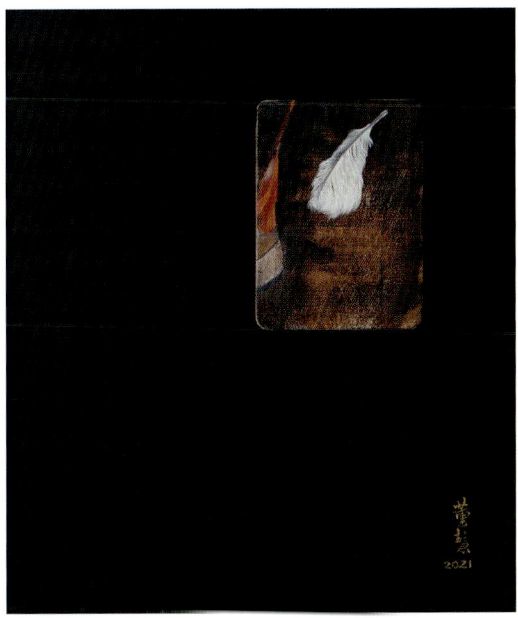

Unchained Melody (8)
2021
Ink and Acrylic on Cowhide Leather
41 cm x 34.5 cm

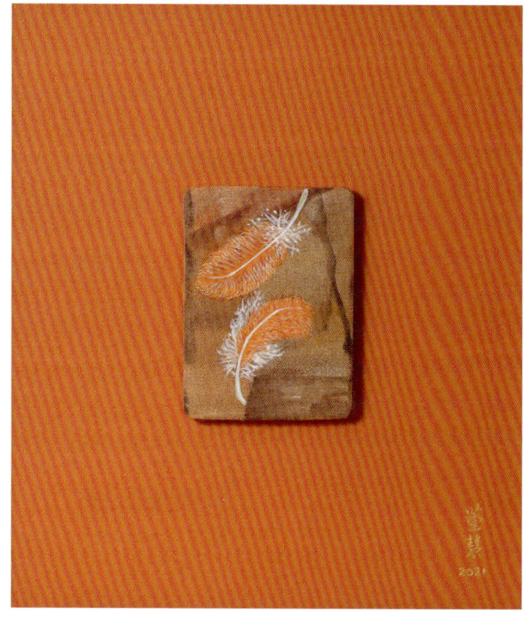

Hold on to Happiness
2021
Ink and Acrylic on Cowhide Leather
41 cm x 34.5 cm

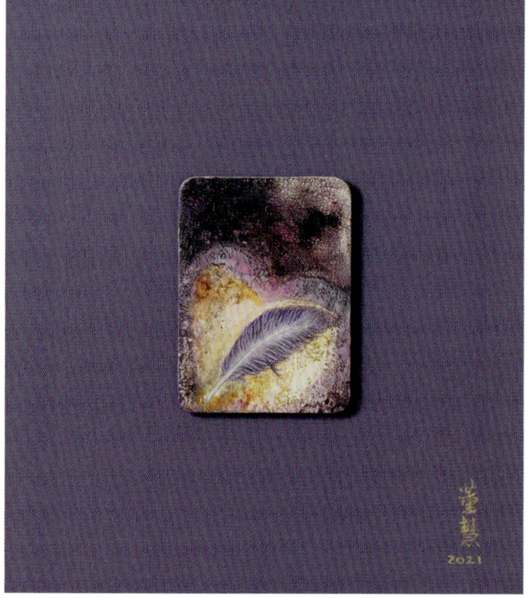

In Trance
2021
Ink and Acrylic on Cowhide Leather
41 cm x 34.5 cm

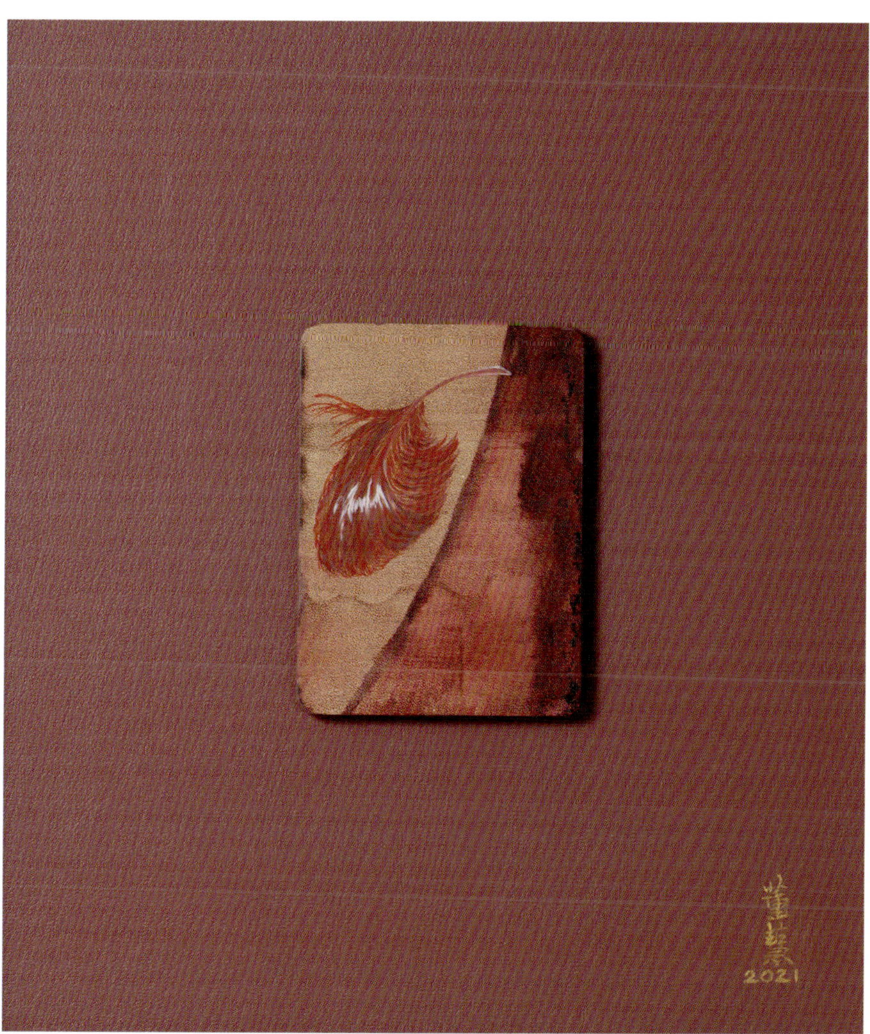

Amor
2021
Ink and Acrylic on Cowhide Leather
41 cm x 34.5 cm

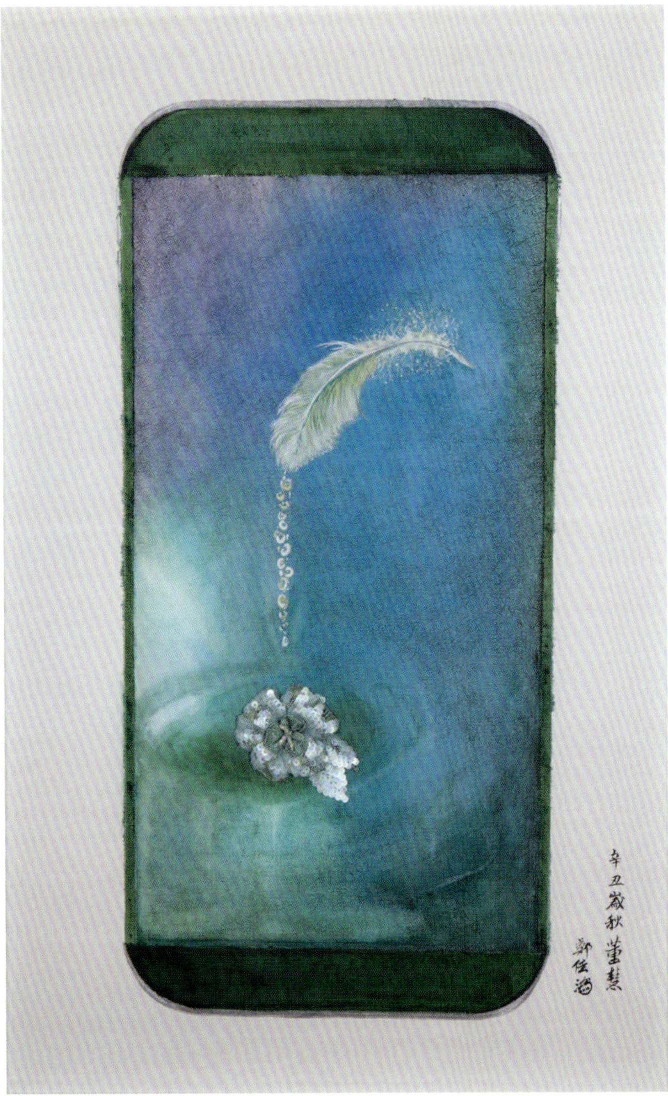

Art on Screen (1)
2021
Christina Tung Wai and Ava Cheng
Camellia Embroidery Jewellery Piece
Ink and Acrylic on Cowhide Leather
68.5 cm x 43.5 cm

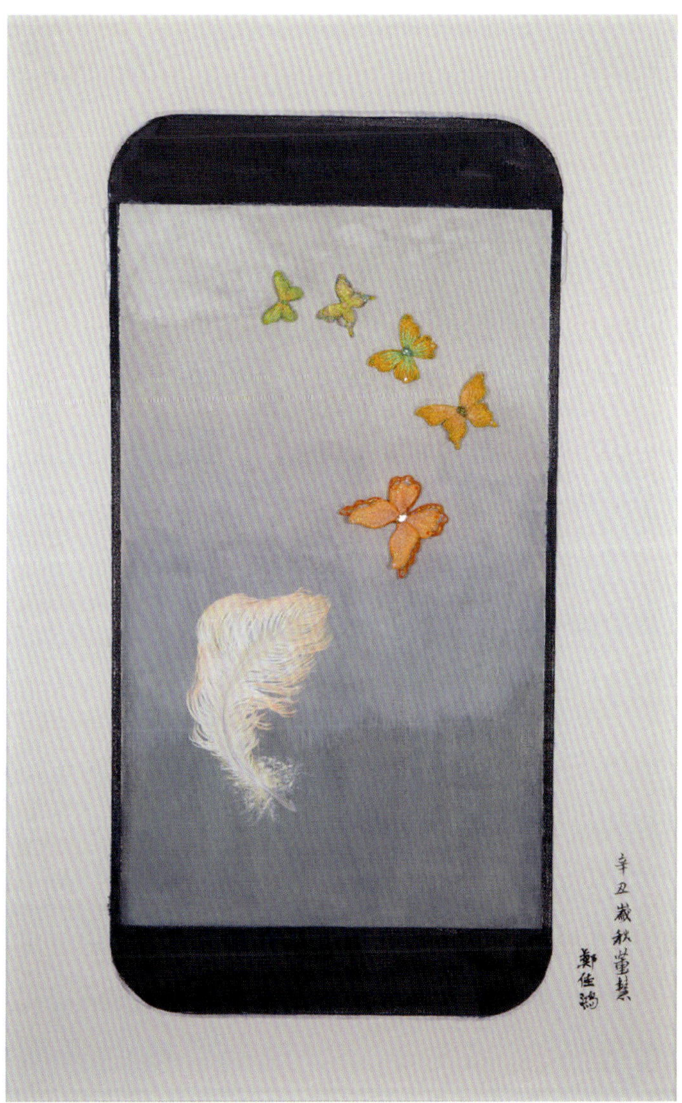

Art on Screen (2)
2021
Christina Tung Wai and Ava Cheng
Butterfly Embroidery Jewellery Piece
Ink and Acrylic on Cowhide Leather
68.5 cm x 43.5 cm

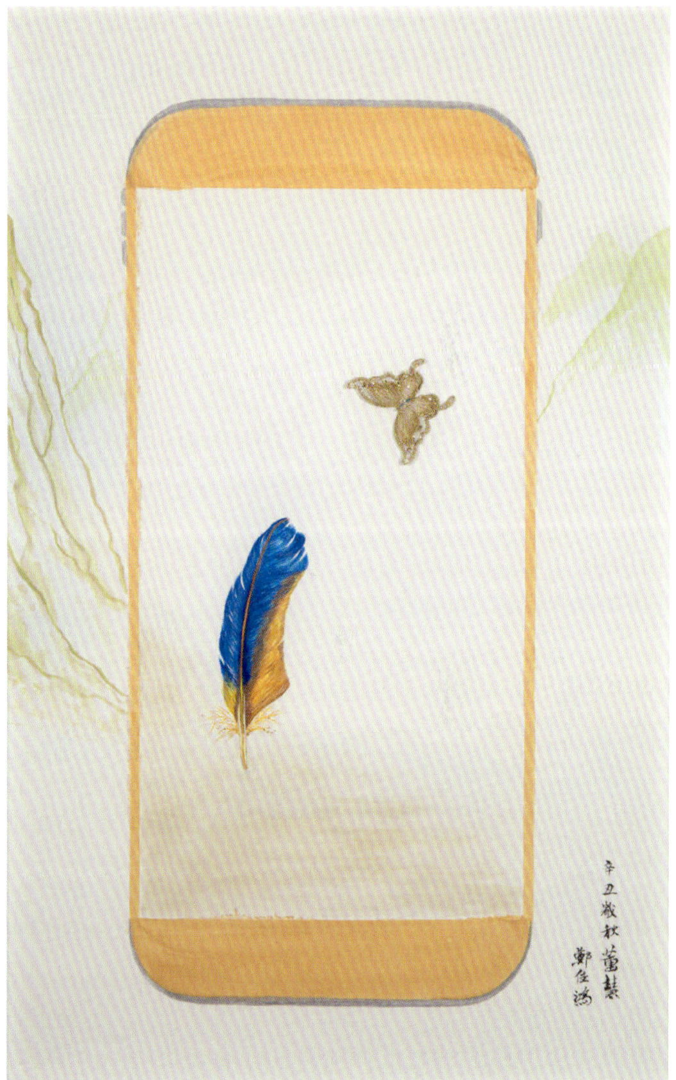

Art on Screen (3)
2021
Christina Tung Wai and Ava Cheng
Butterfly Embroidery Jewellery Piece
Ink and Acrylic on Cowhide Leather
68.5 cm x 43.5 cm

All I Have to Do is Dream
2021
Ink and Acrylic on Cowhide Leather
123 cm x 153 cm

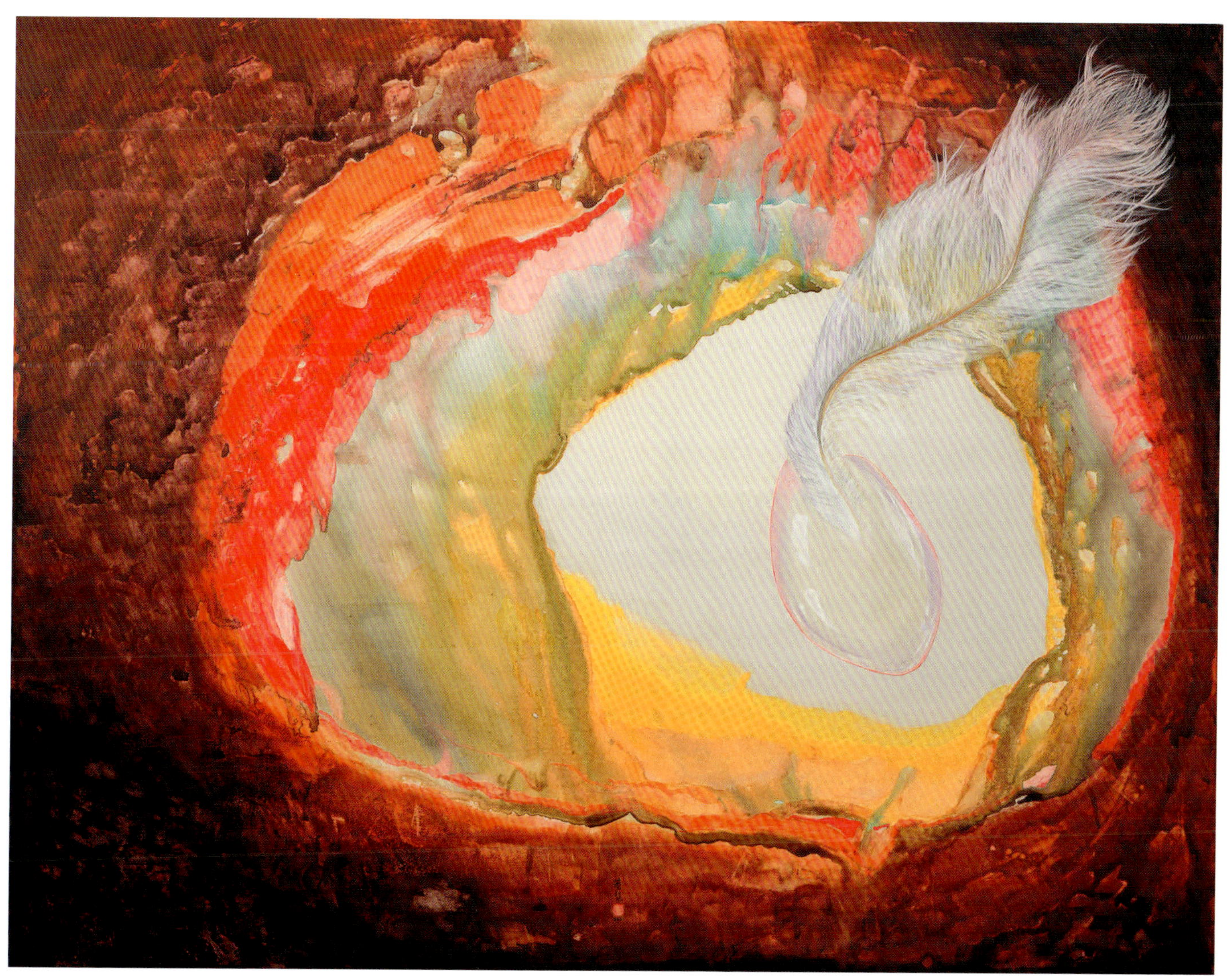

A Wintry Ballet (1) (2) (4) (3) (Clockwise)
2021
Ink and Acrylic on Cowhide Leather
31.5 cm x 31.5 cm each

During the pandemic, Christina Tung Wai created 'A Wintry Ballet' series for her own entertainment while being confined at home. She transformed feathers into ballet dancers and staged a production of *Swan Lake* ballet, satisfying her craving for watching theatrical performances.

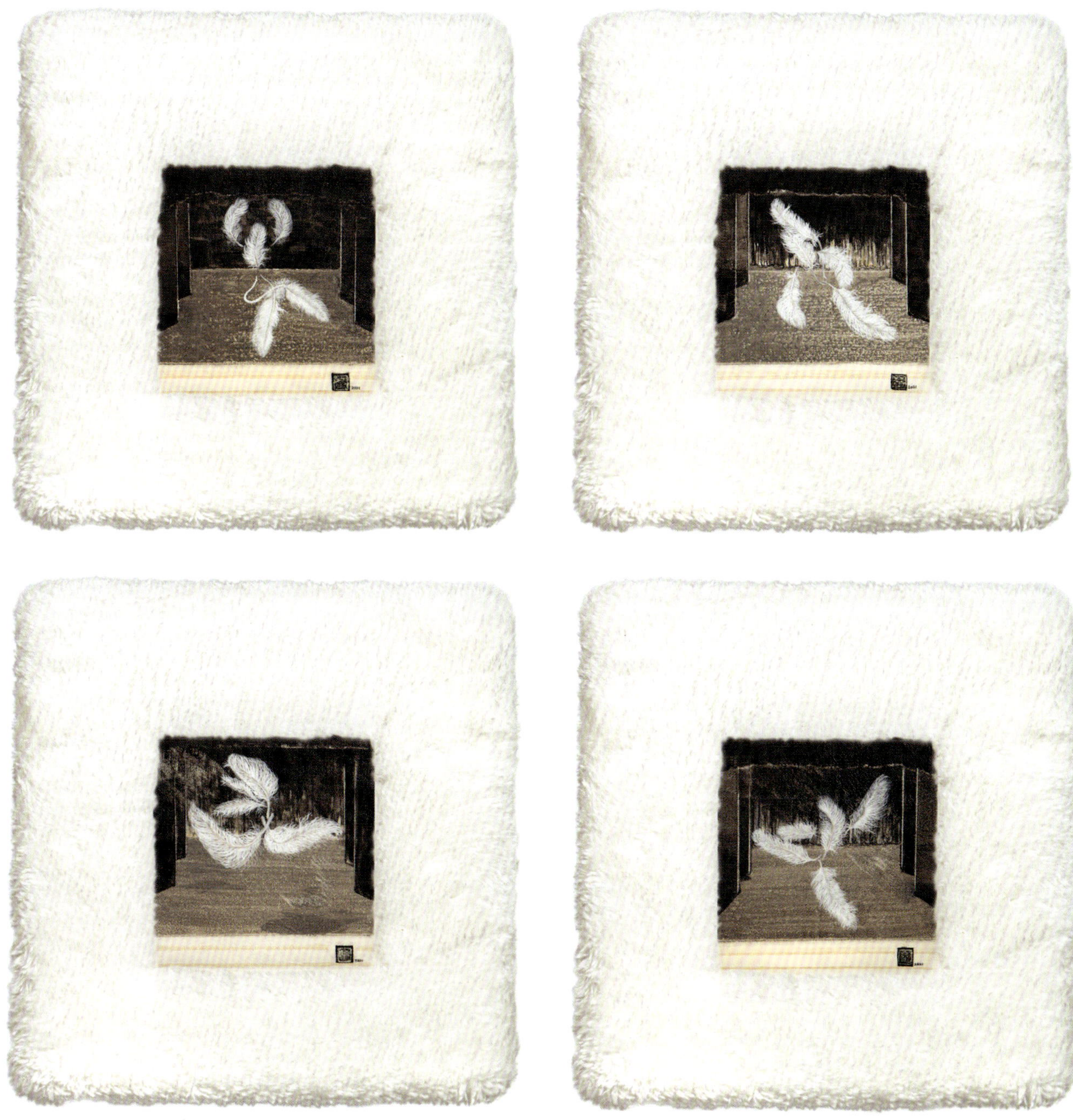

Home Is Where The Heart Is – Tides at Qiantang River Series
2024
Mixed Media on Paper
125 cm x 74 cm

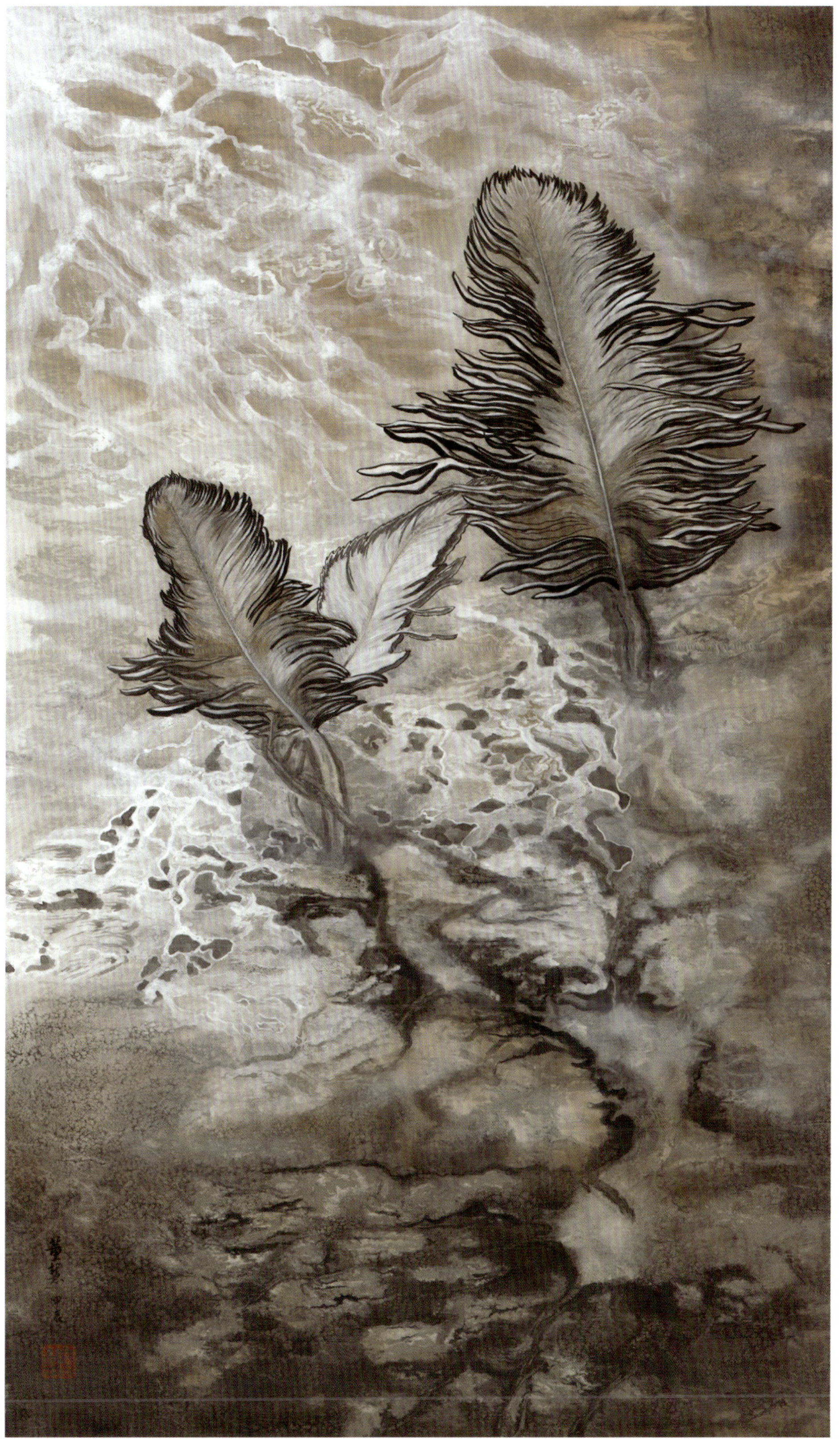

Resonance – Tides at Qiantang River Series
2024
Mixed Media on Paper
28 cm x 46 cm

Artworks: Flimsy Paper

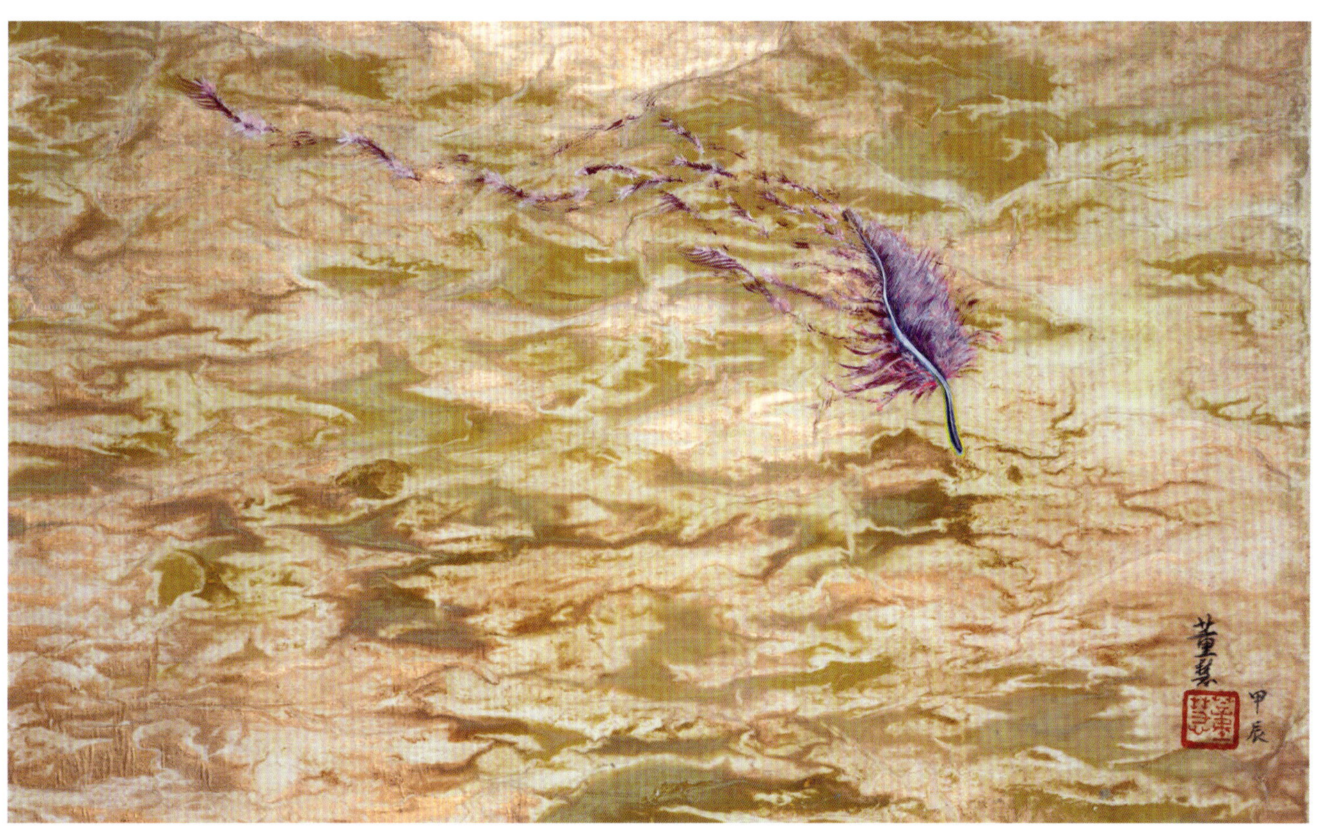
甲辰

Metamorphosis – Tides at Qiantang River Series
2024
Mixed Media on Paper
60 cm x 58 cm

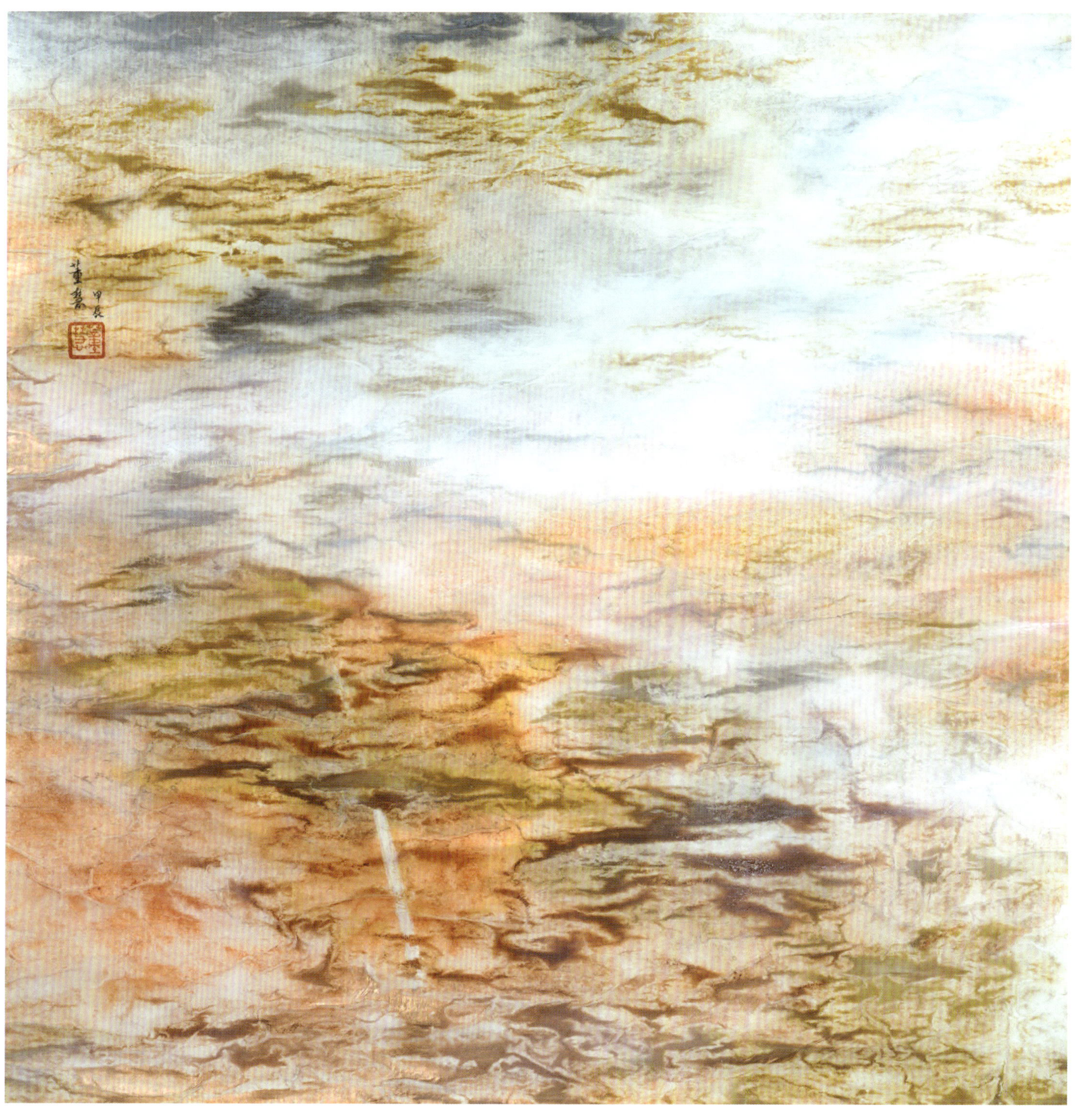

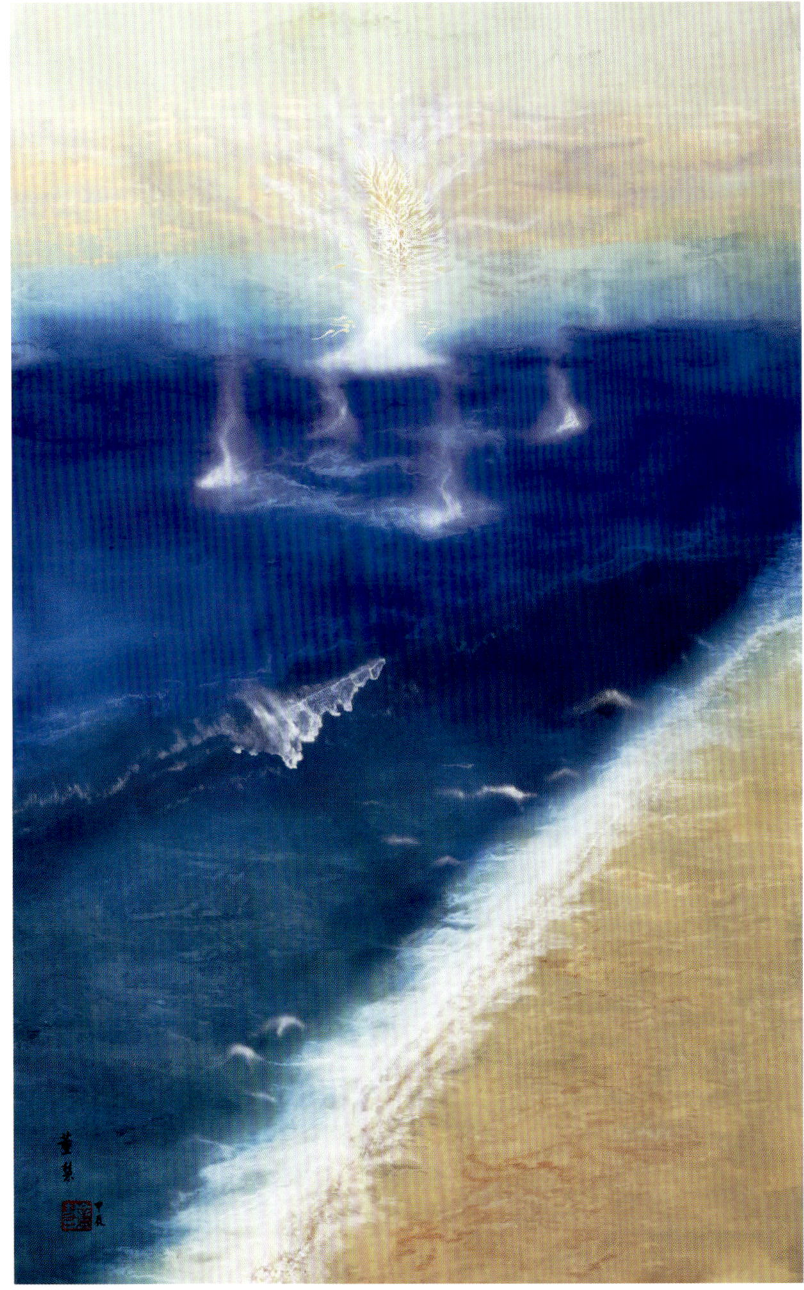

Tribulations
2024
Mixed Media on Paper
117 cm x 77 cm

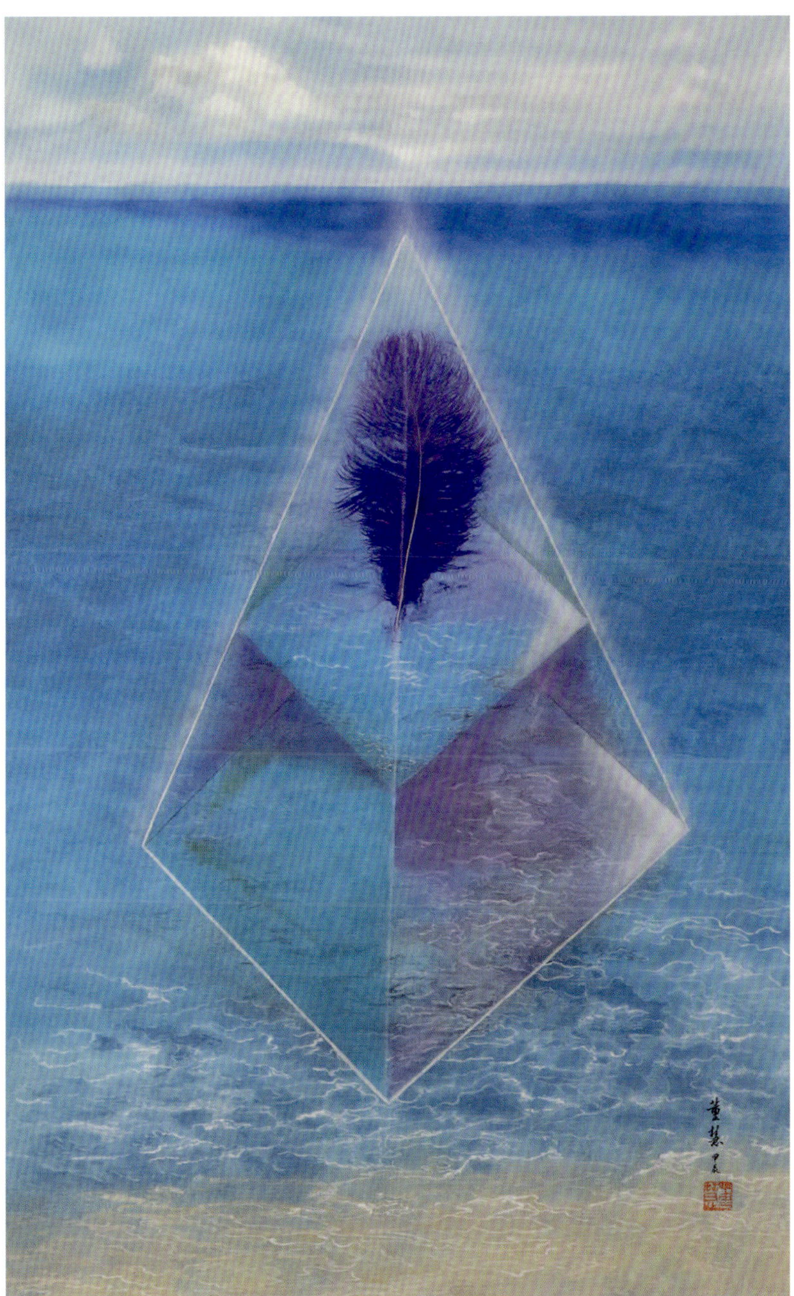

Virtues of Water
2024
Mixed Media on Paper
117 cm x 71 cm

Close to You
2022
Mixed Media on Paper
50 cm x 64 cm

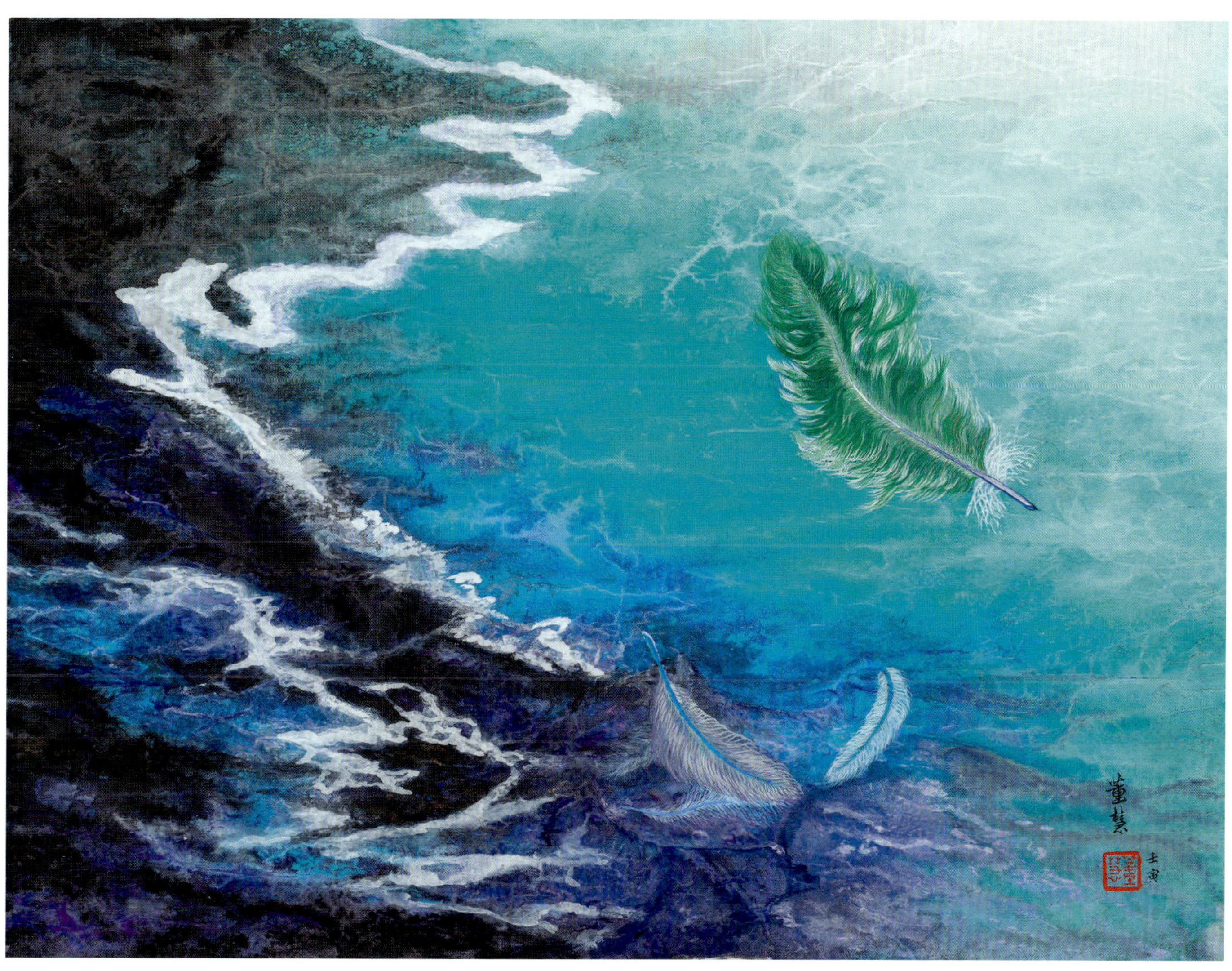
董慧
壬寅

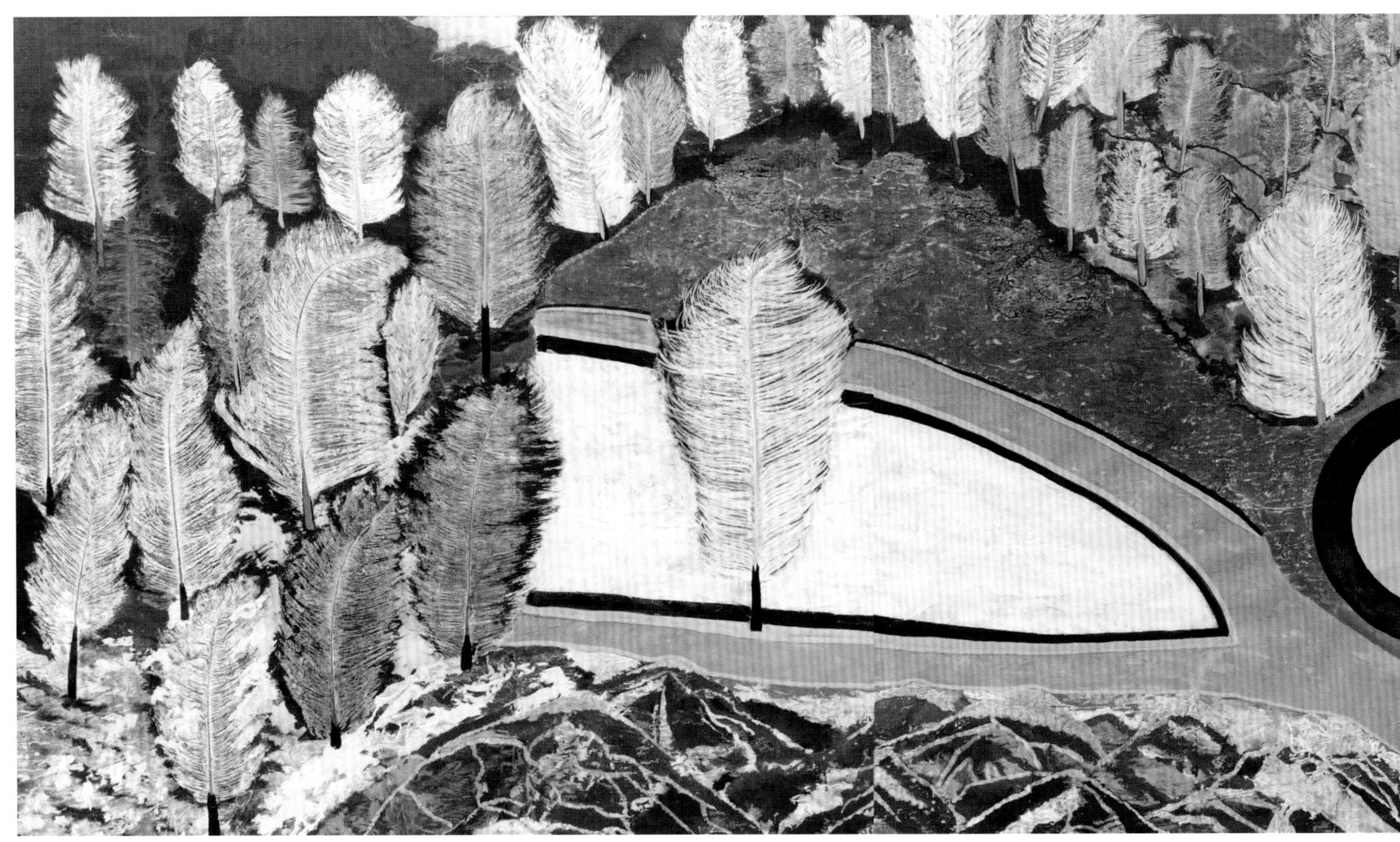

Paving New Paths
2022
Mixed Media on Paper
Quadriptych: 120 cm x 406 cm

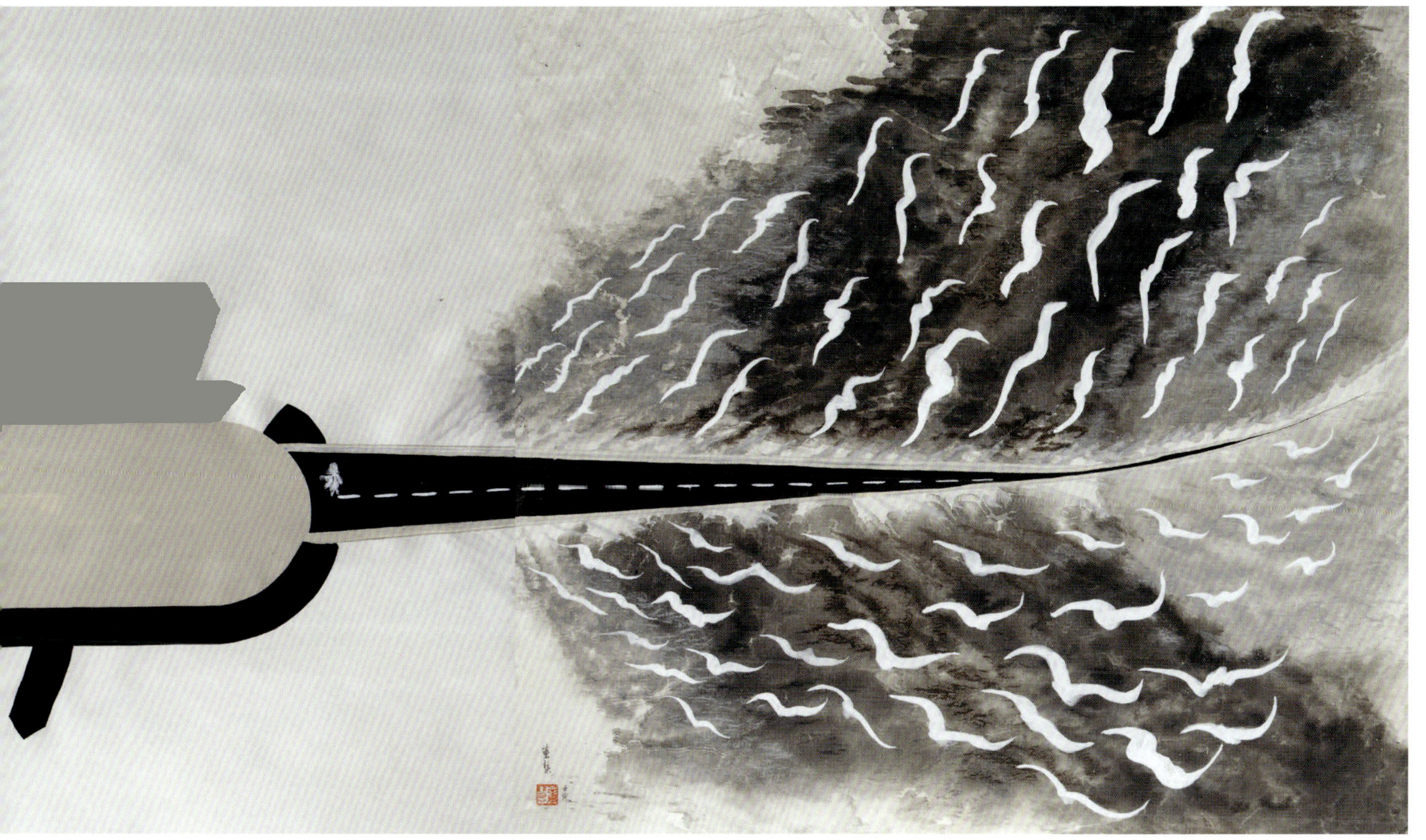

Reflection from Christina

The heaven and the earth, and everything between them is destined to follow a certain order, while we as humans have the luxury of making our own choices and paths. When faced with adversity, we have to pull through and carve out a niche of our own.

Frozen Echoes
2022
Mixed Media on Paper
73 cm x 102 cm

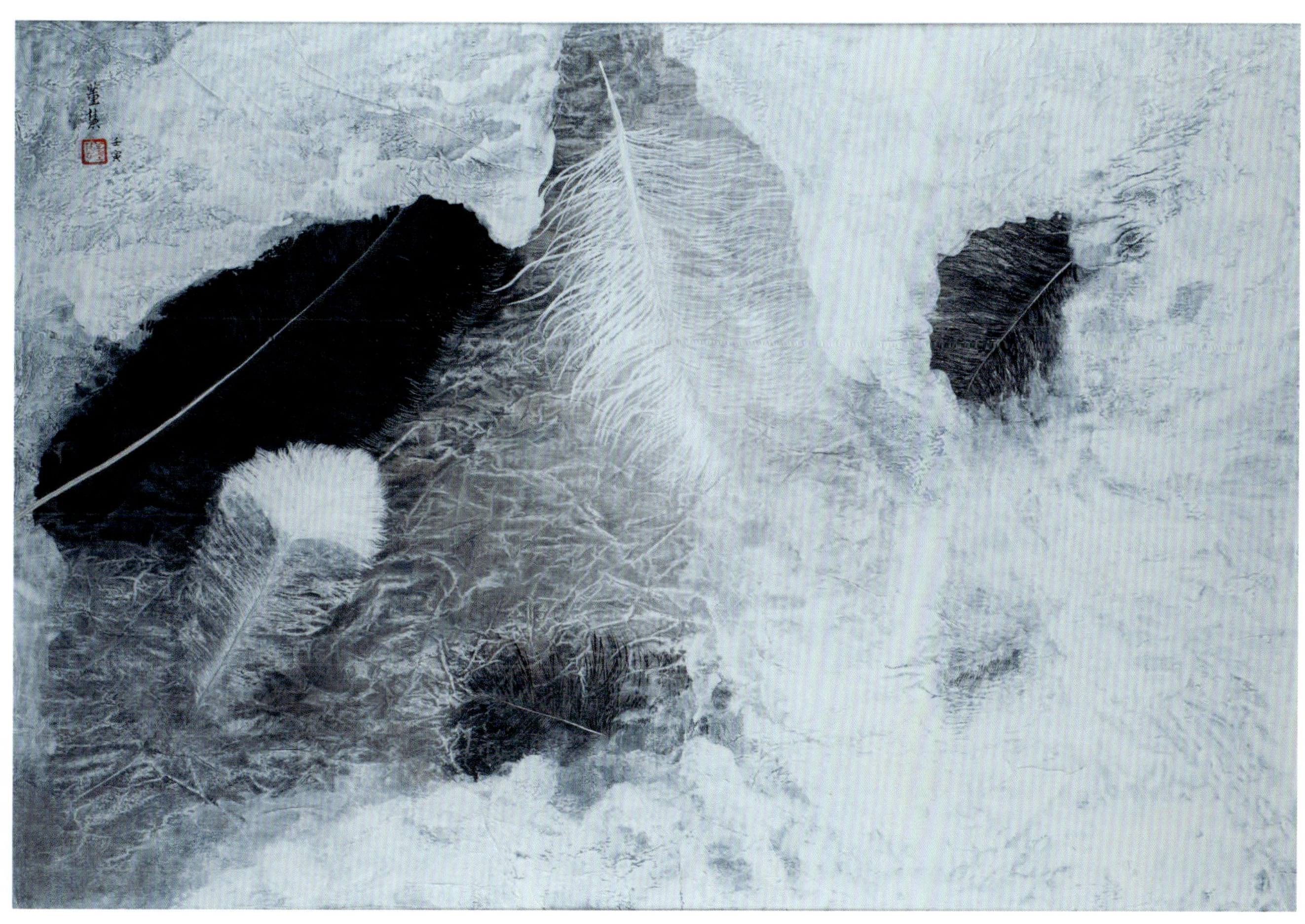

Beyond
2022
Mixed Media on Paper
127 cm x 95 cm

The work 'Beyond' is inspired by the Beijing 2022 Winter Olympics. Christina Tung Wai took the initiative to personify the feather and portrayed it as a forest. If feathers can go beyond their limitations and realise their potential, why can't humans do the same? This work reflects how humans are nothing but specks of dust in the universe, encouraging viewers to push themselves no matter what.

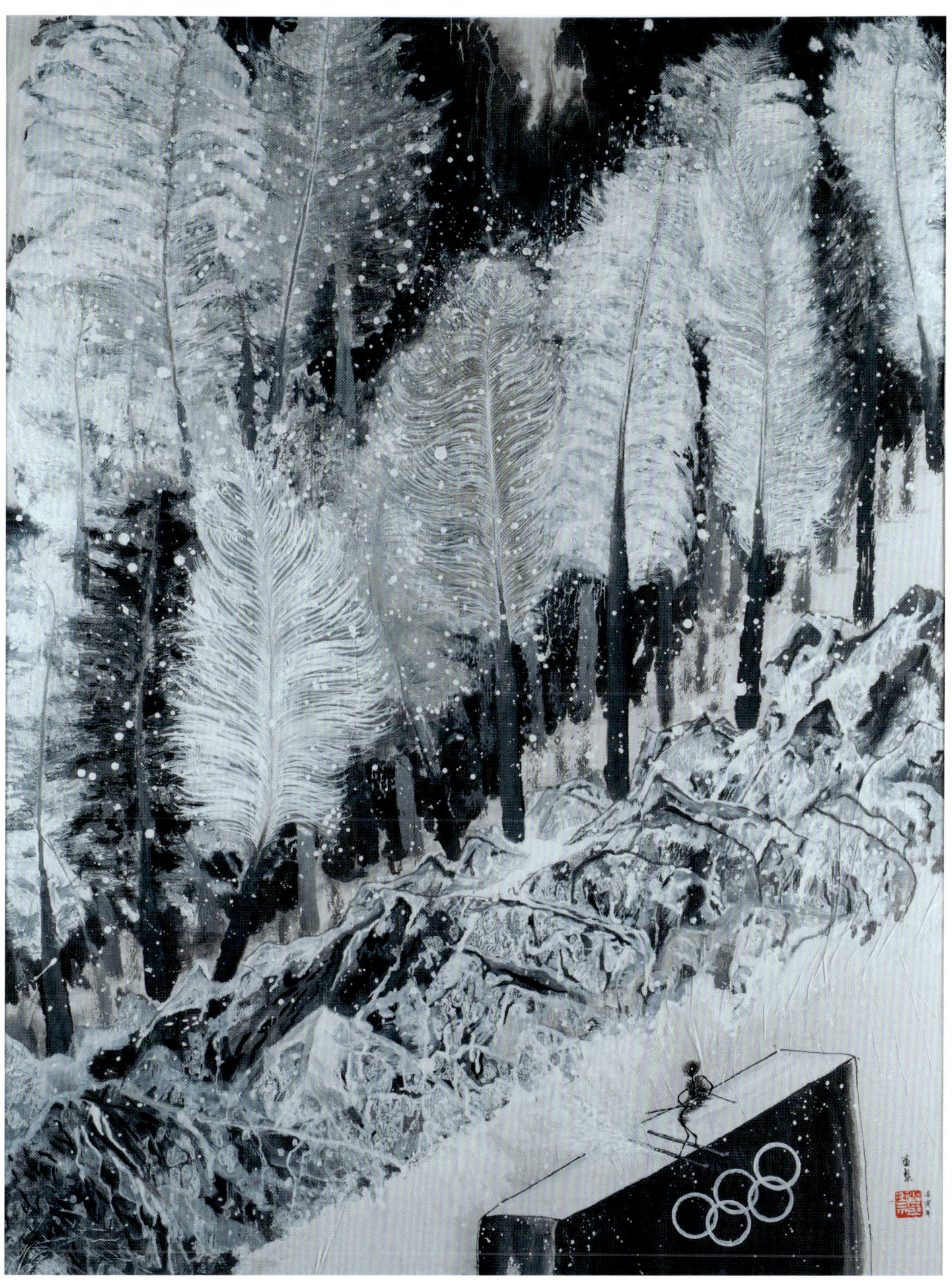

Blissful
2021
Ink, Colour and Feather on Paper
88 cm x 52 cm

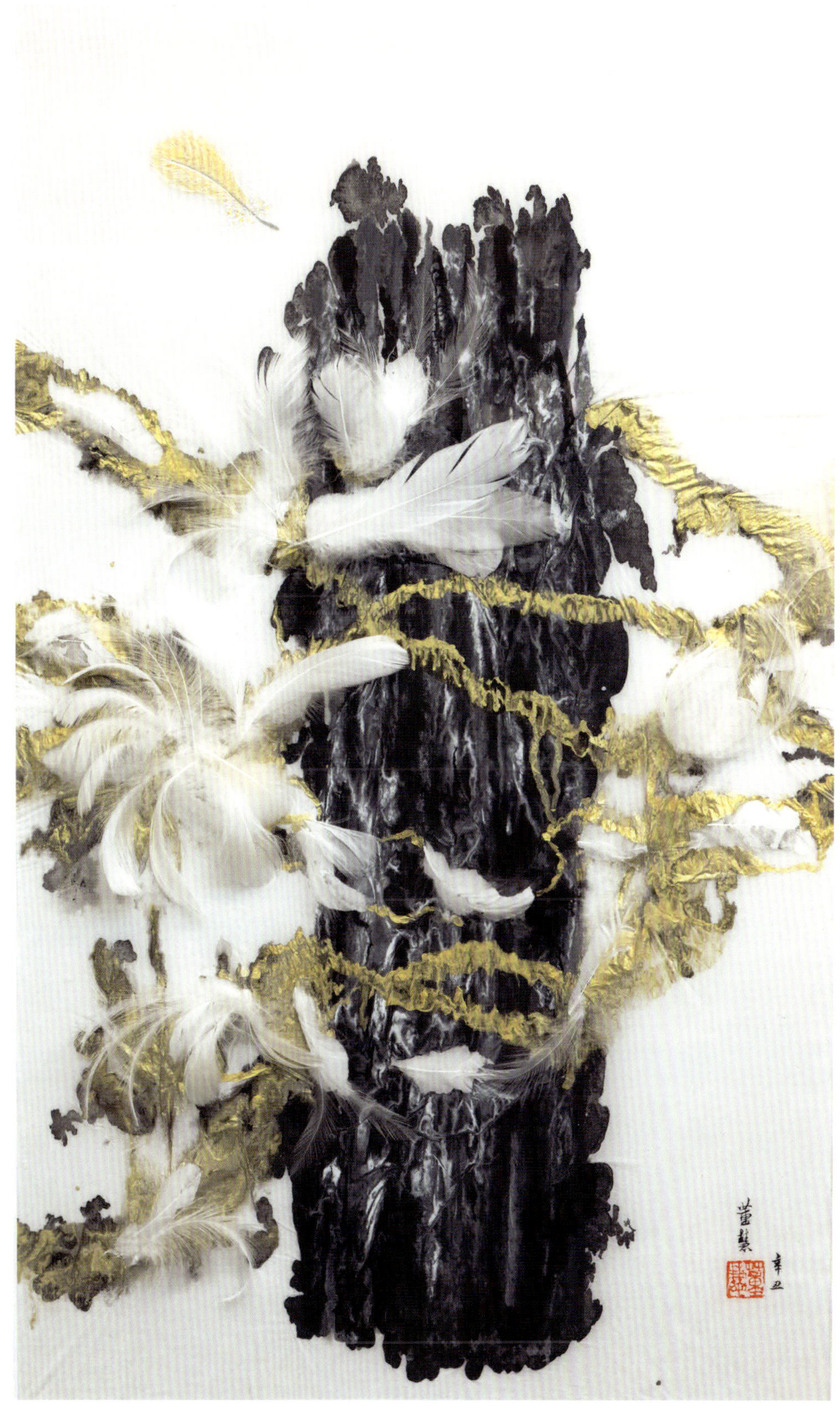

My Precious Love
2021
Ink, Colour and Feather on Paper
101 cm x 73 cm

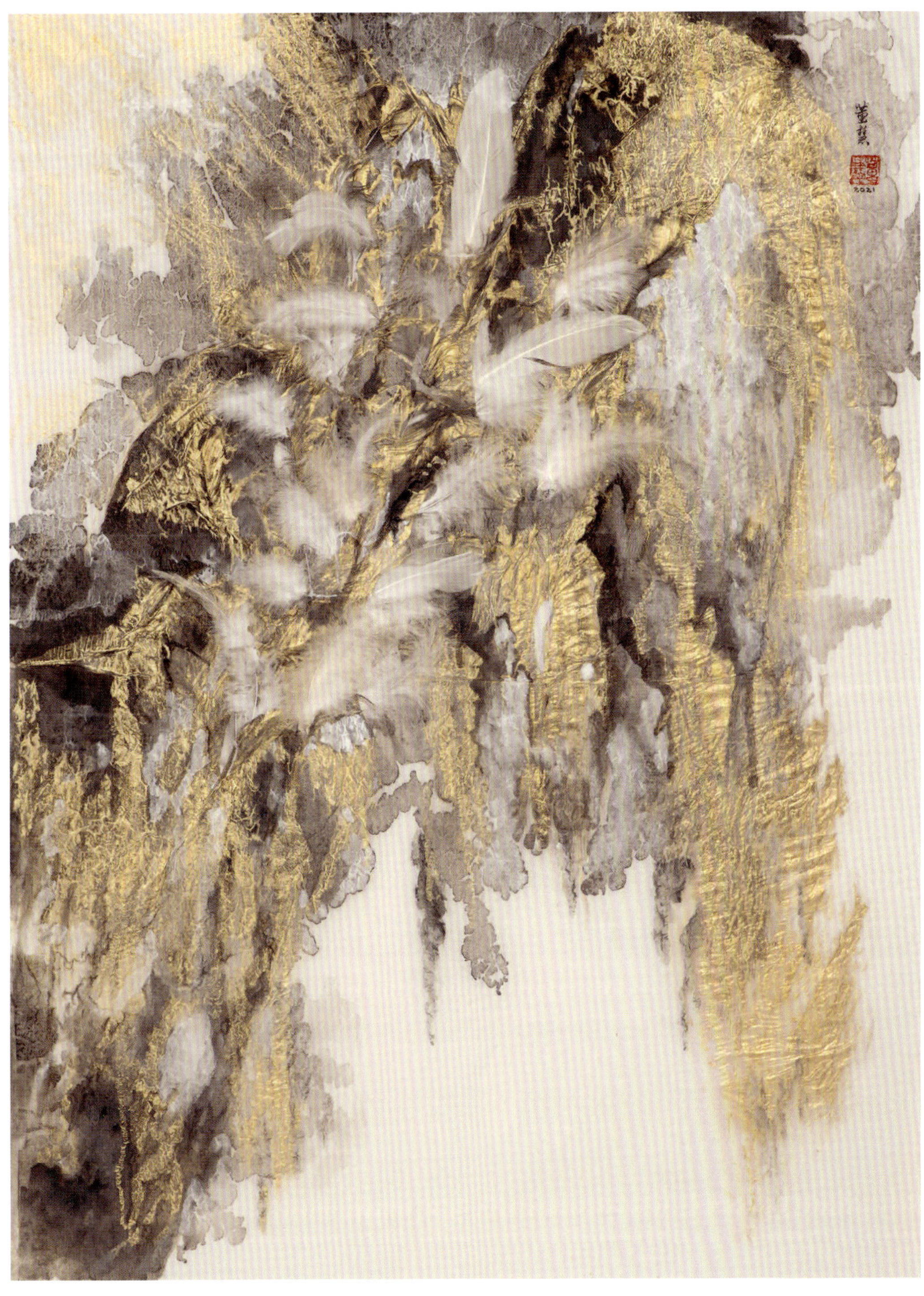

Reflection from Christina

I can always fly higher than an eagle
for you are the wind beneath my wings

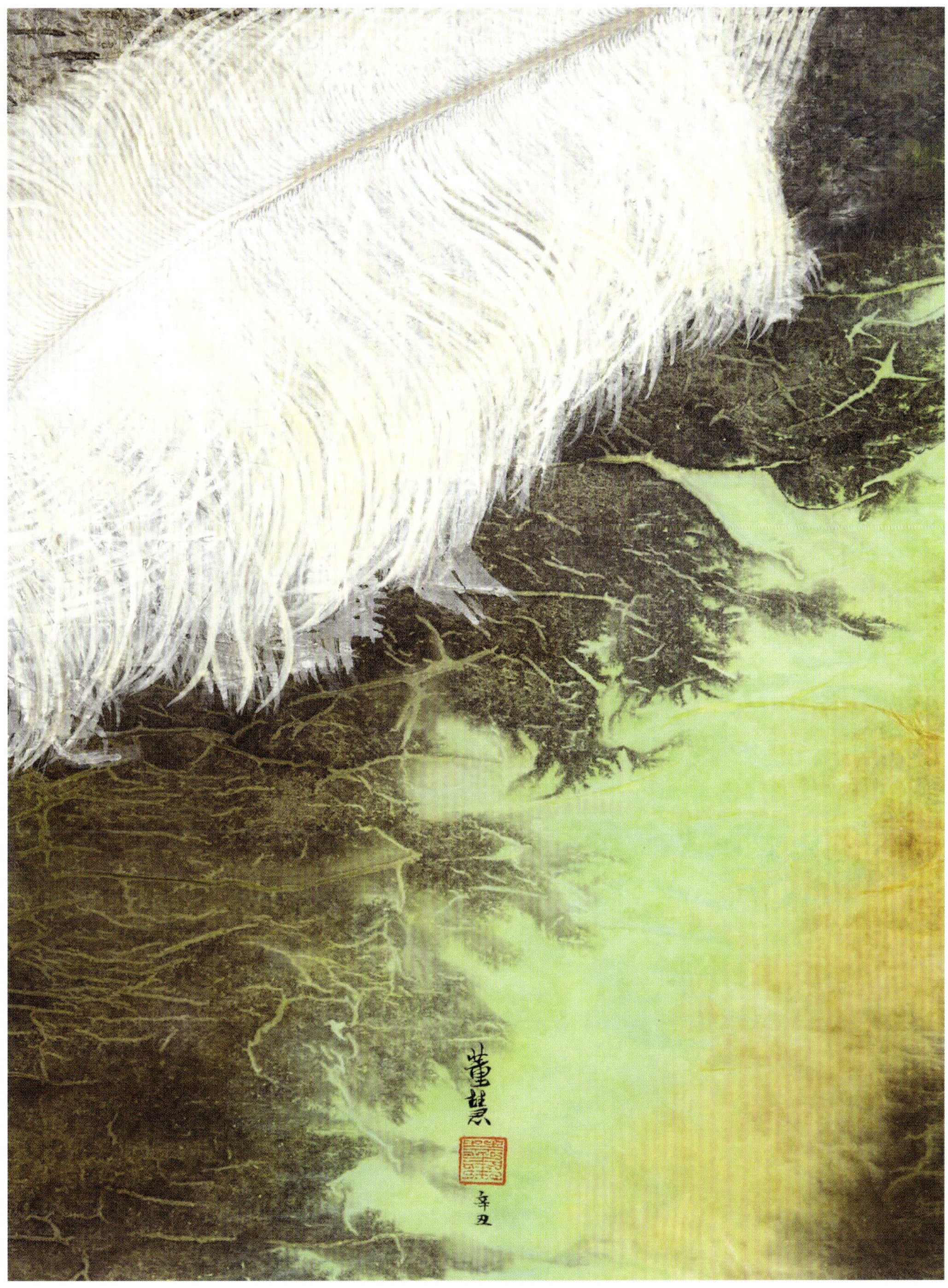

Wind Beneath My Wings
2021
Mixed Media on Paper
42 cm x 30 cm

Reflection from Christina

Been through it all
Ups and downs; thick and thin
Take My Hand
My Dear Friend

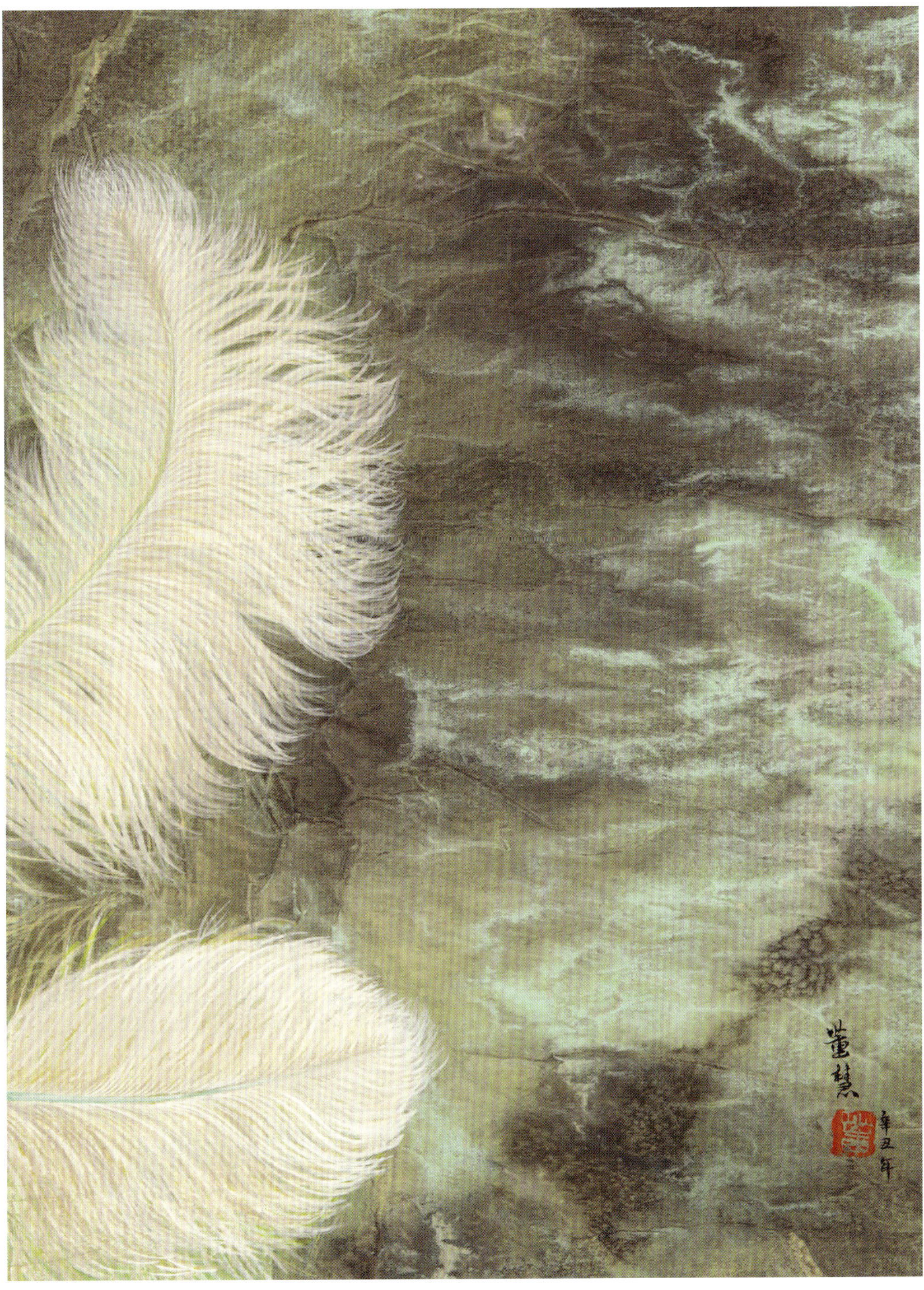

Company
2021
Mixed Media on Paper
42 cm x 30 cm

Reflection from Christina

Sunset glow and hazy smoke
Like a tired bird returning home
Through the paddy fields there I roam

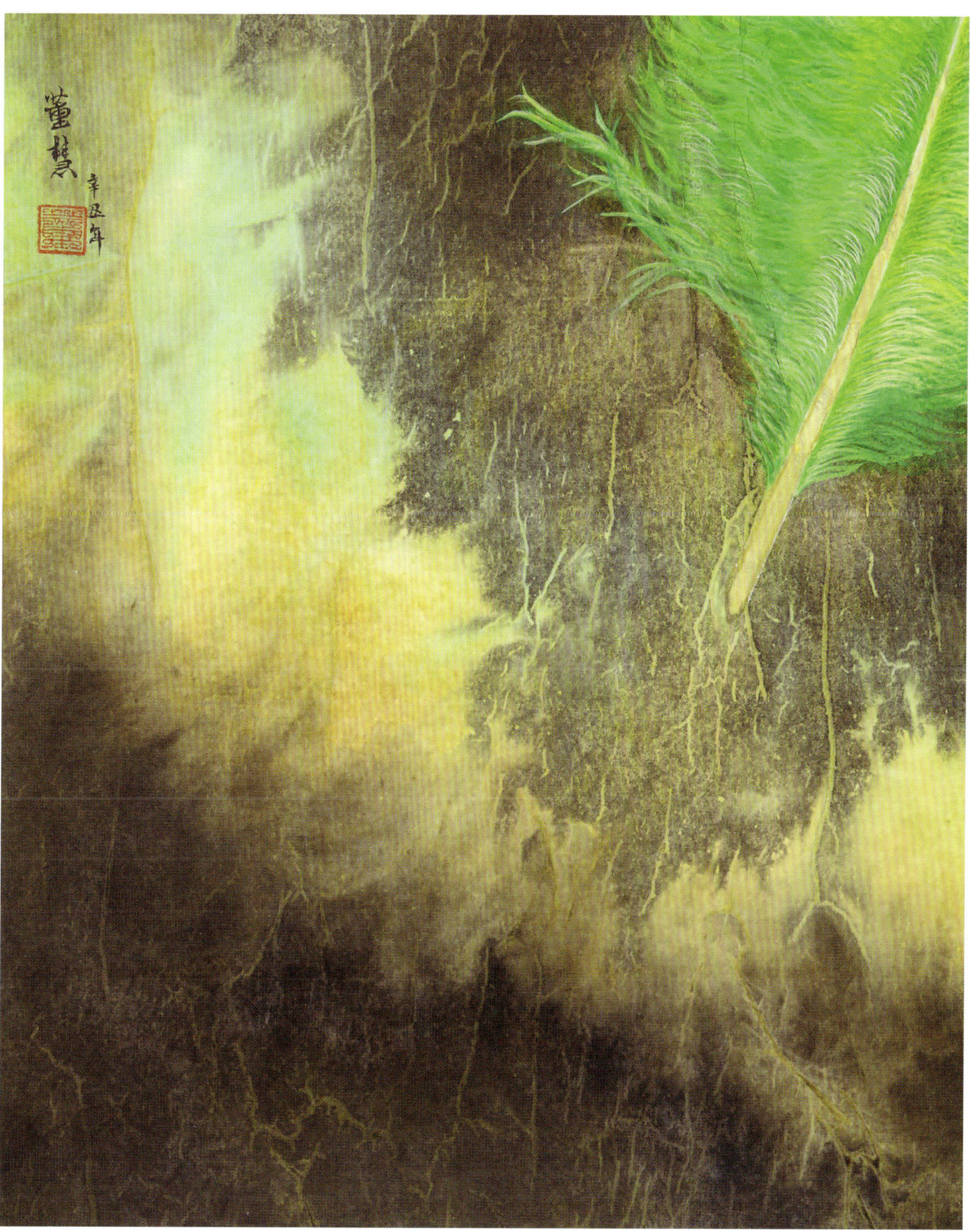

The Road to Home
2021
Mixed Media on Paper
40 cm x 31.5 cm

FROM THE ARTIST'S HEART, PLUMES IN THOUSANDS

From the artist's heart arose,
Plumes in thousands of layers;
Some like clouds wispily float,
Some like pines uprightly stand.
Dazzling hues and charming sway,
Dancing away with the dreams;
We all ought to meet one day,
Up above the highest sky.

Lavender

(Translated by Allen Zhuang)

Pin Siu Ying, whose pseudonym is Lavender. Current positions include executive president of the Pearl of the Orient Cultural Association, vice president of the Greater China Poetry Association Hong Kong, executive supervisor of the International Contemporary Chinese Poetry Study Association, executive secretary-general of the Hong Kong Poetry Society, and vice president of the Hong Kong Book Reviewers Association, Editor in Chief of *Hong Kong Book Reviewers*, deputy secretary-general of the Hong Kong Literature Promoted Association, director of the Hong Kong Women Writers Association, director of the Hong Kong World Culture and Art Association, and Executive Editor of the Xiang Jiang Information Network.

Artworks: Flimsy Paper

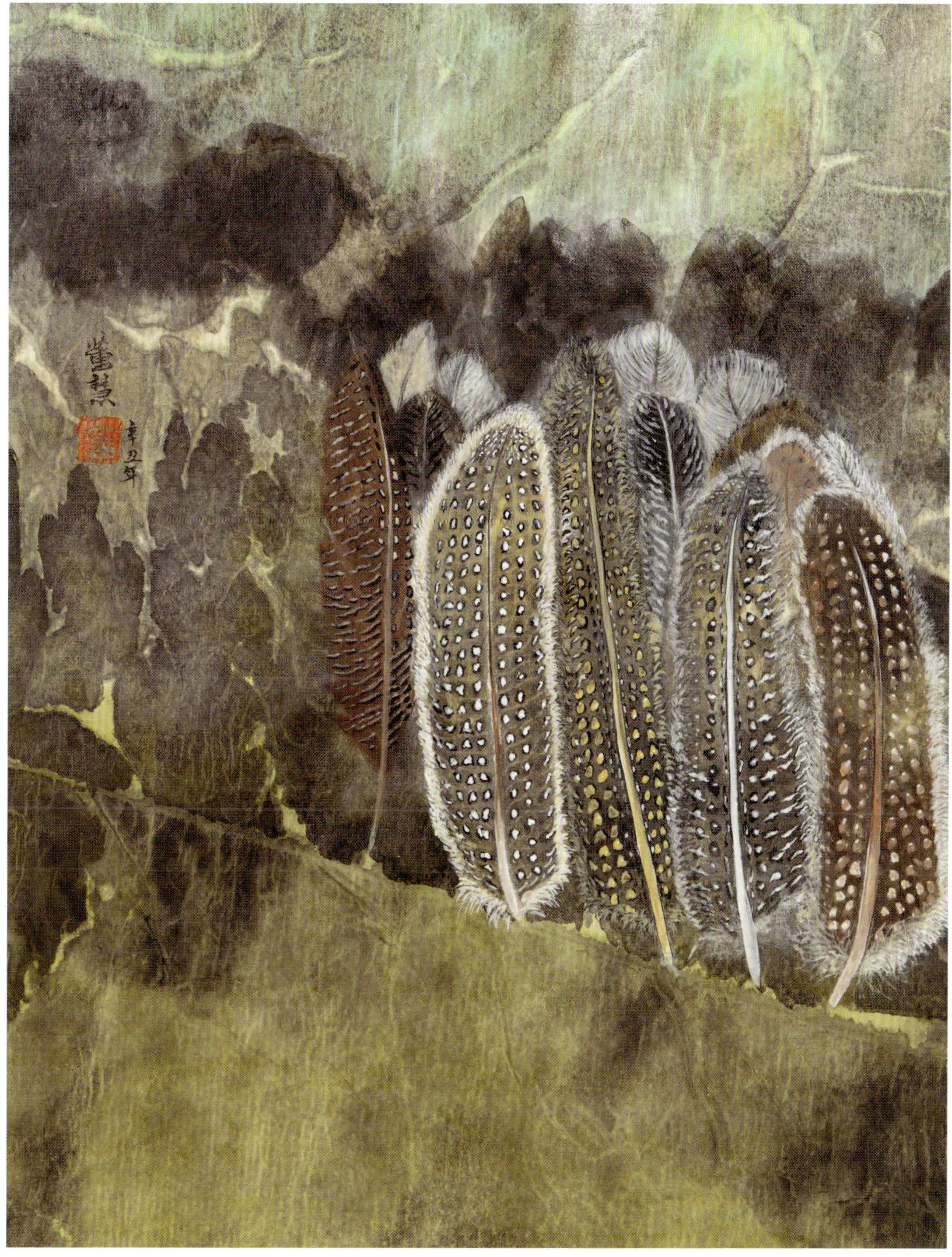

Flock
2021
Mixed Media on Paper
40 cm x 31 cm

THE SELF UNBOUND

It awaits good news from a thousand miles away.
It believes that each glass of glory's wine is brewed by God personally.
Even if twilight's not yet gone,
The Self, Unbound—that's the luminous ray of light within you.
Dawn will always break.

He Jialin

(Translated by Allen Zhuang)

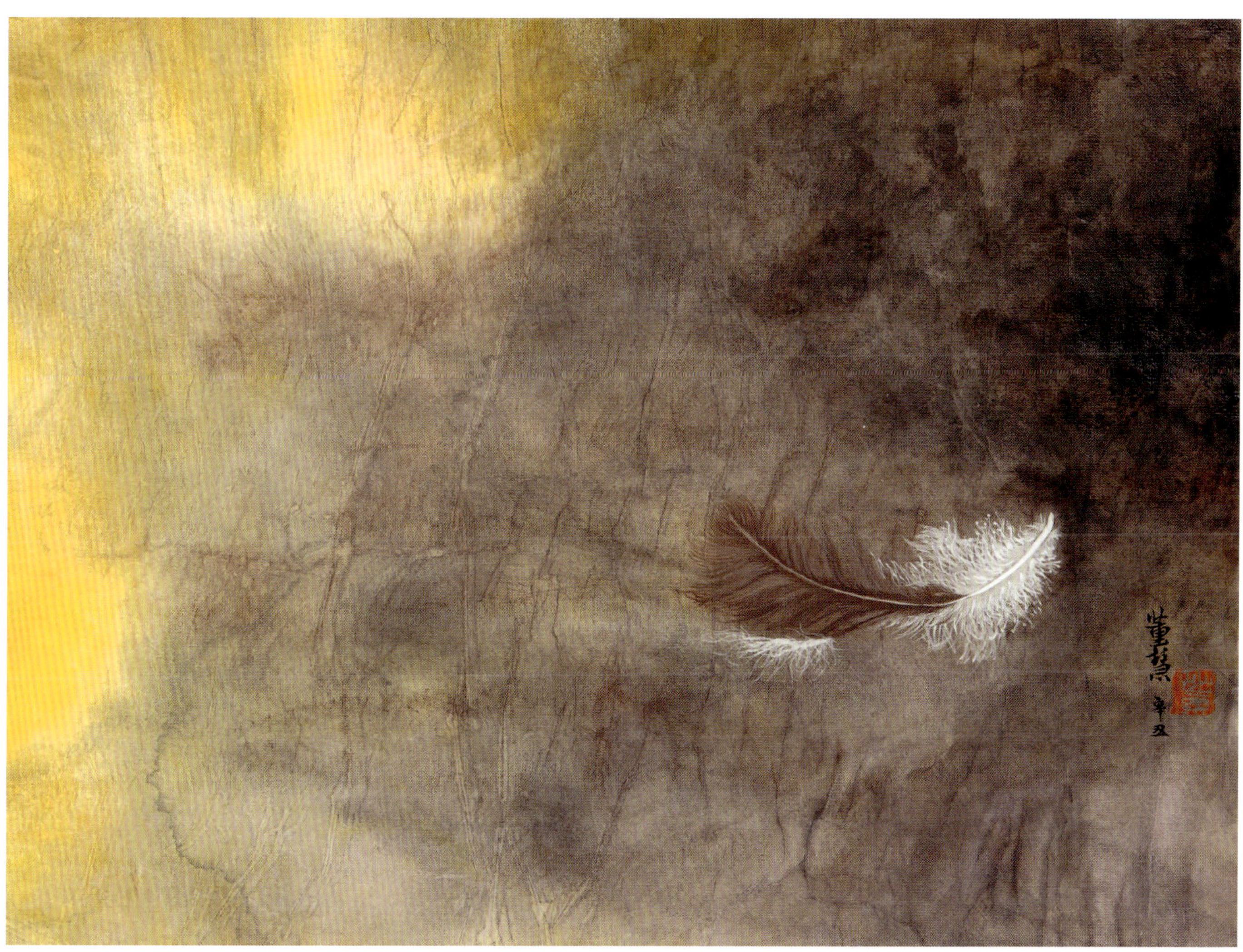

At Ease
2021
Mixed Media on Paper
30 cm x 40 cm

Everlasting Love
2021
Mixed Media on Paper
43 cm x 43 cm

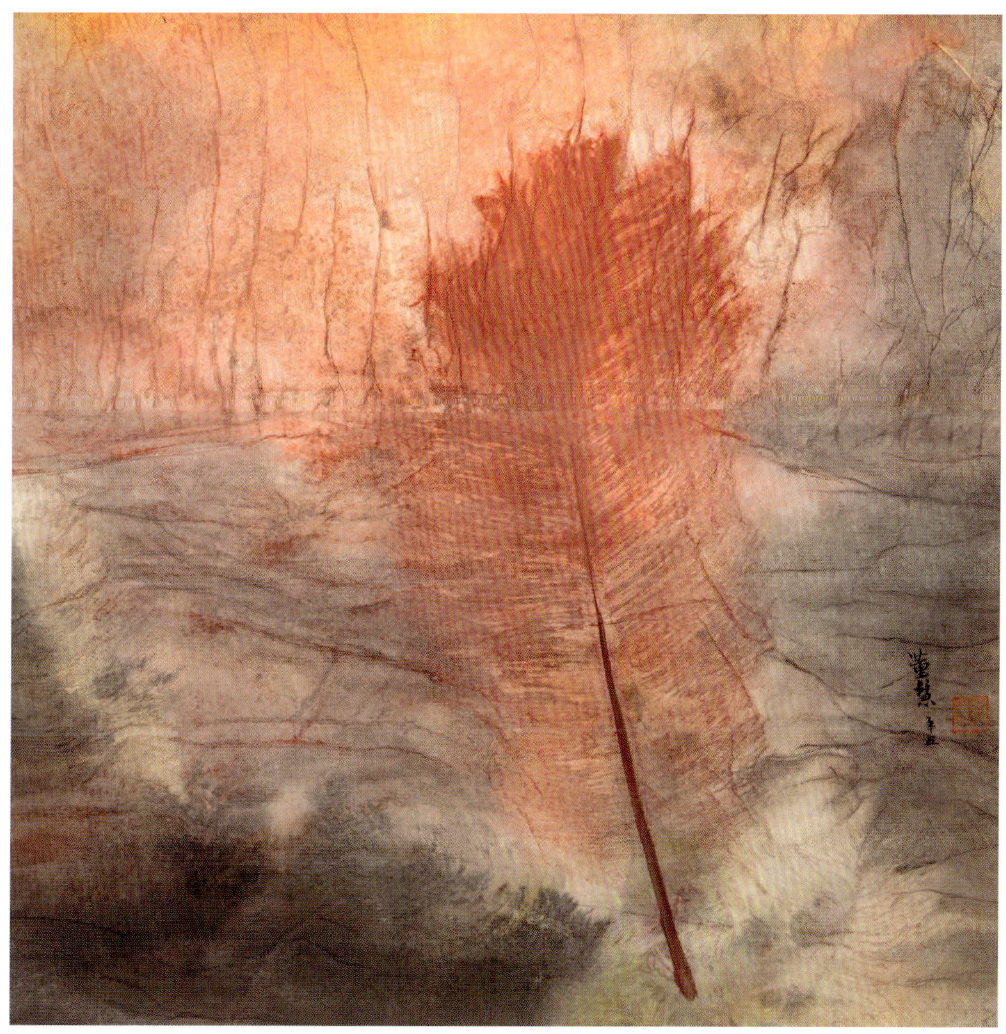

EVERLASTING LOVE

In whose field they're fated to land, picked at the wind's whim.
Like seeds, we're taken along by migrant birds flying from South to North,
or o'er thousands of mountains.
Where'er the fate of a tree is carried to settle,
It takes root—for its whole lifetime.

If love is no longer a reason good enough,
Then what else is there,
That leaves you laid low in the dust, light as feathers,
counting plumules strewn o'er the land.

He Jialin

(Translated by Allen Zhuang)

LIGHTWEIGHT PLUMAGE

Is that the plumage of a sacred bird, or a mountain spirit,
Dwelling in the depths of groves in the Age of Chaos.
Its crimson breath pervades the hills and rivers' indigo topknots;
Its veins and the ridgelines knit up the world's warp and weft.

What a puny little thing,
And yet remains mysterious and afar.
Under the night's dome that hangs myriads of stars,
It's decoding endless allegories of Life and Divinity.

Wang Huijuan

(Translated by Allen Zhuang)

Wang Huijuan, a Doctor of Literature from Nanjing University and a postdoctoral fellow in drama from Mei Lanfang Memorial Hall, is a writer, poet and media reporter. She began publishing works at the age of five and is engaged in research on Chinese language and art.

FEATHERY LIGHTNESS O'ER BLOOD-STAINED SEASONS

There's a kind of lightness,
flitting through the flowers
like a dream high o'er the latitudes, bothering no men.
There's a kind of lightness,
rooted in life but severed from it;
that's Weightiness by the name of Lightness.
Like a brush's touch, it skims o'er
the blood-stained chain of seasons.

He Jialin

(Translated by Allen Zhuang)

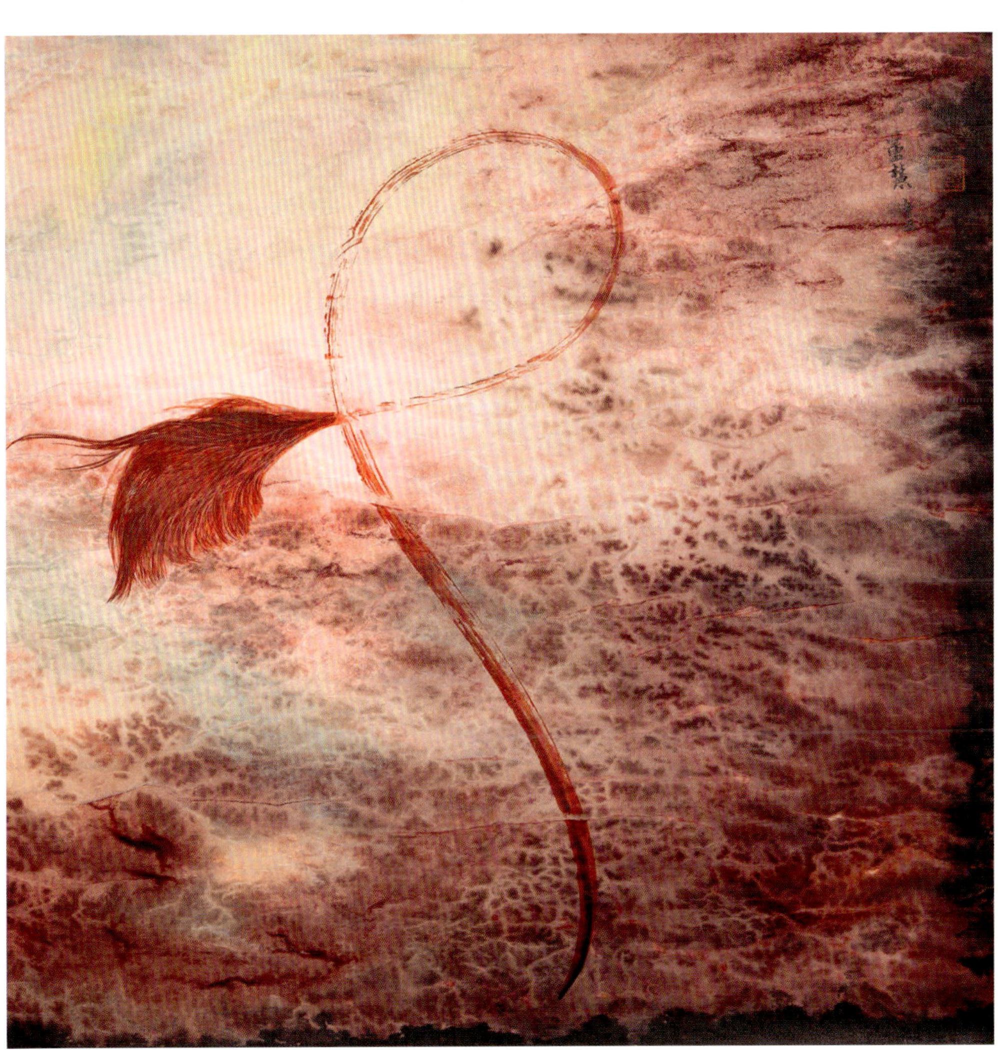

Woman Flower
2021
Mixed Media on Paper
45 cm x 43.5 cm

BREATH OF THE UNIVERSE – A FEATHER'S TALE

Underneath a feather,
A flock of twittering birdies nests.
The single feather measures time and space.

It is more like a gift from Heaven.
In an unknowing moment,
You came across it.
That feather, grows larger and larger,
Look afar beyond the birdies you will see,
There lies a band of dream chasers beneath the feather.

He Jialin

(Translated by Allen Zhuang)

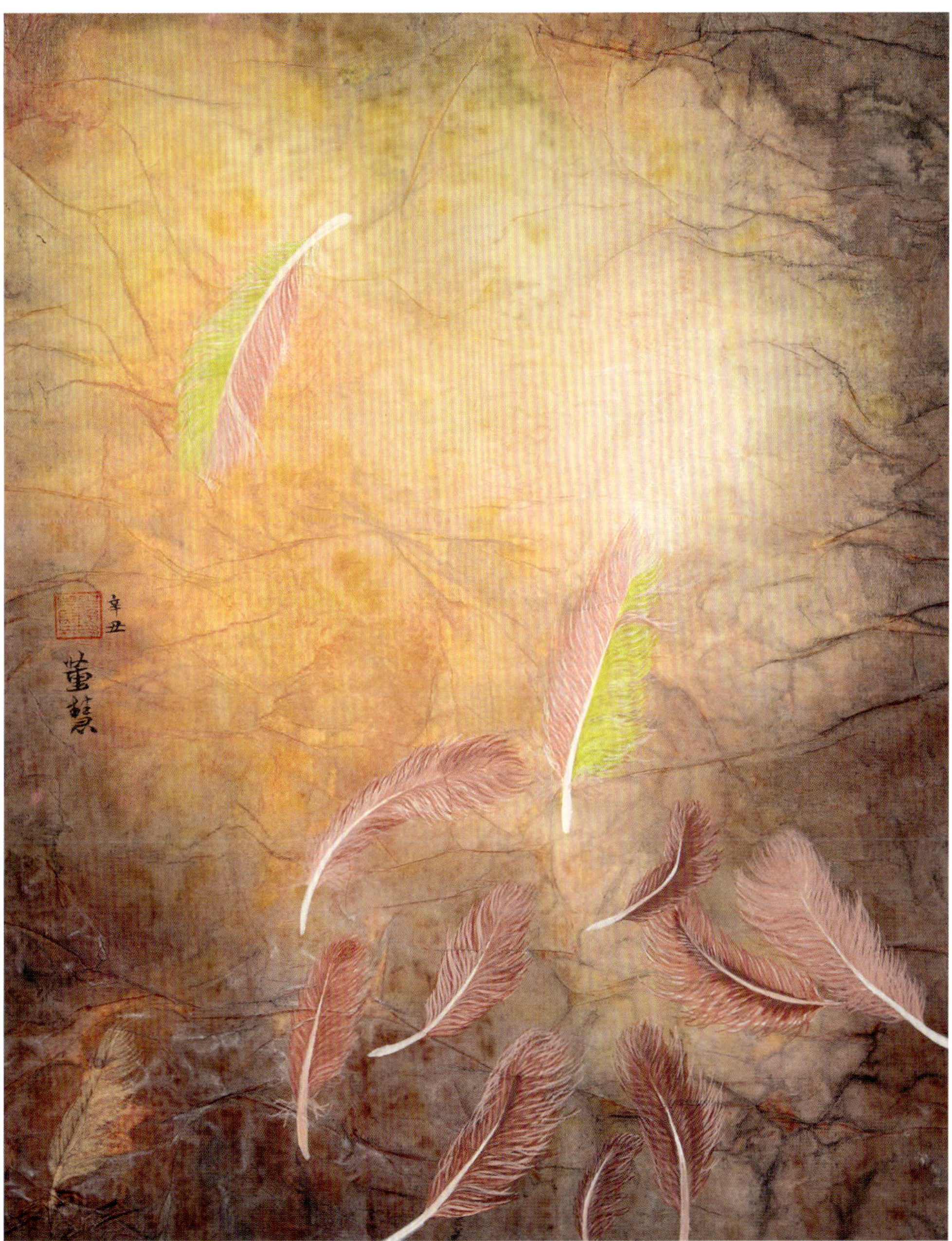

Reminiscence
2021
Mixed Media on Paper
40 cm x 30 cm

Reflection from Christina

I try to hold on to you but you vanish
Maybe some things are better left unsaid
That way everything would stay the same

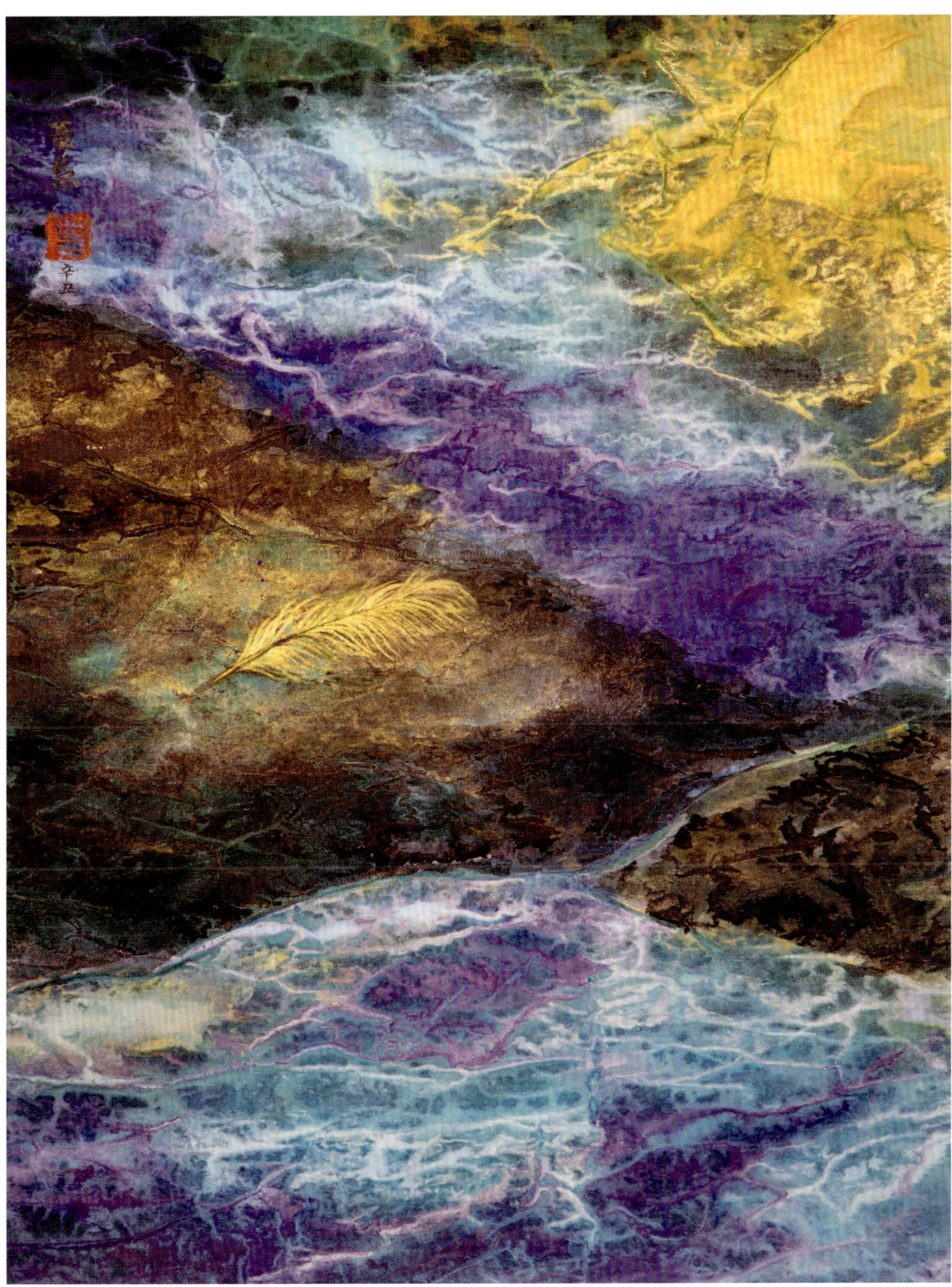

How Did We Fall Apart
2021
Mixed Media on Paper
41 cm x 30 cm

Reflection from Christina

There are places I'll remember
All my life though some have changed
Some forever not for better
Some have gone and some remain

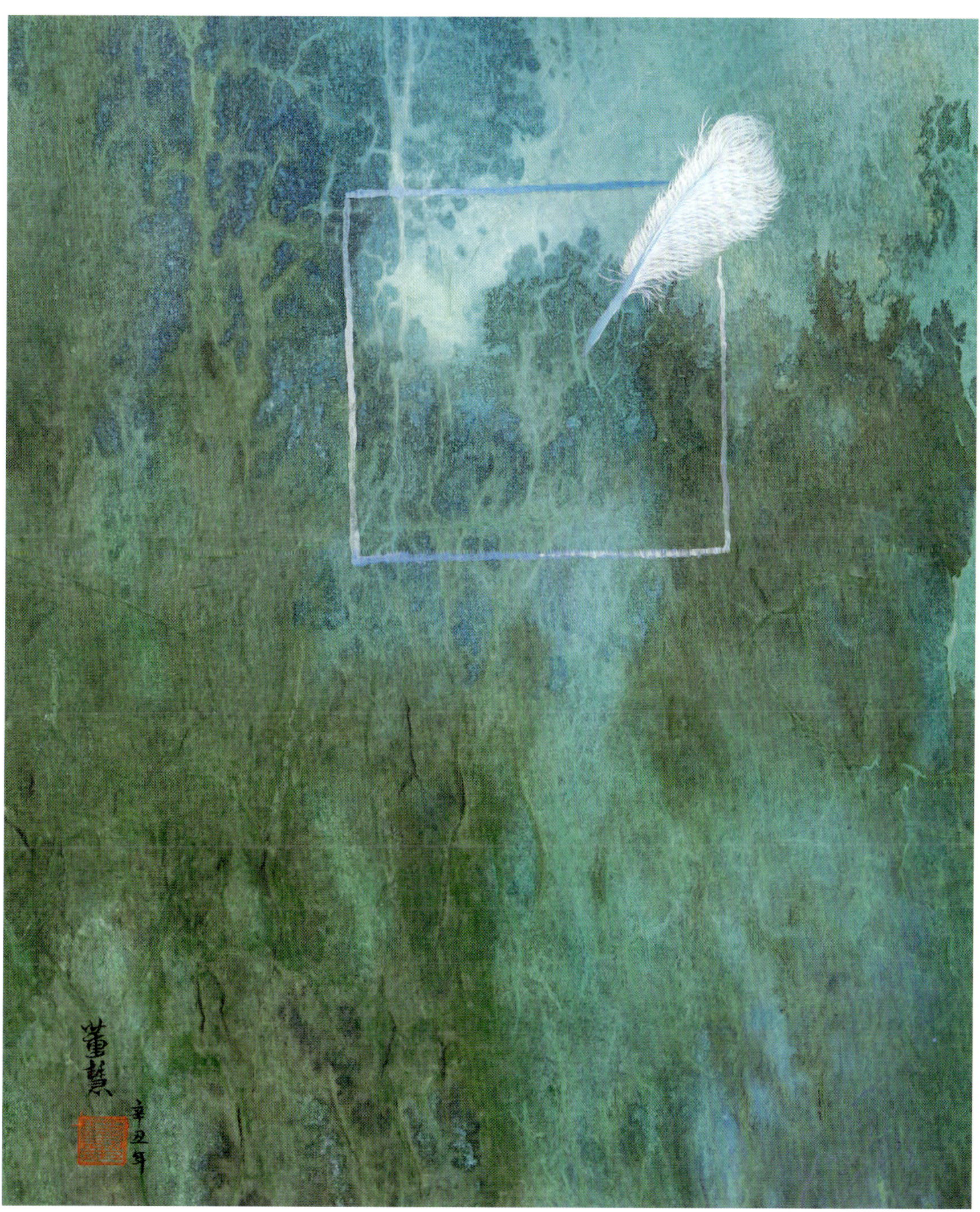

In My Life
2021
Mixed Media on Paper
38.5 cm x 31 cm

Reflection from Christina

You raise me up, so I can stand on mountains
You raise me up to more than I can be...

Artworks: Flimsy Paper

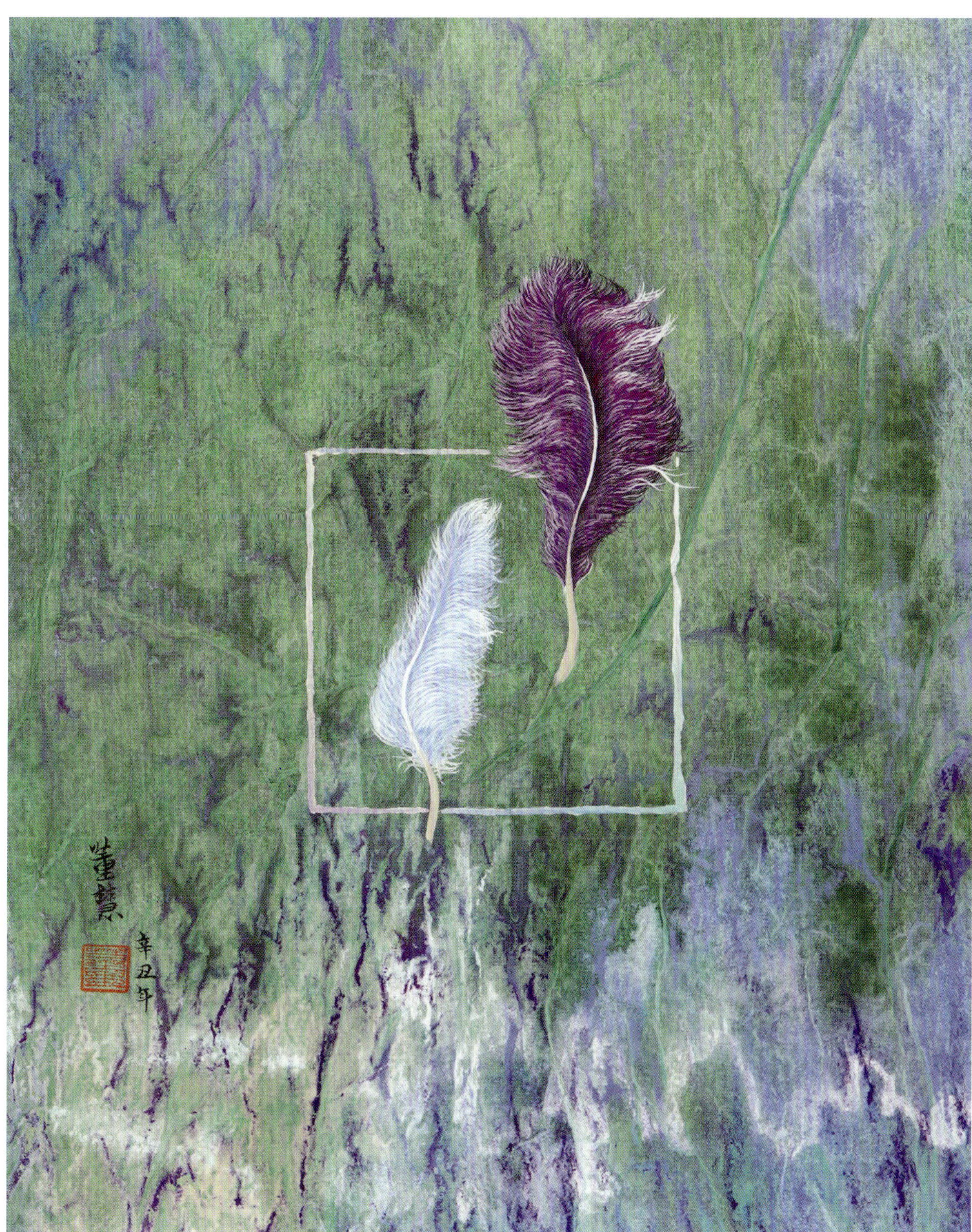

You Raise Me Up
2021
Mixed Media on Paper
40 cm x 31 cm

Reflection from Christina

Ocean glimmering with glamorously dazzling plumes
As though seeing the peafowl fairy
bestowing life upon us with her iridescent coat

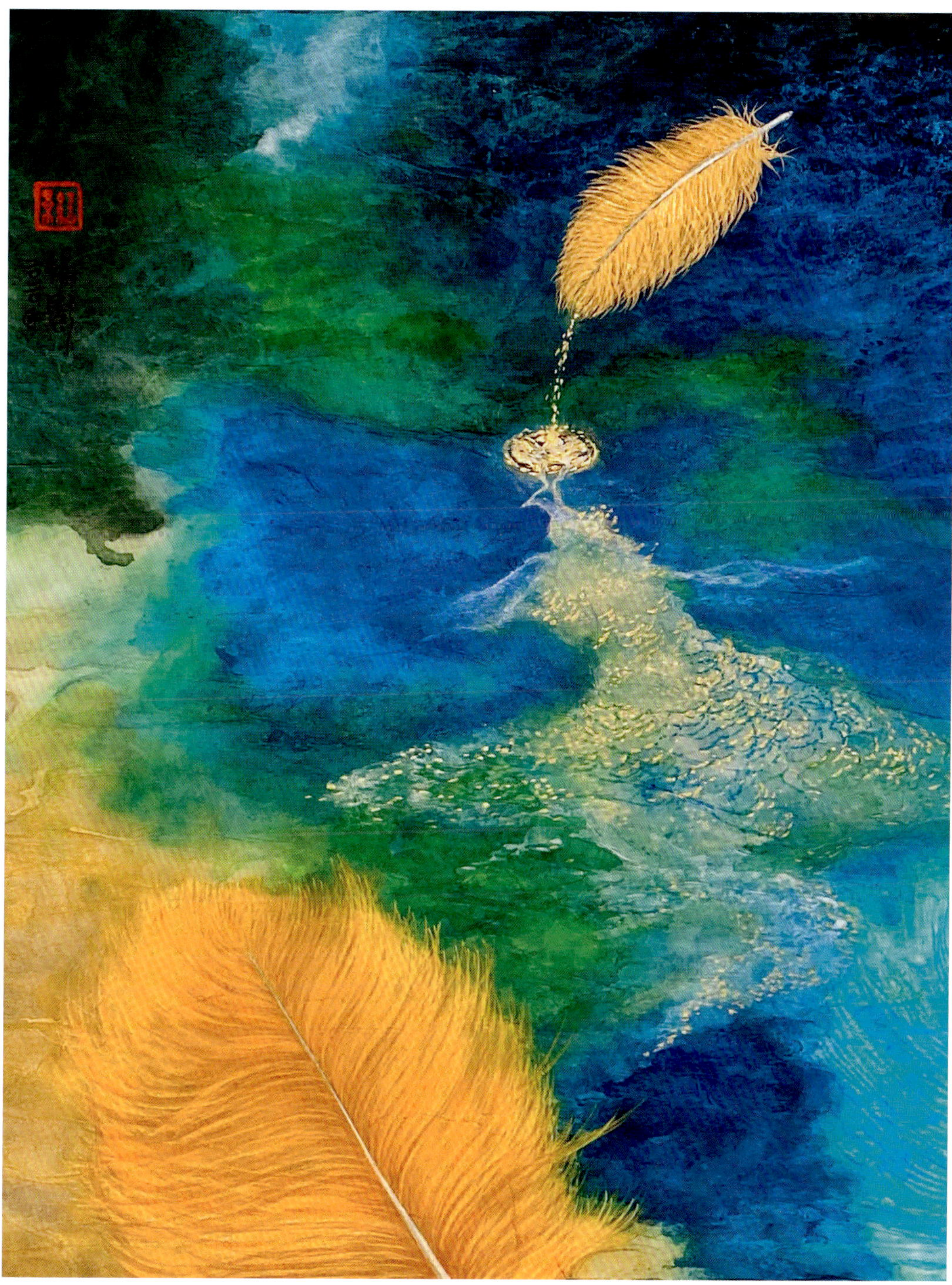

Fountain of Life
2020
Mixed Media on Paper
40 cm x 30 cm

Reflection from Christina

A rainbow is a promise, of sunshine after rain,
of calm after storms, of joy after sadness,
of peace after pain, of love after loss.

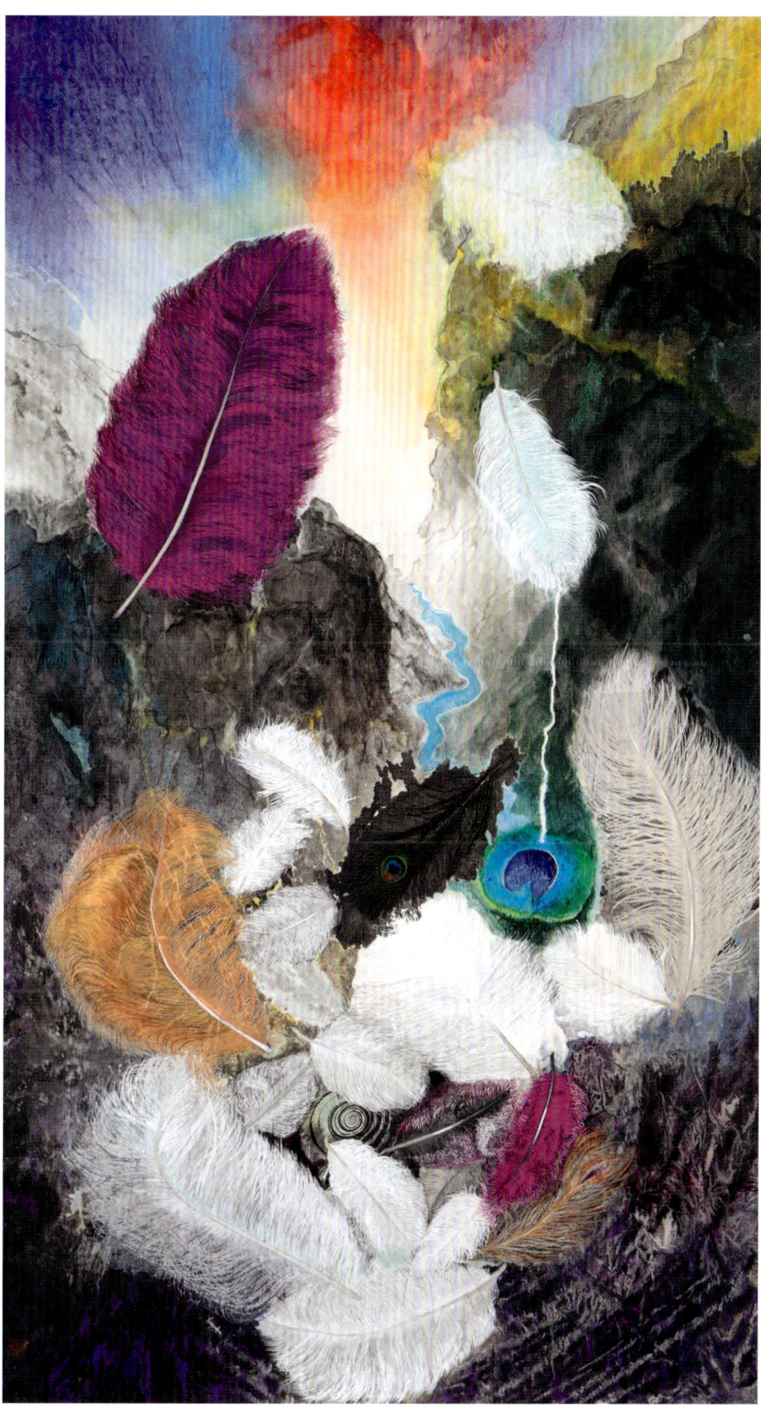

Dynasty
2020
Mixed Media on Paper
180 cm x 102 cm

Propitious Portent
2019
Ink, Colour and Feather on Paper
98 cm x 98 cm

Selected as one of the 500 ink masterpieces worldwide in '*Ink Global*' 2020

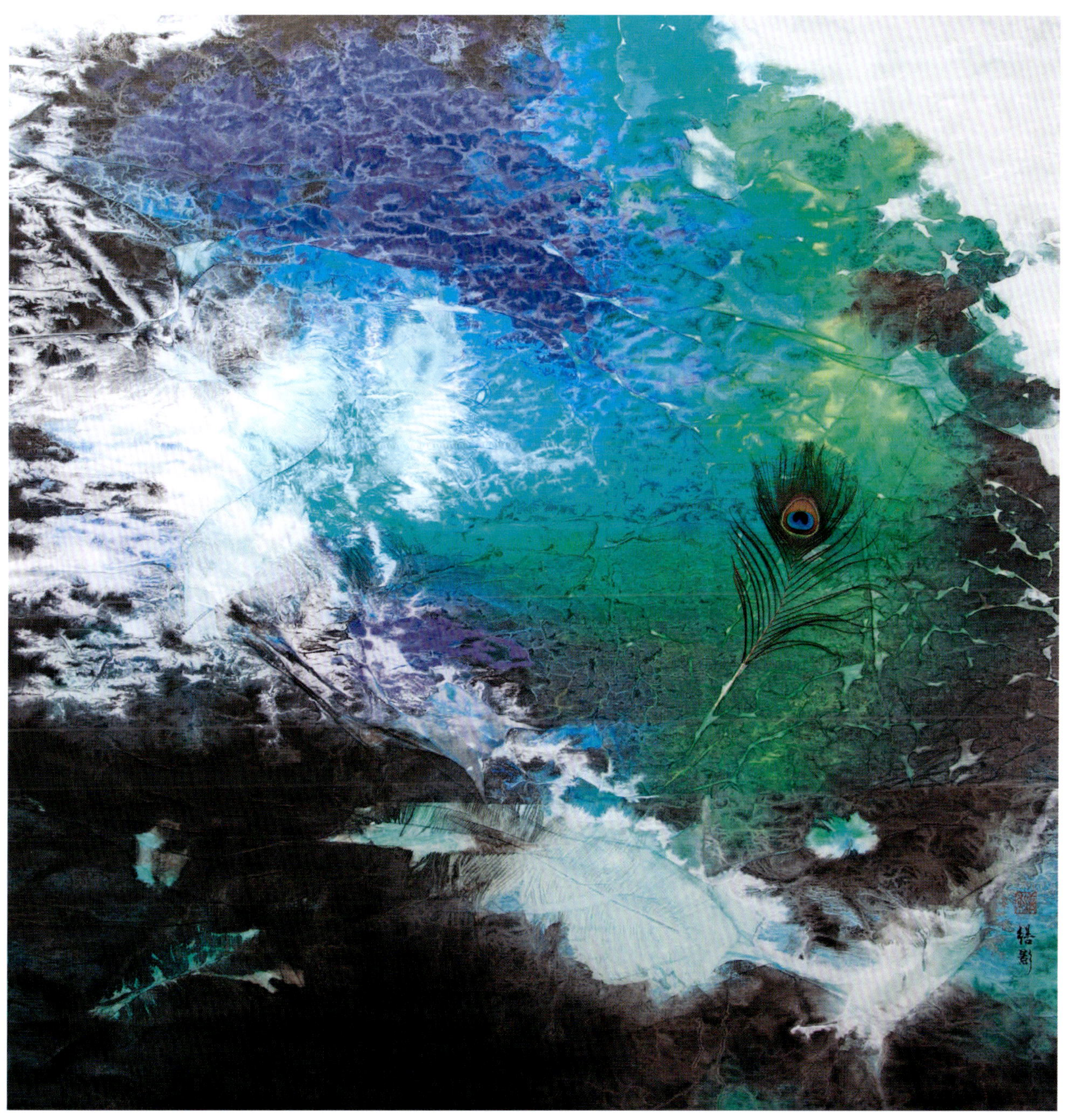

Abstraction
2019
Ink and Colour on Paper
76 cm x 104 cm

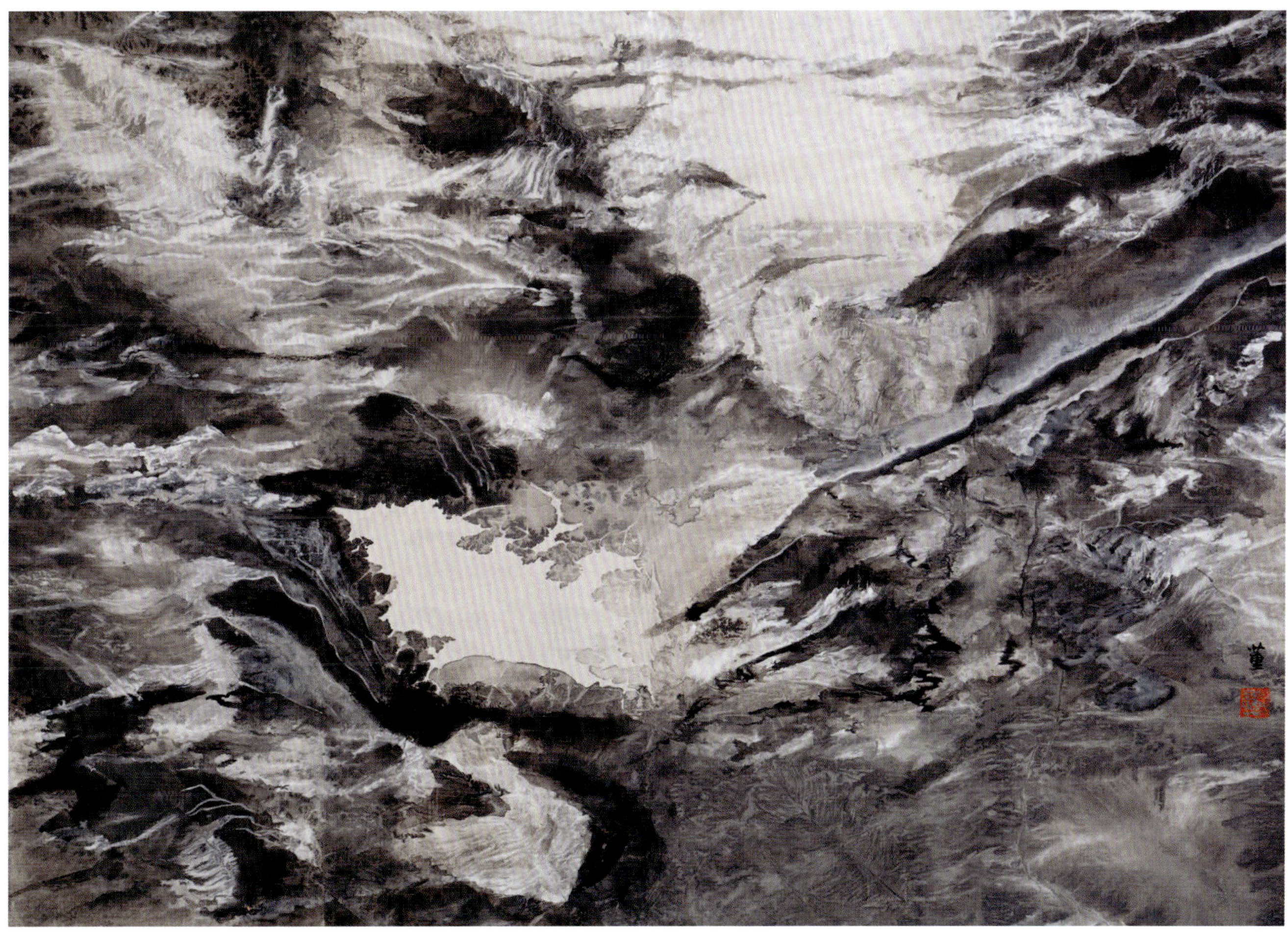

REVERIE OF A FEATHER

Bereft of the tip,
It flows out of primal chaos.
Expectantly, a faint glimmer from where the tip split off,
Has been quietly drifting out to the dome of the sky.

The world remains as it was,
But where's the feather gone, crippled and yet flying?
Nothing can I remember but its muddled innocence,
Against the primordial first light of creation.

Wen Rong

(Translated by Allen Zhuang)

Wen Rong, the vice chairperson of the Hong Kong Women Writers Association, the executive vice president of the Hong Kong Prose Poetry Society and Editor in Chief of the *Poetry Journal of Olive Leaves* in Hong Kong. She has won awards in recognition of excellent Chinese poetry in four places on both sides of the Strait Chinese poetry Summit Forum, the award of excellent female poetry creation in 2020 and the third Tianma Award of Chinese prose poetry. She has published a number of collections of poems and her works have been selected into dozens of poetry anthologies.

Artworks: Flimsy Paper

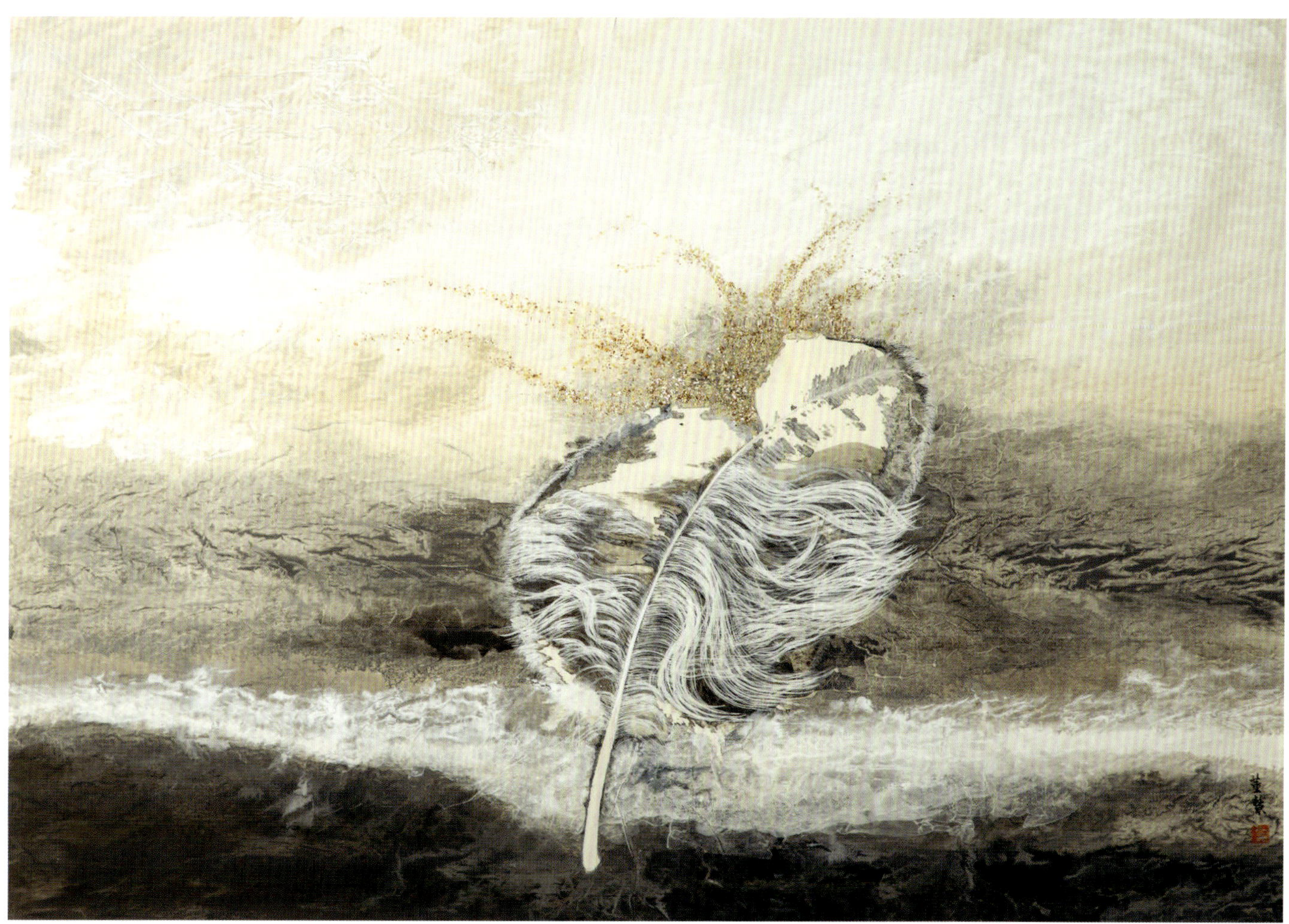

Delight of Freedom (1)
2019
Ink and Colour on Paper
73 cm x 100 cm

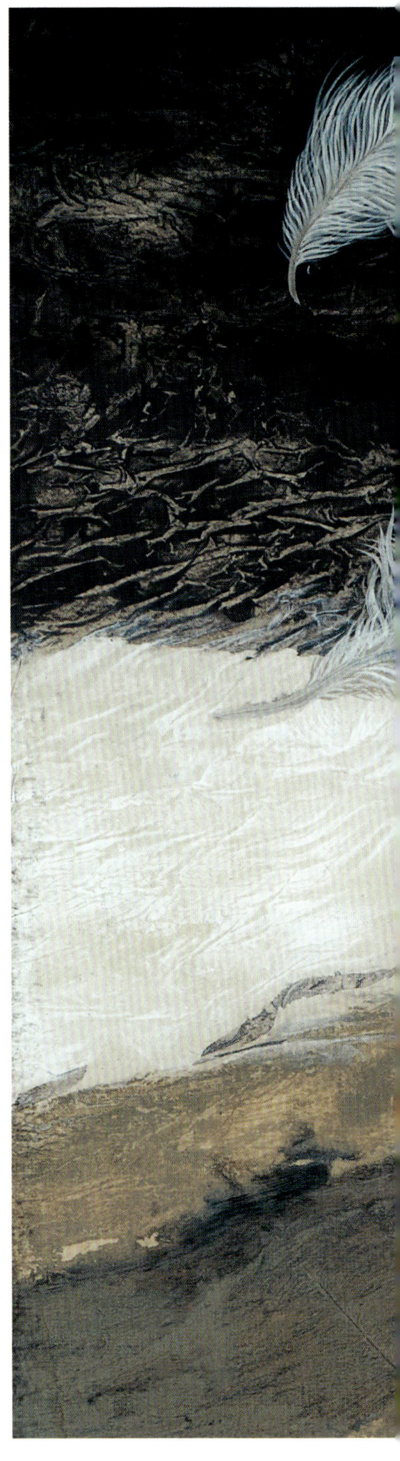

Delight of Freedom (2)
2019
Ink, Colour and Feather on Paper
73 cm x 101 cm

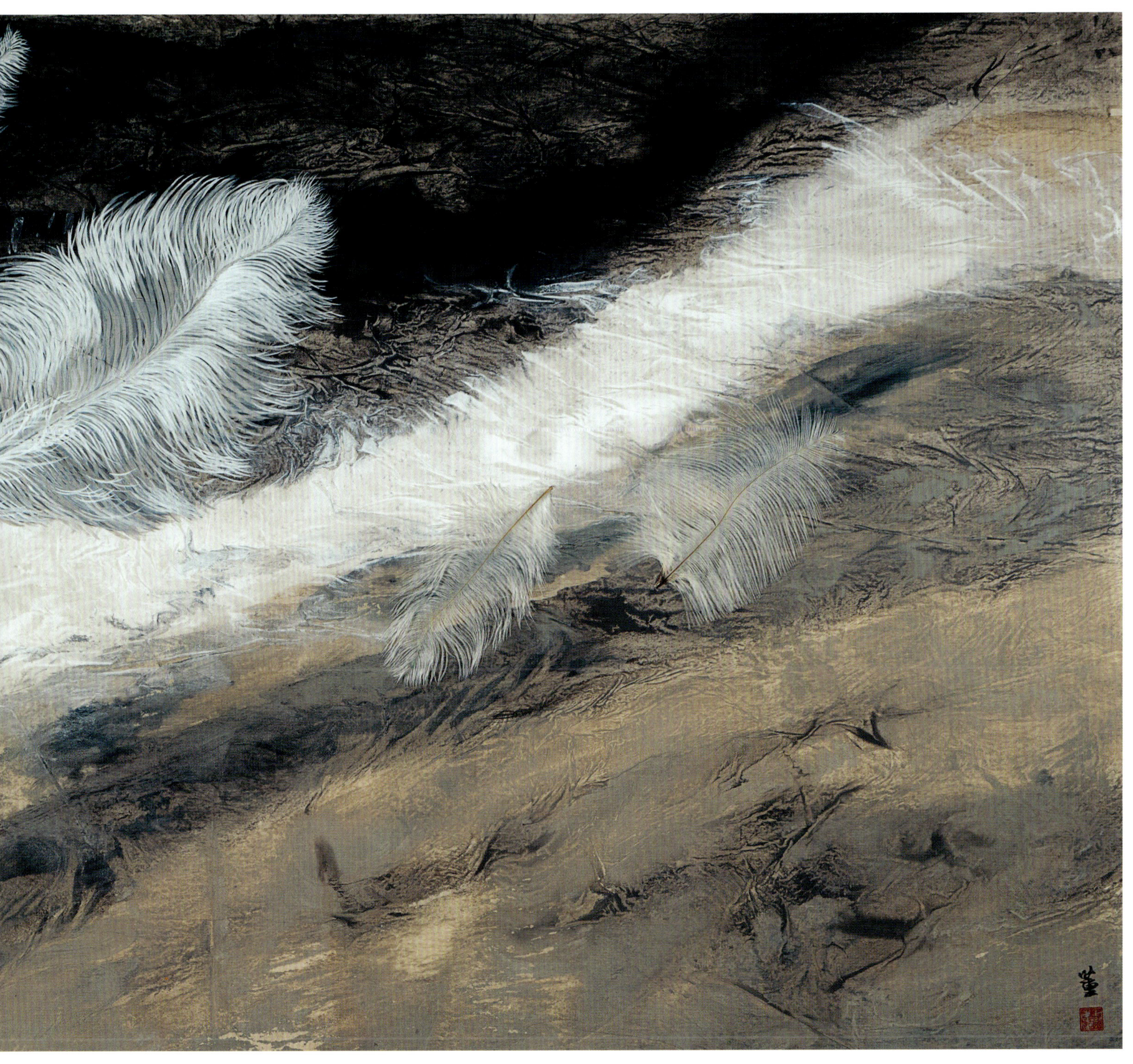

Delight of Freedom (3)
2019
Ink, Colour and Feather on Paper
74.5 cm x 44.5 cm

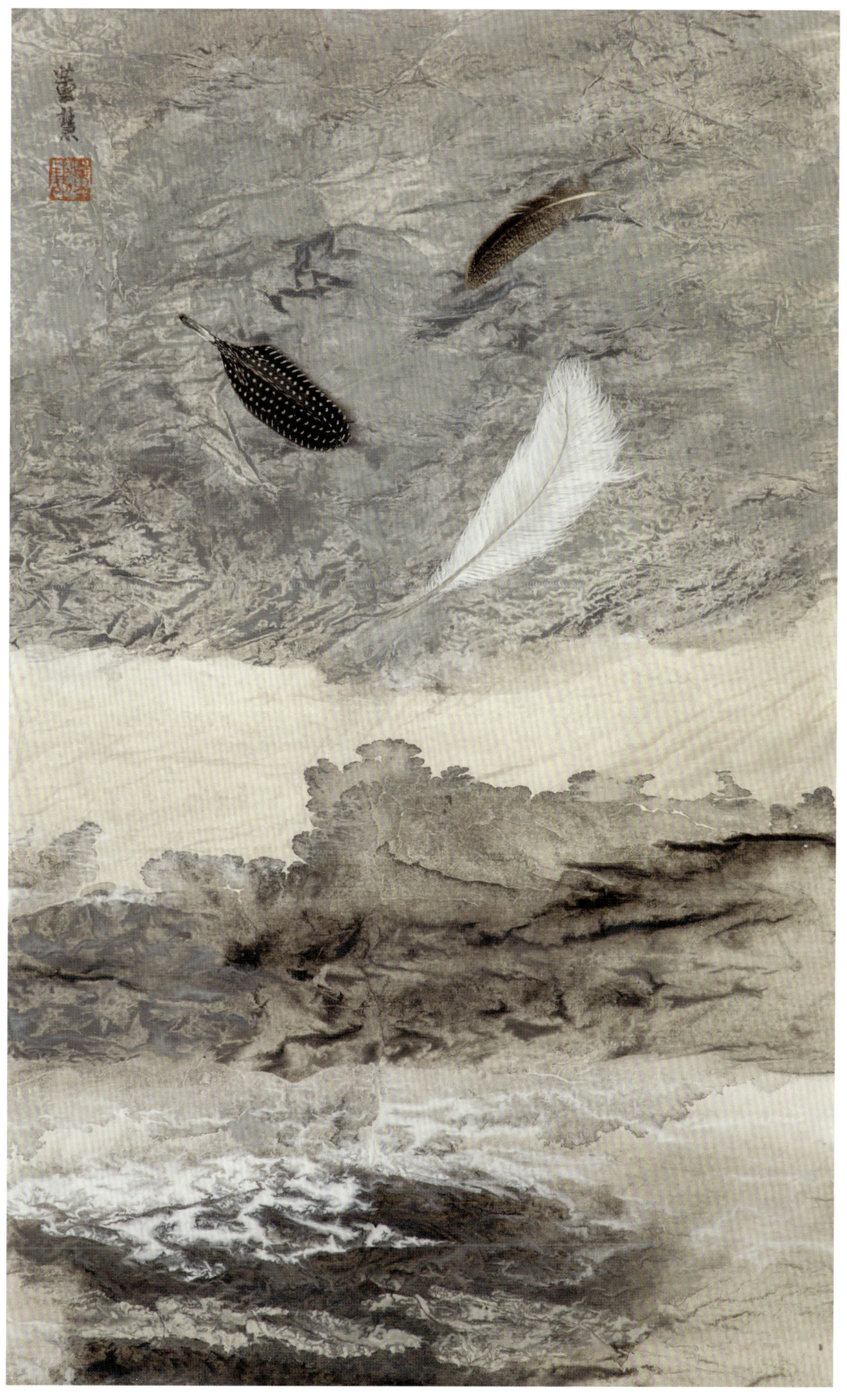

Delight of Freedom (4)
2019
Ink, Colour and Feather on Paper
75 cm x 44 cm

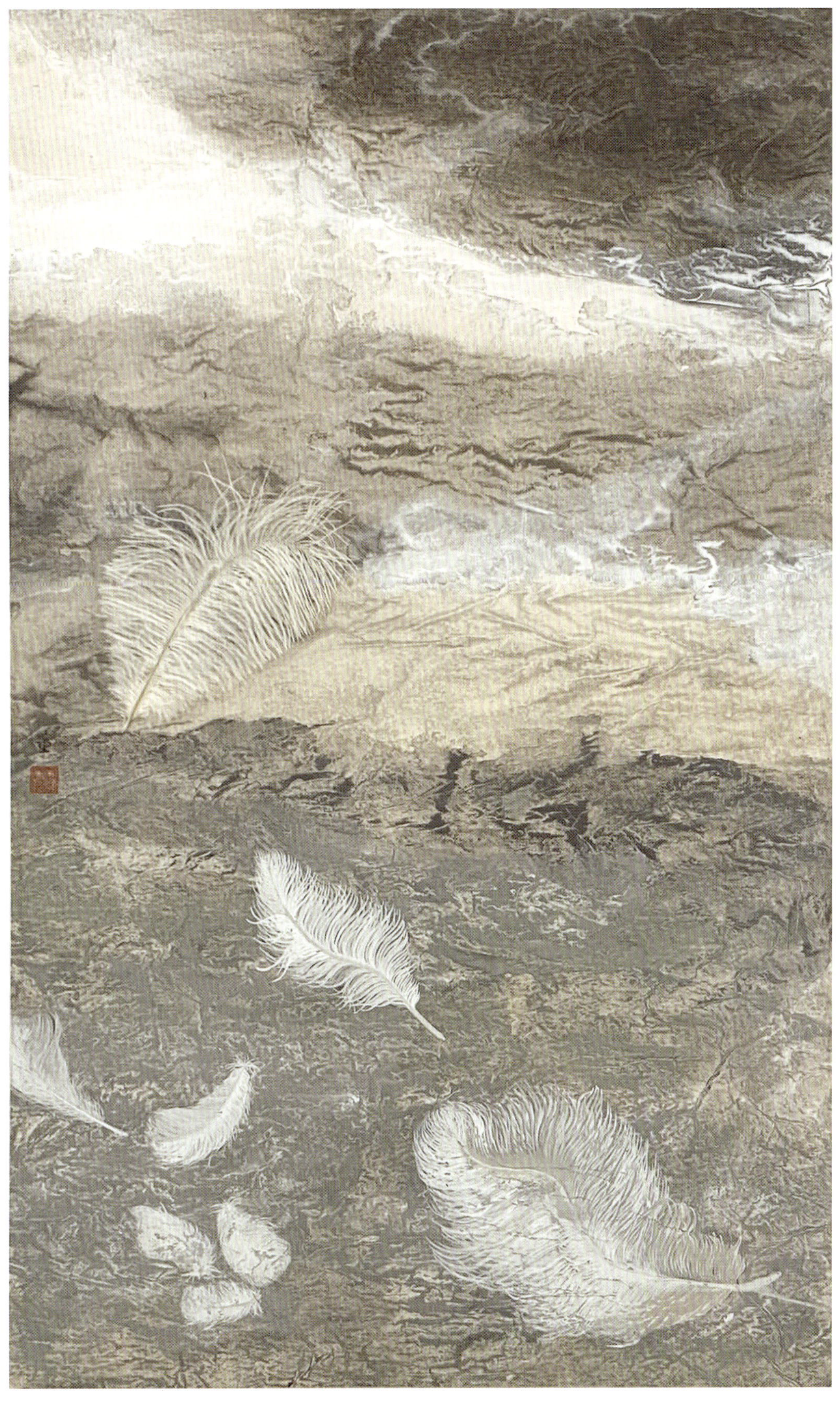

Delight of Freedom (5)
2019
Ink, Colour and Feather on Paper
54 cm x 15.5 cm

Delight of Freedom (6)
2019
Ink, Colour and Feather on Paper
54 cm x 15.5 cm

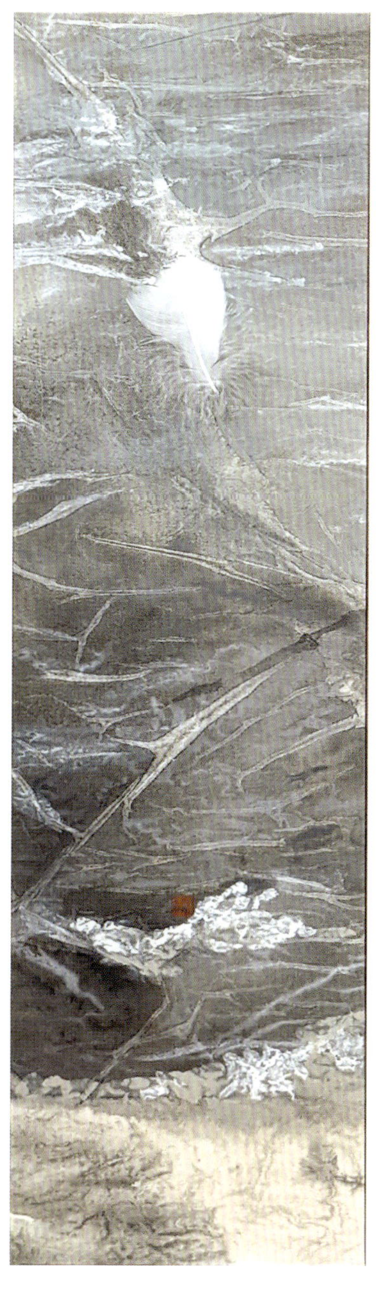

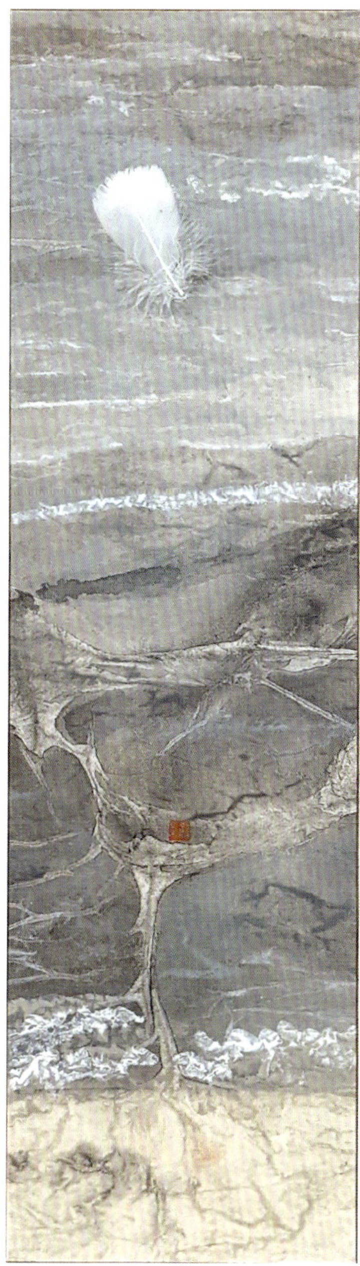

Reflection from Christina

You are never on your own
Every cloud has a silver lining

Artworks: Flimsy Paper

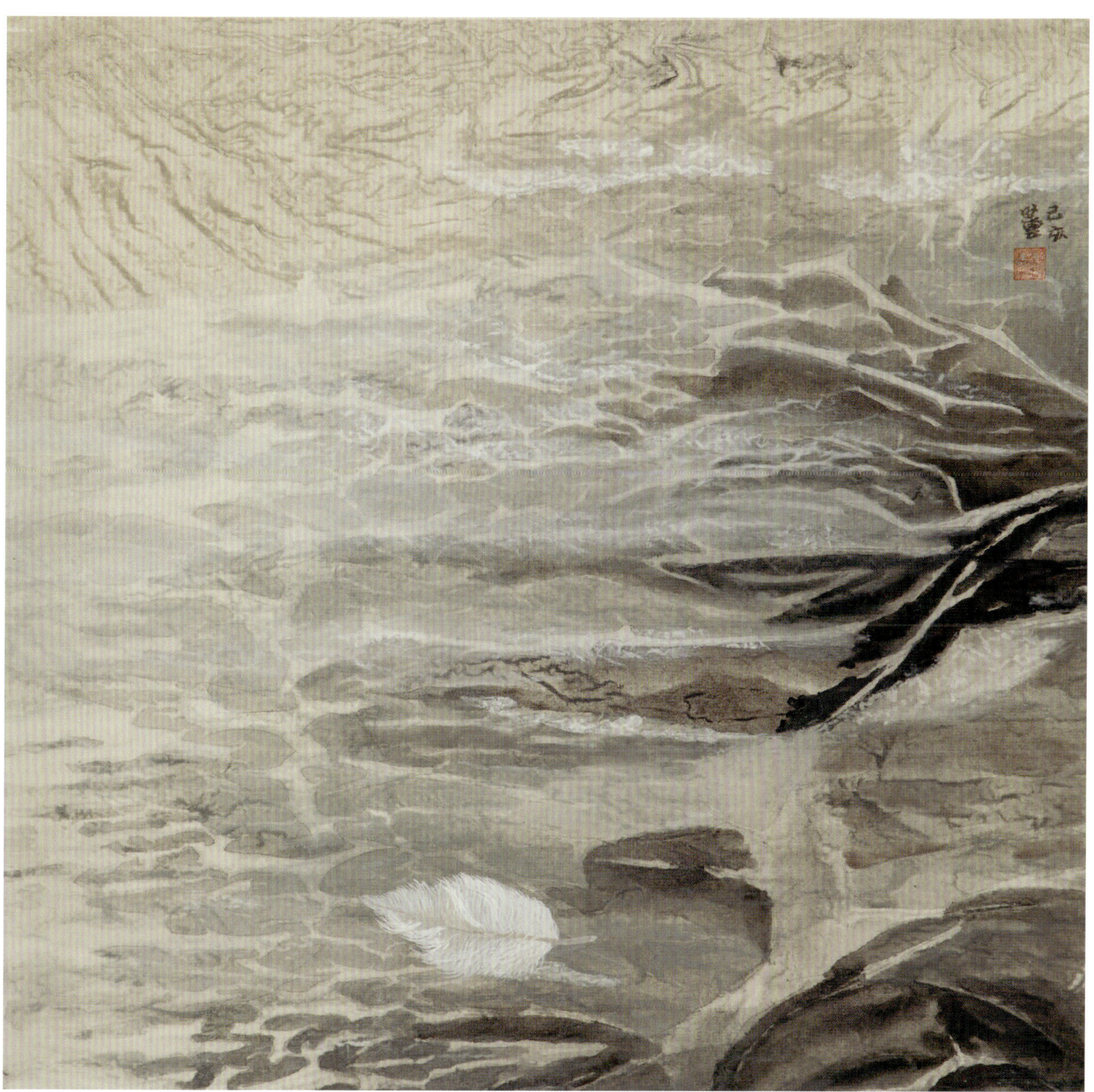

I am Alone but not Lonely
2019
Ink and Colour on Paper
49 cm x 48.5 cm

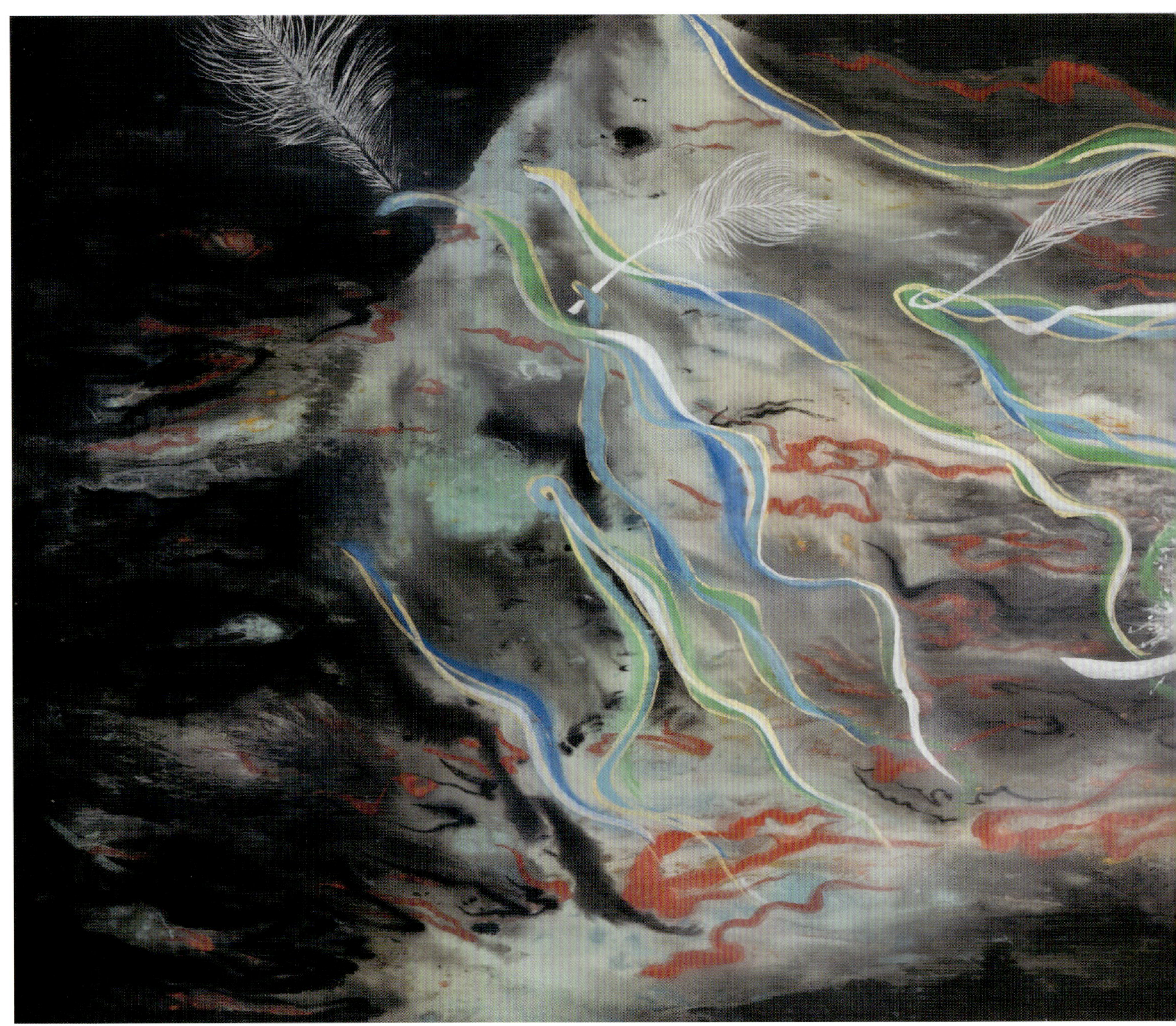

Eternal Encounters
2024
Ink and Colour on Rice Paper
40 cm x 94 cm

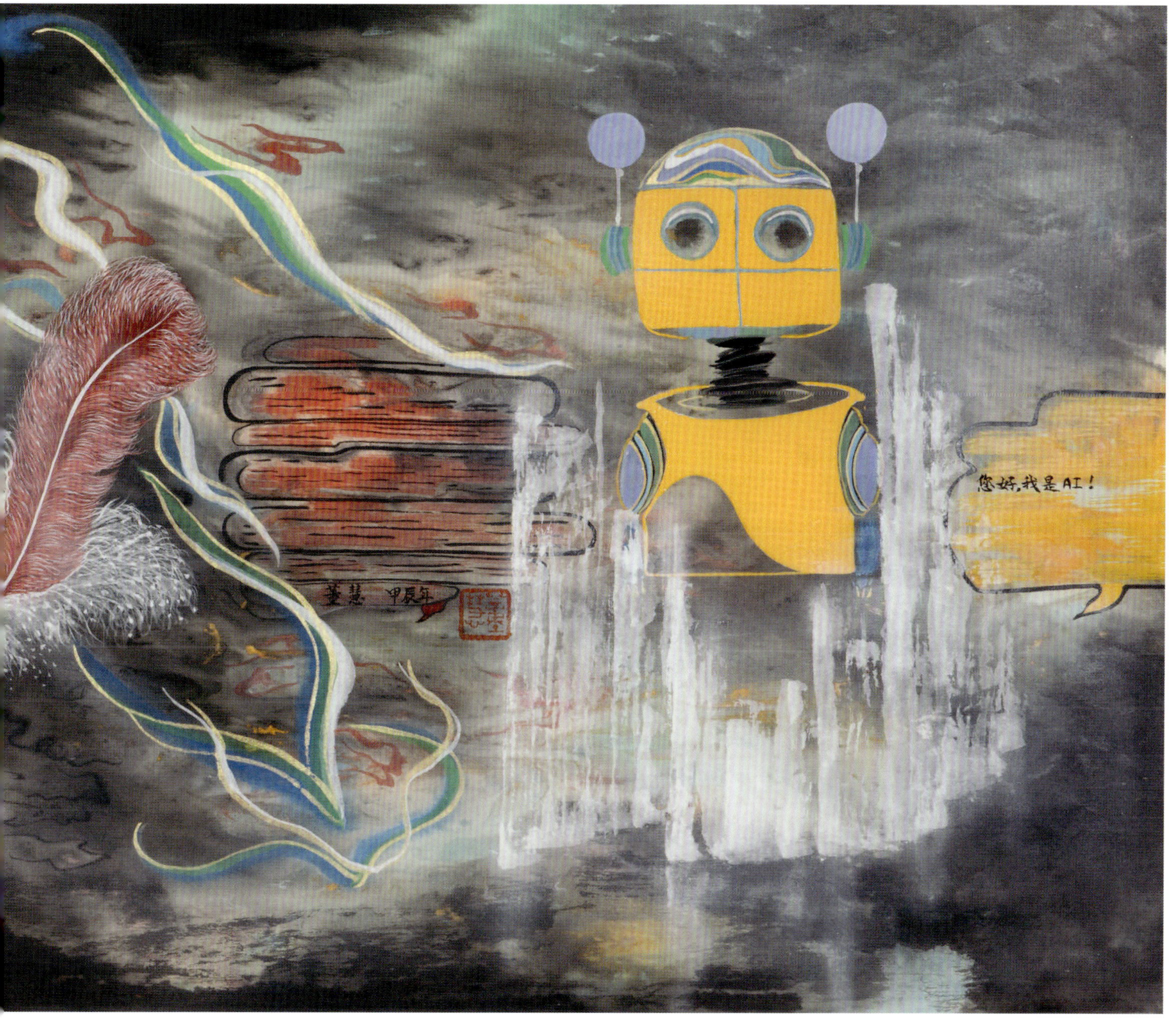
董慧 甲辰年
您好,我是AI!

Longing
2024
Ink and Colour on Rice Paper
77 cm x 40 cm

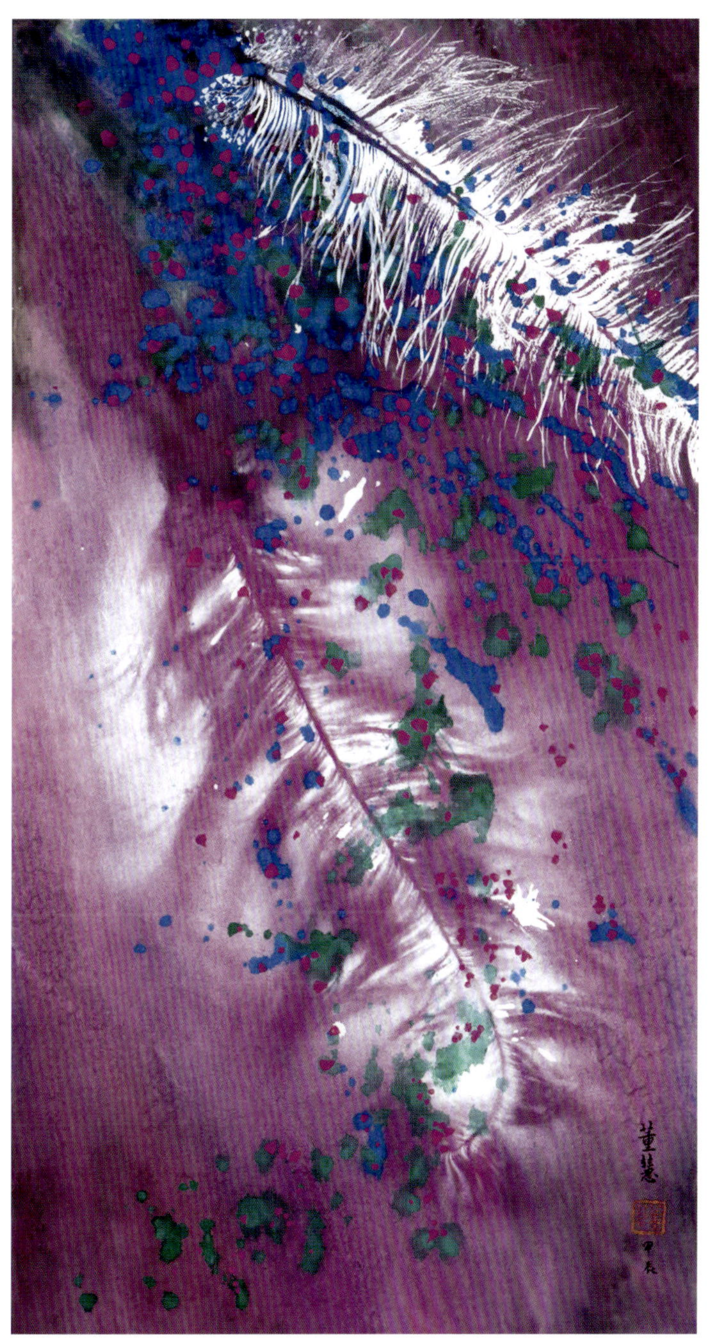
董慧

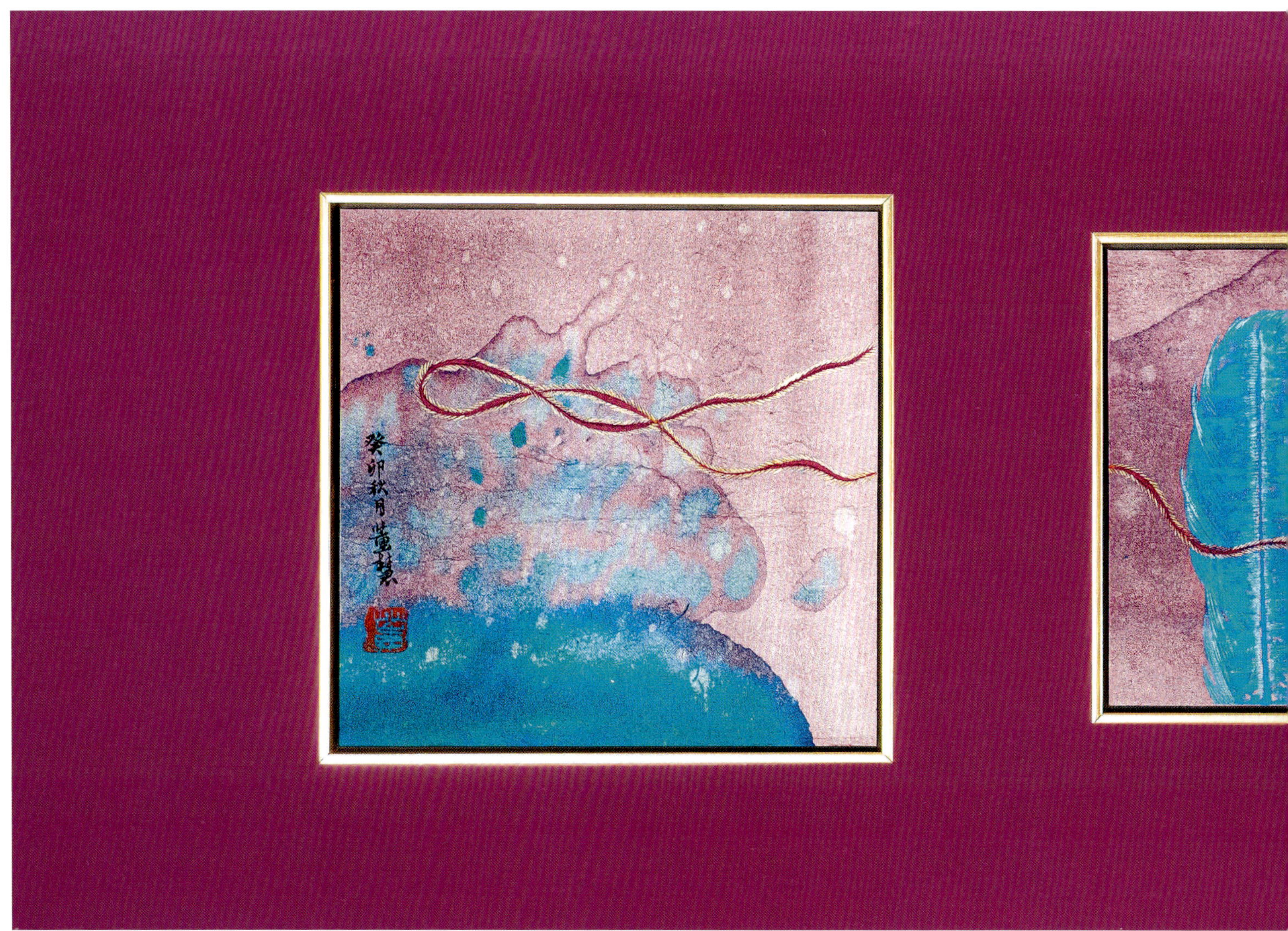

Drifting
2023
Ink and Colour on Rice Paper
31 cm x 88 cm

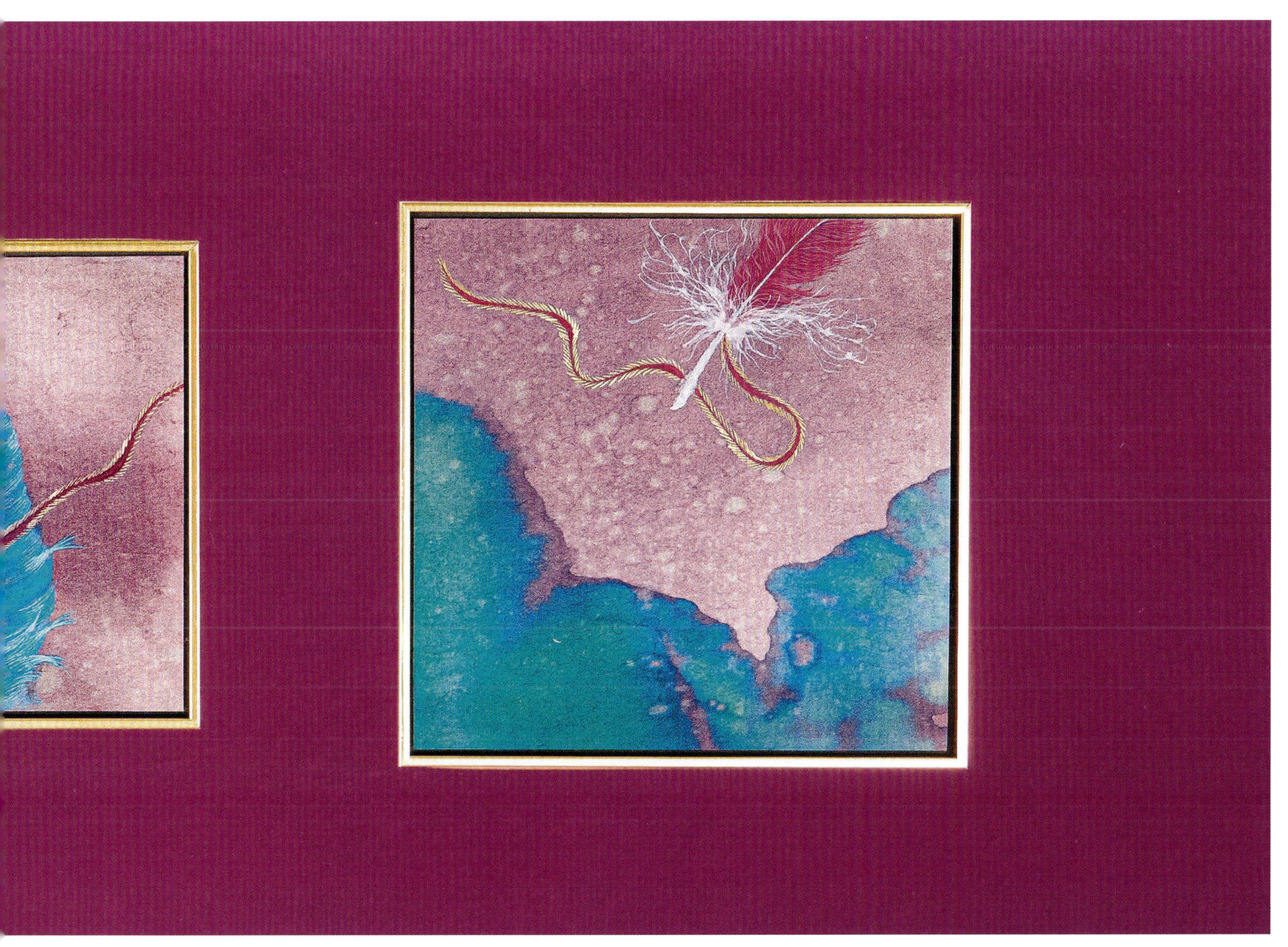

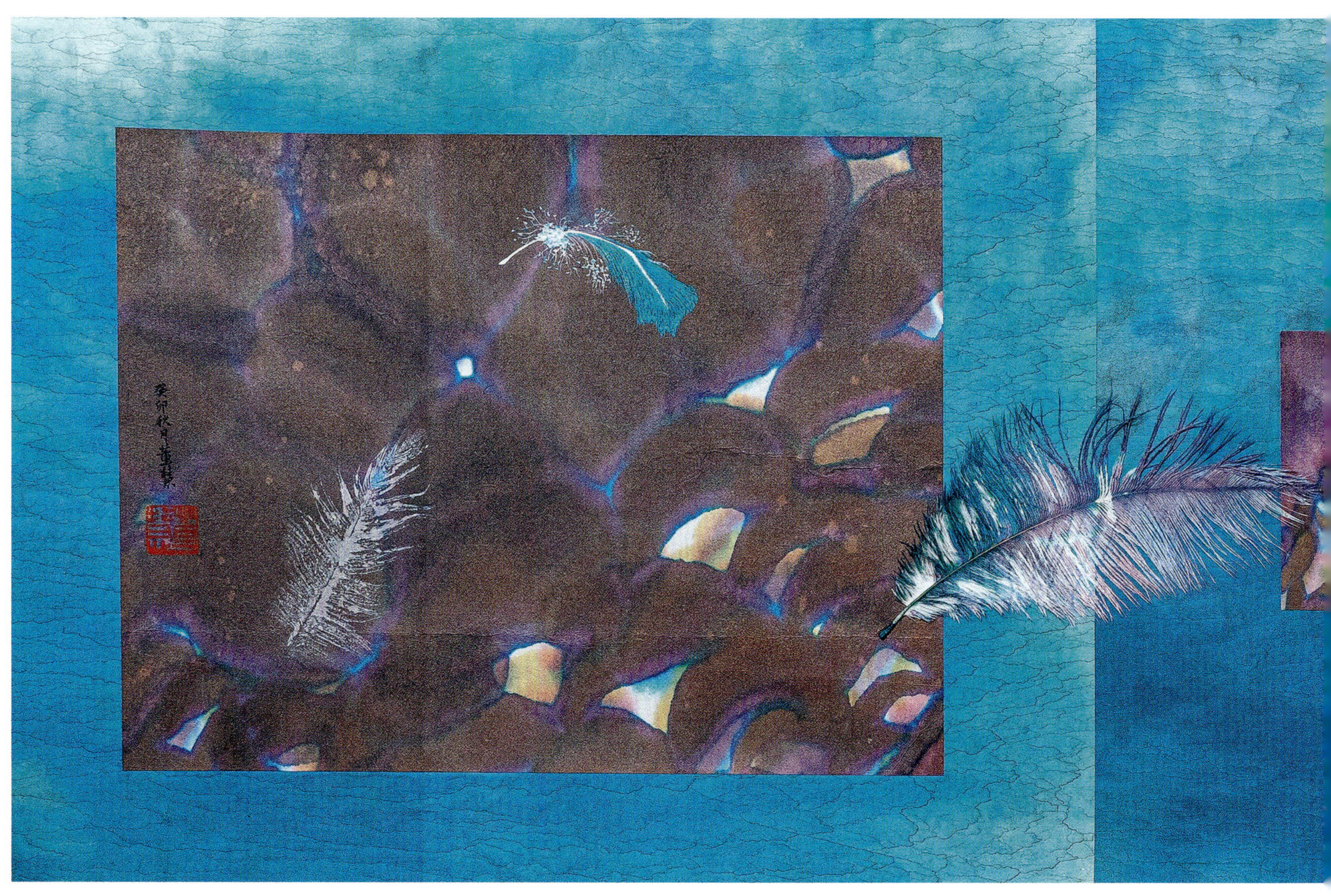

The Cutting-Edge
2023
Ink, Colour and Feather on Rice Paper
47 cm x 143.5 cm

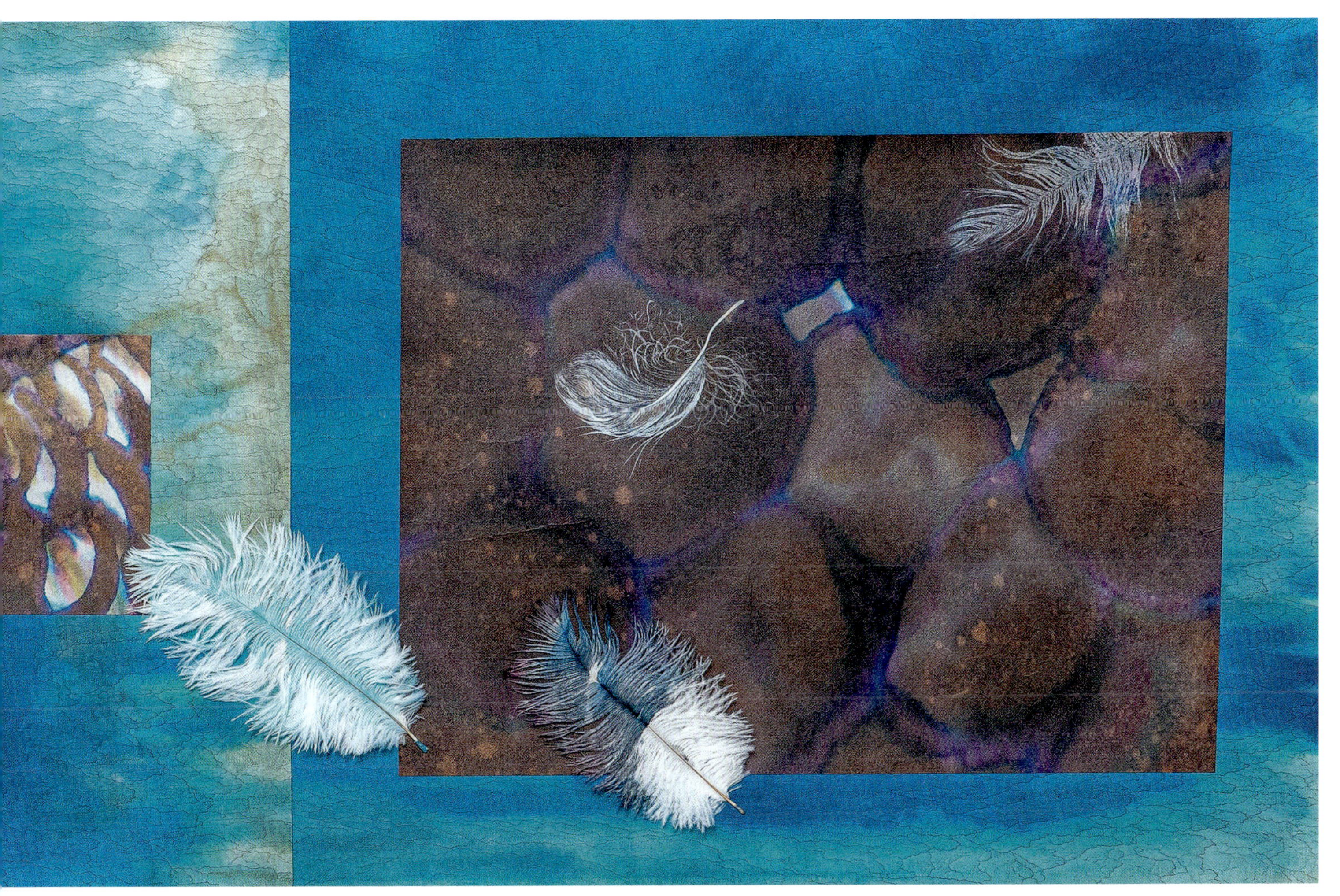

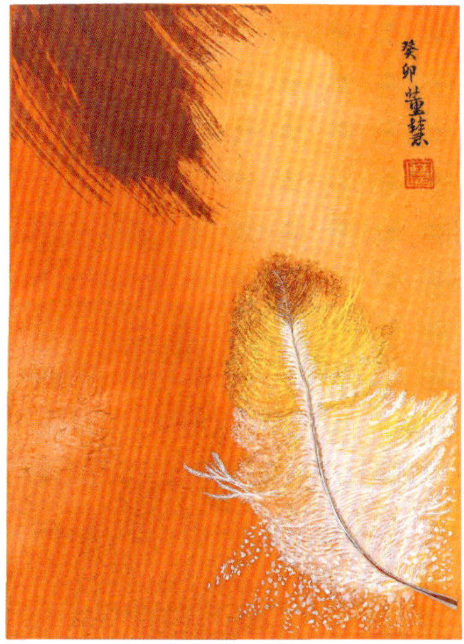

Breath of the Universe –
A Feather's Tale (1)
2023
Ink and Colour on Rice Paper
28 cm x 20 cm

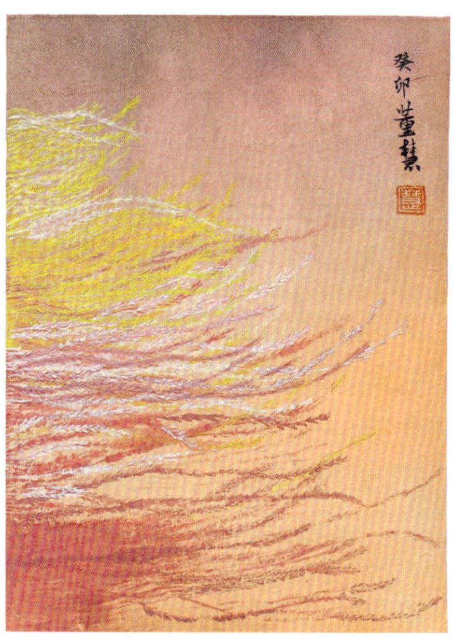

Breath of the Universe –
A Feather's Tale (2)
2023
Ink and Colour on Rice Paper
28 cm x 20 cm

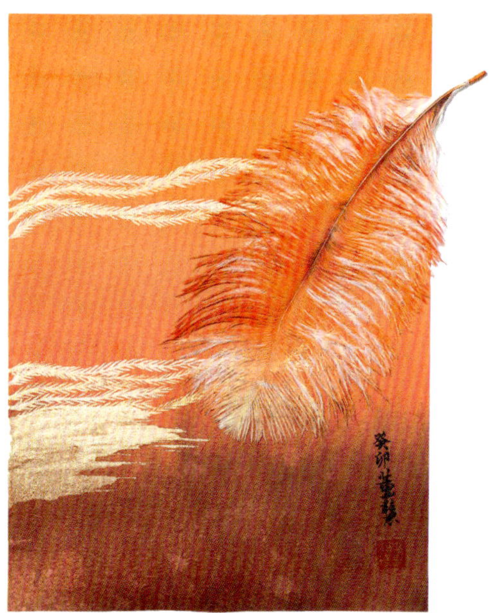

Breath of the Universe –
A Feather's Tale (3)
2023
Ink, Colour and Feather on Rice Paper
28 cm x 20 cm

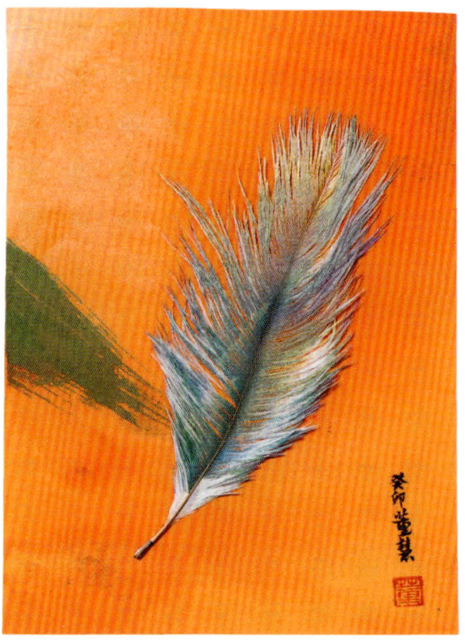

Breath of the Universe –
A Feather's Tale (4)
2023
Ink, Colour and Feather on Rice Paper
28 cm x 20 cm

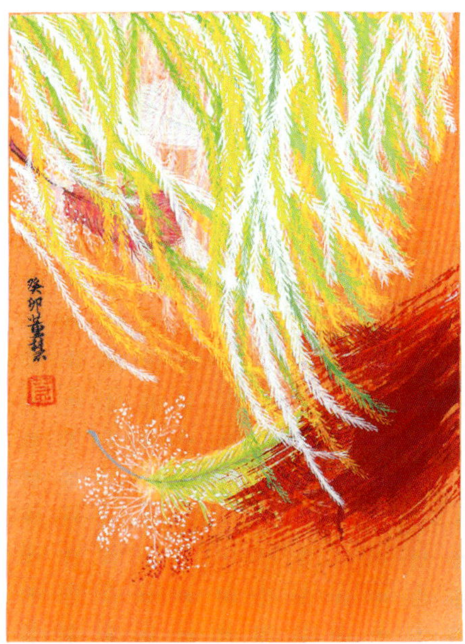

Breath of the Universe –
A Feather's Tale (5)
2023
Ink and Colour on Rice Paper
28 cm x 20 cm

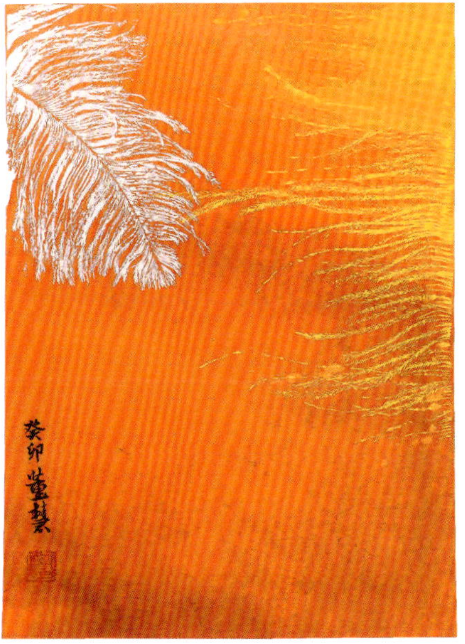

Breath of the Universe –
A Feather's Tale (6)
2023
Ink and Colour on Rice Paper
28 cm x 20 cm

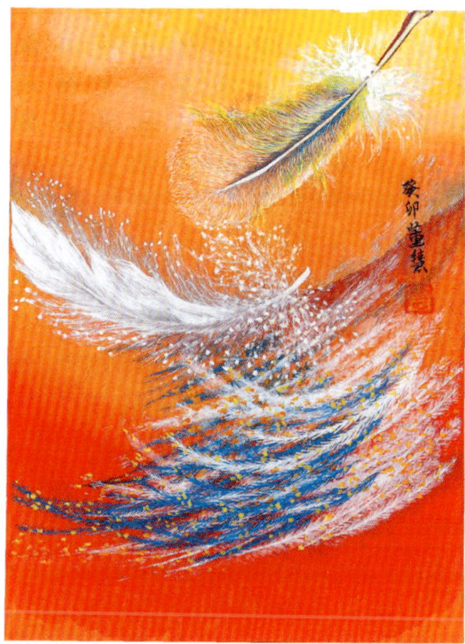

Breath of the Universe –
A Feather's Tale (7)
2023
Ink and Colour on Rice Paper
28 cm x 20 cm

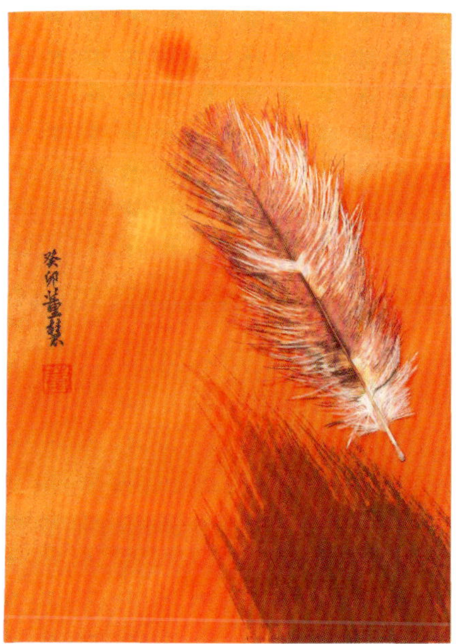

Breath of the Universe –
A Feather's Tale (8)
2023
Ink, Colour and Feather on Rice Paper
28 cm x 20 cm

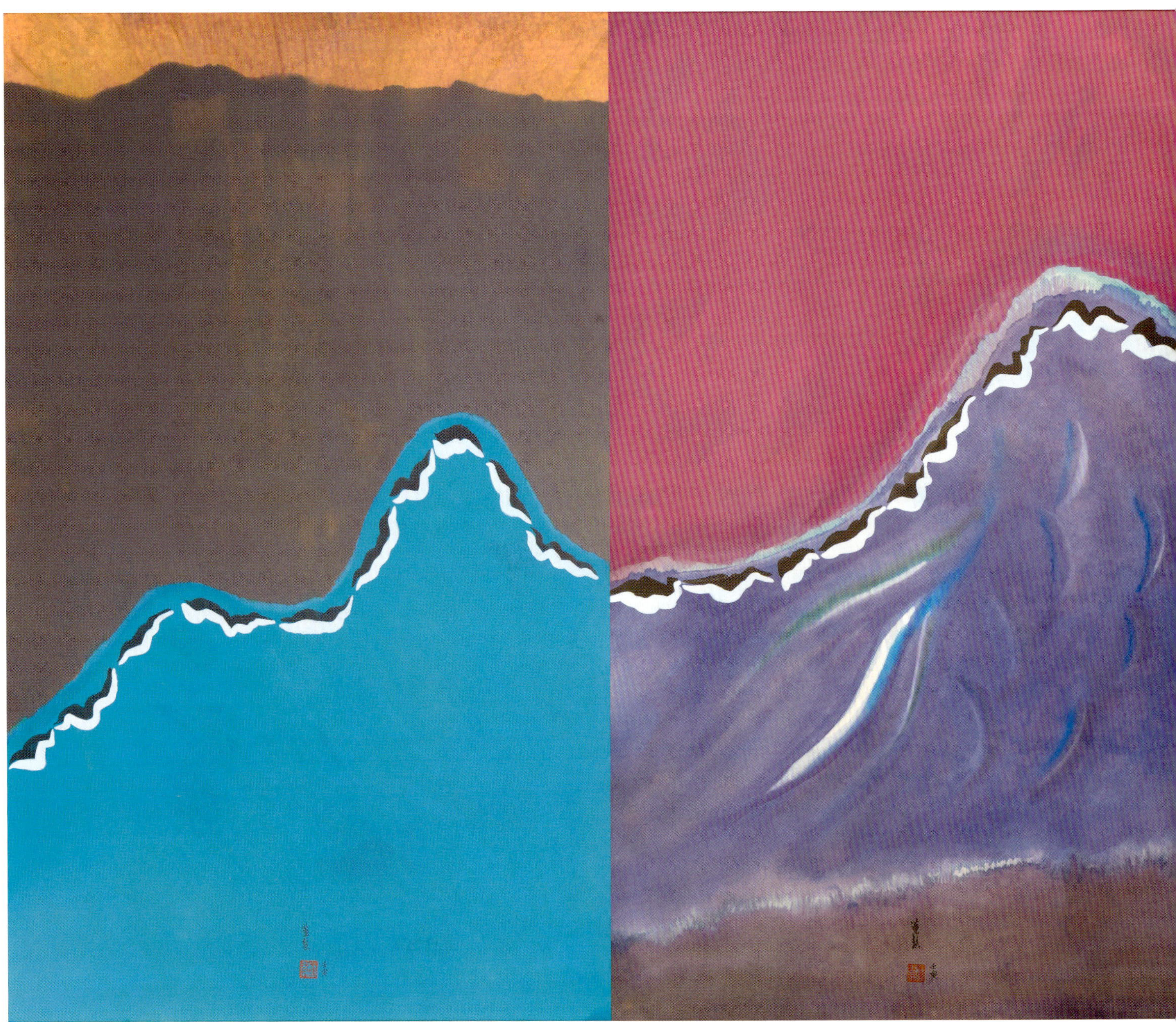

Extravaganza
2022
Mixed Media on Rice Paper
Quadriptych: 156 cm x 380 cm

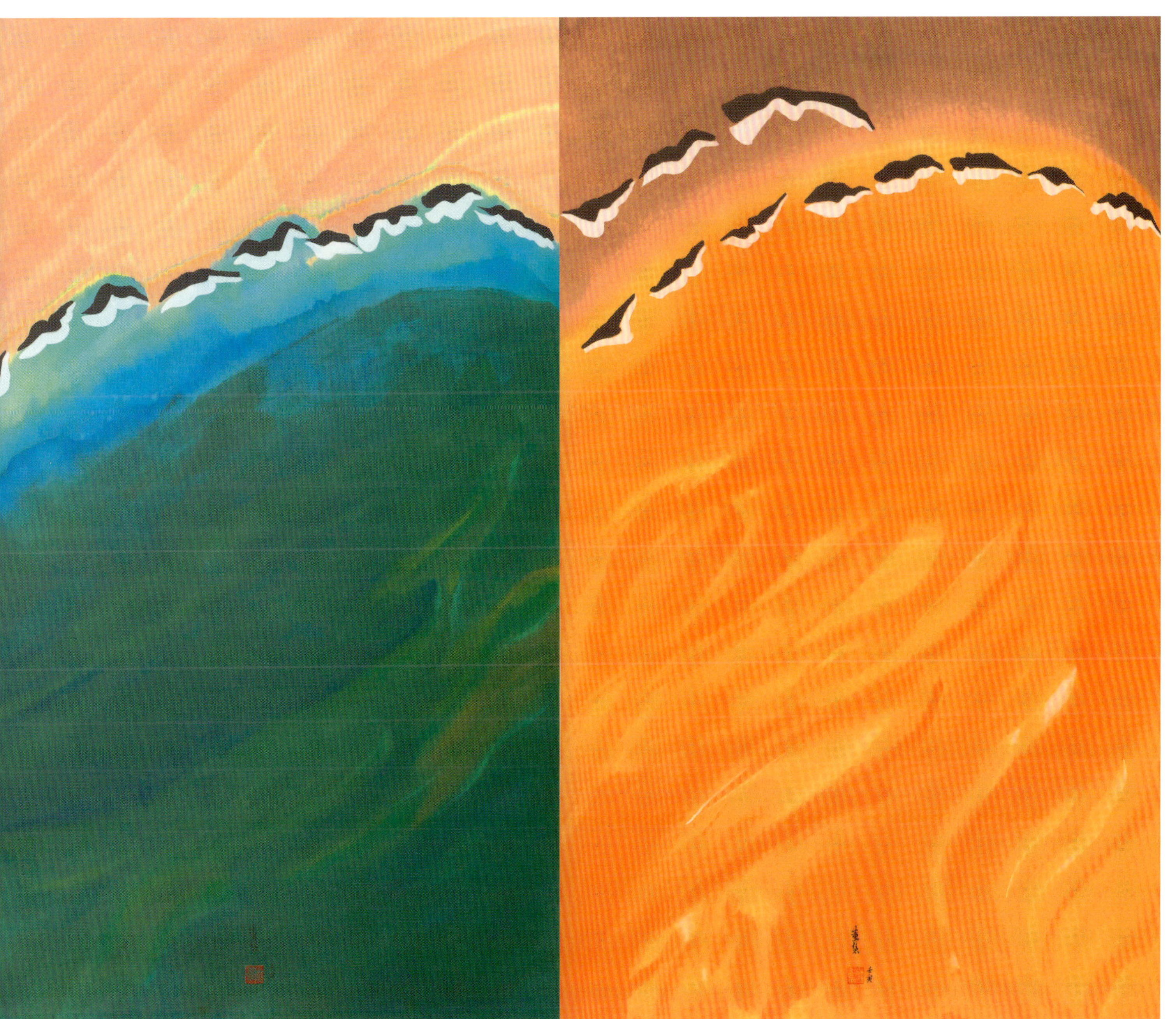

In this work 'Love of My Life', the spirits of two lovers transformed into pheasant feathers, gently drifting through misty mountains, representing their eternal love and devotion to each other during the forced separations of the pandemic. It reflects the unyielding desire for companionship – the universal human need for love and closeness, even in the face of death.

Love of My Life
2022
Mixed Media on Rice Paper
96.5 cm x 188 cm

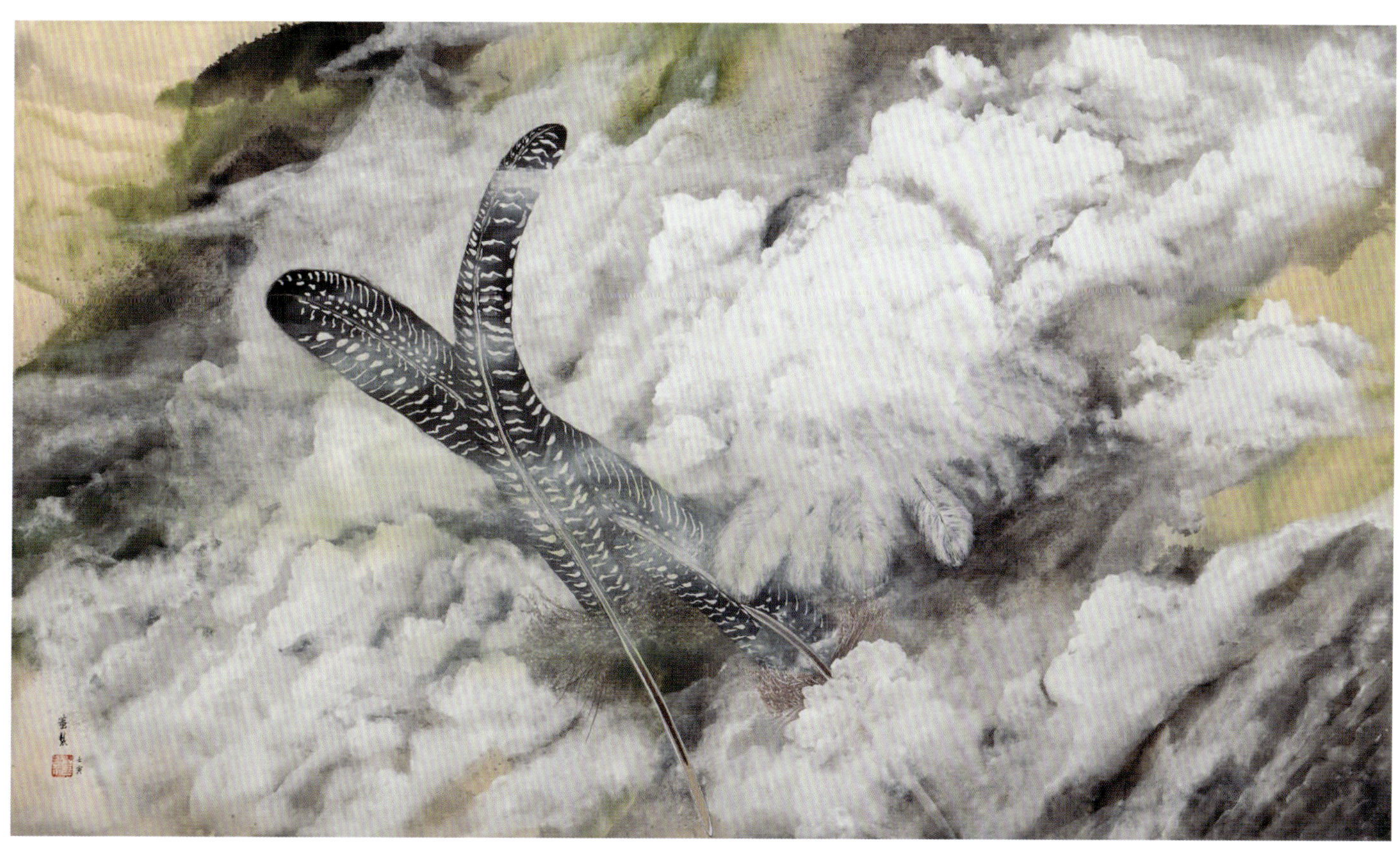

Connectivity
(A New Era under the 25th Anniversary of the Establishment of the Hong Kong Special Administrative Region)
2022
Mixed Media on Rice Paper
96 cm x 124 cm

Discover the landmarks of the West Kowloon Cultural District in Hong Kong – the Hong Kong Palace Museum, Xiqu Centre, and M+ art museum. It only takes 28 minutes to get to the District from the Hong Kong–Zhuhai–Macao Bridge.

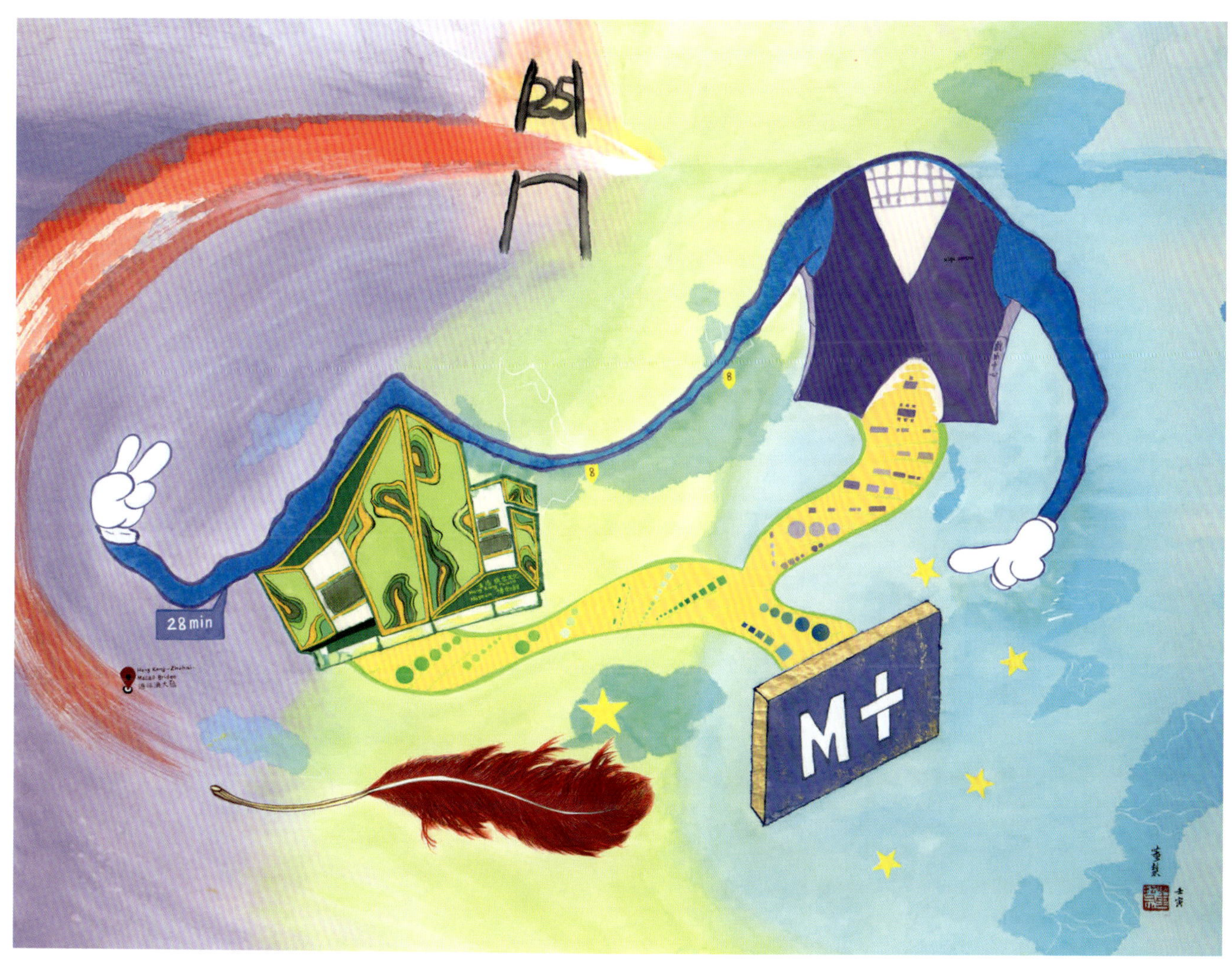
28min
M+

Still (1)
2021
Ink and Colour on Rice Paper
40 cm x 30 cm

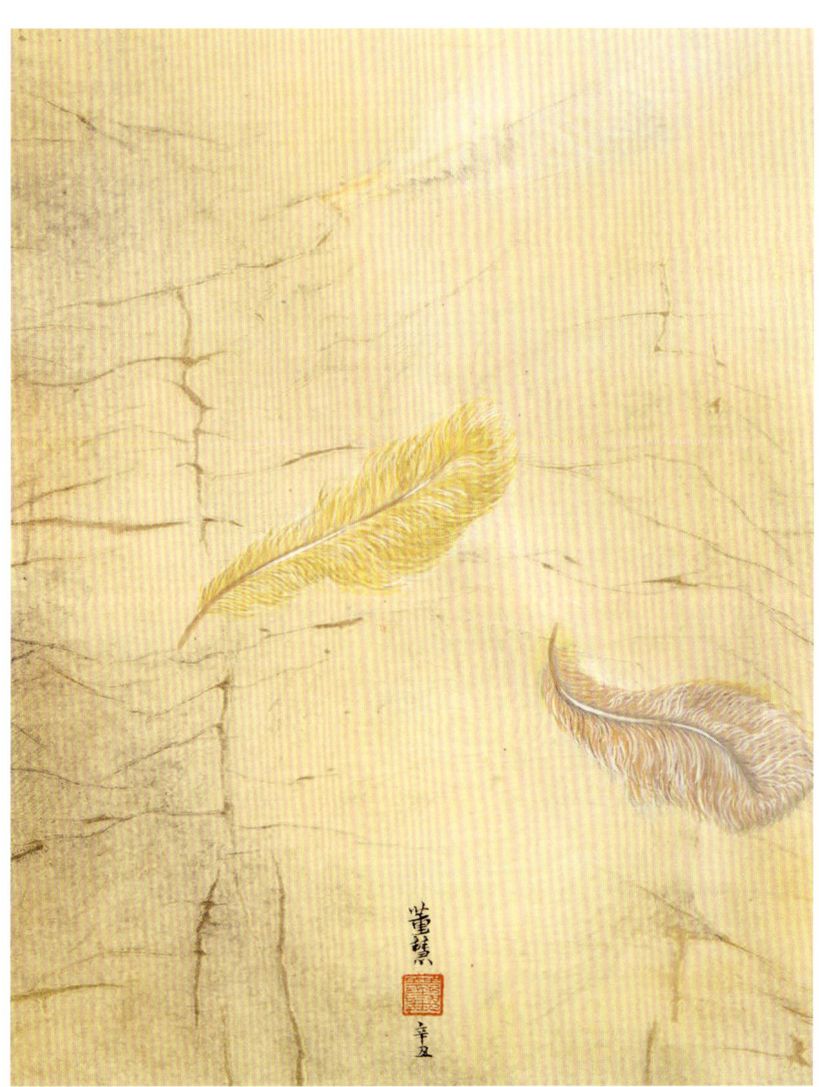
辛丑

Still (2)
2021
Ink and Colour on Rice Paper
40 cm x 32 cm

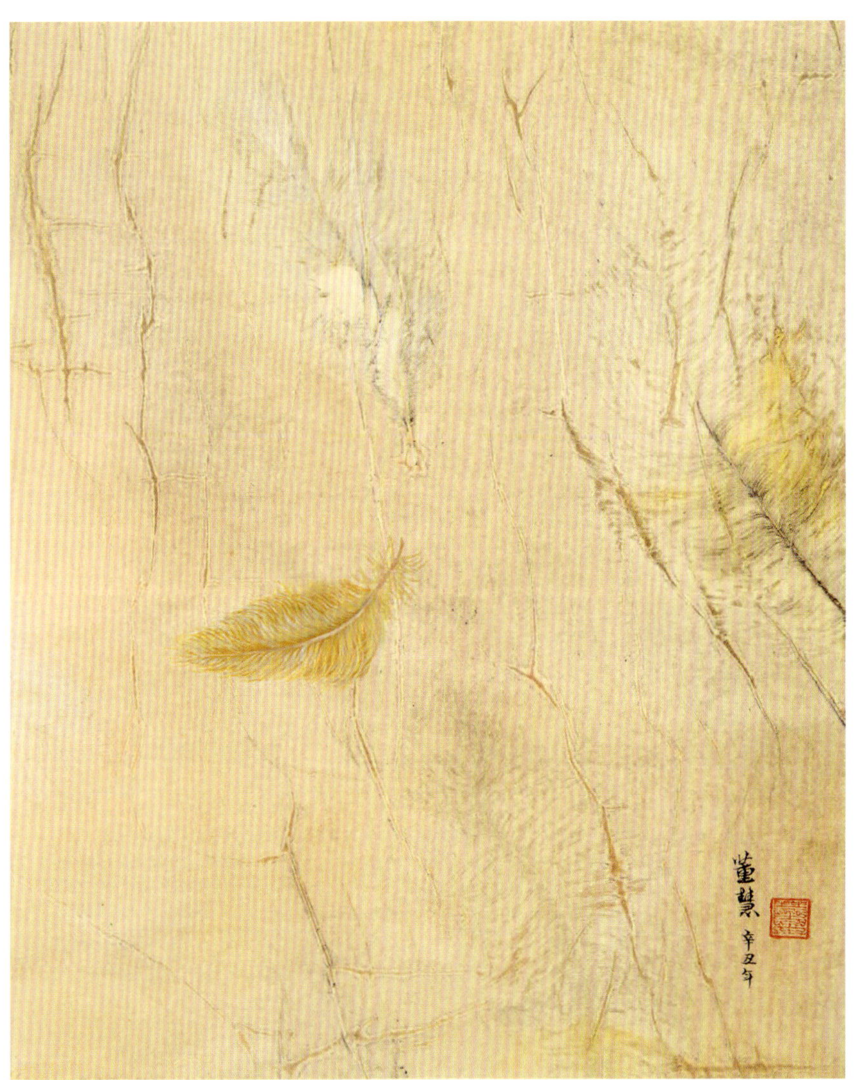
董慧
辛丑年

Anti-coronavirus
2020
Mixed Media on Rice Paper
120 cm x 69 cm

Selected and featured in *'Beijing International Art Biennale 'Fighting with Love' Anti-coronavirus Series (Hong Kong)'*

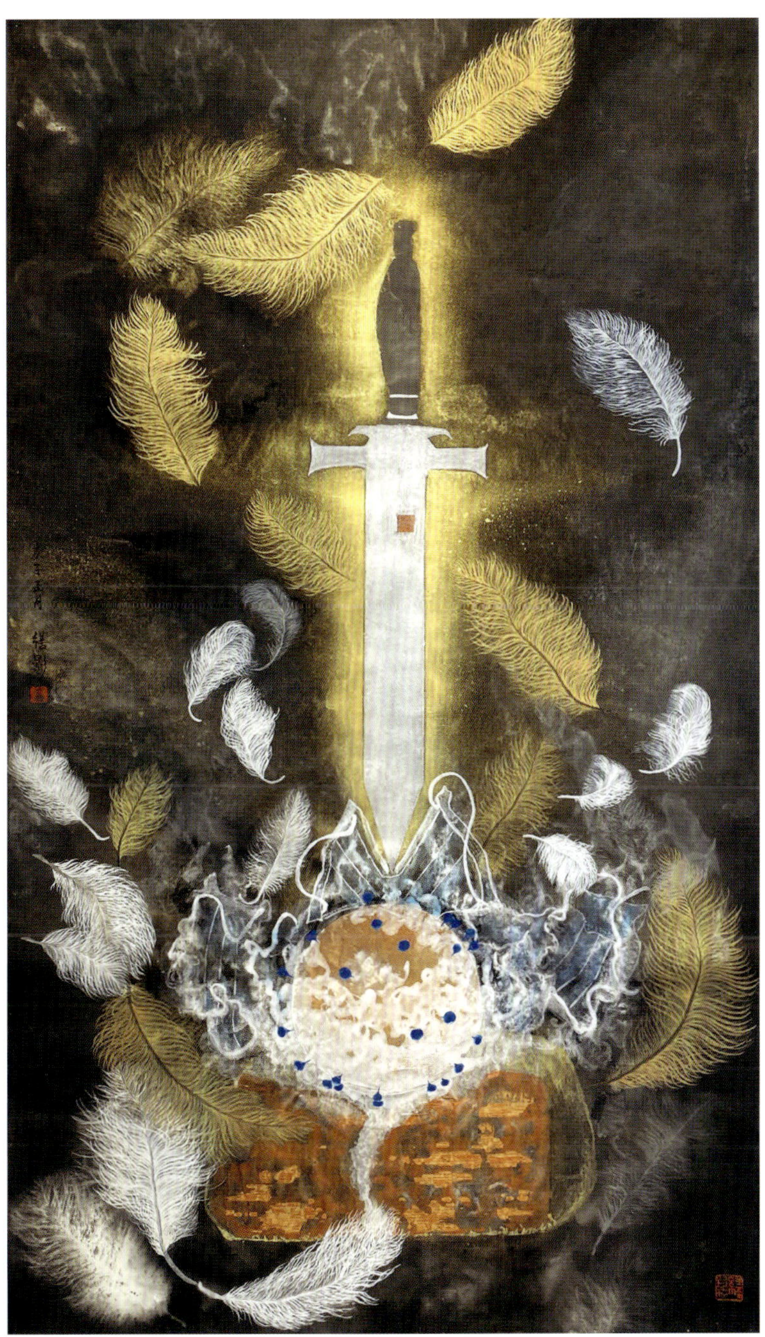

Reflection from Christina

Nothing lasts forever,
even those you hold dear
You lose some to gain more

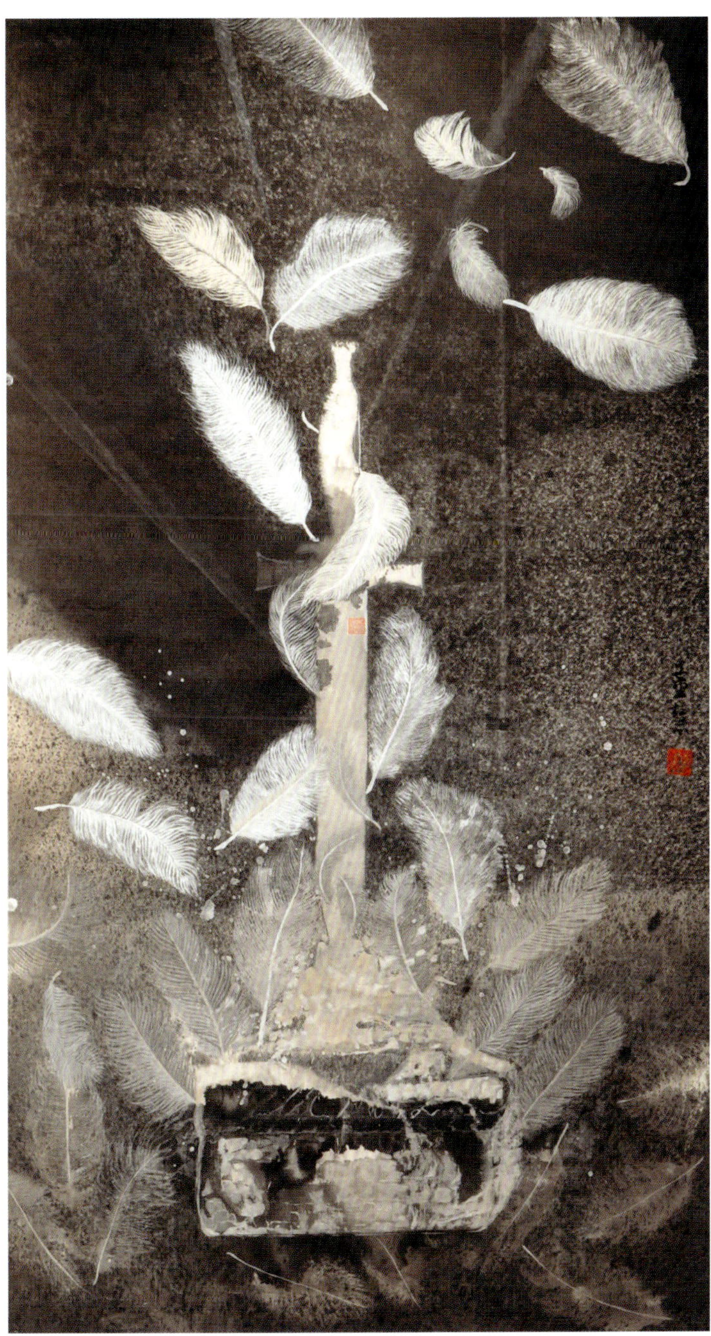

Liberation (1)
2019
Mixed Media on Rice Paper
123 cm x 65 cm

Reflection from Christina

Phoenix rising from the ashes

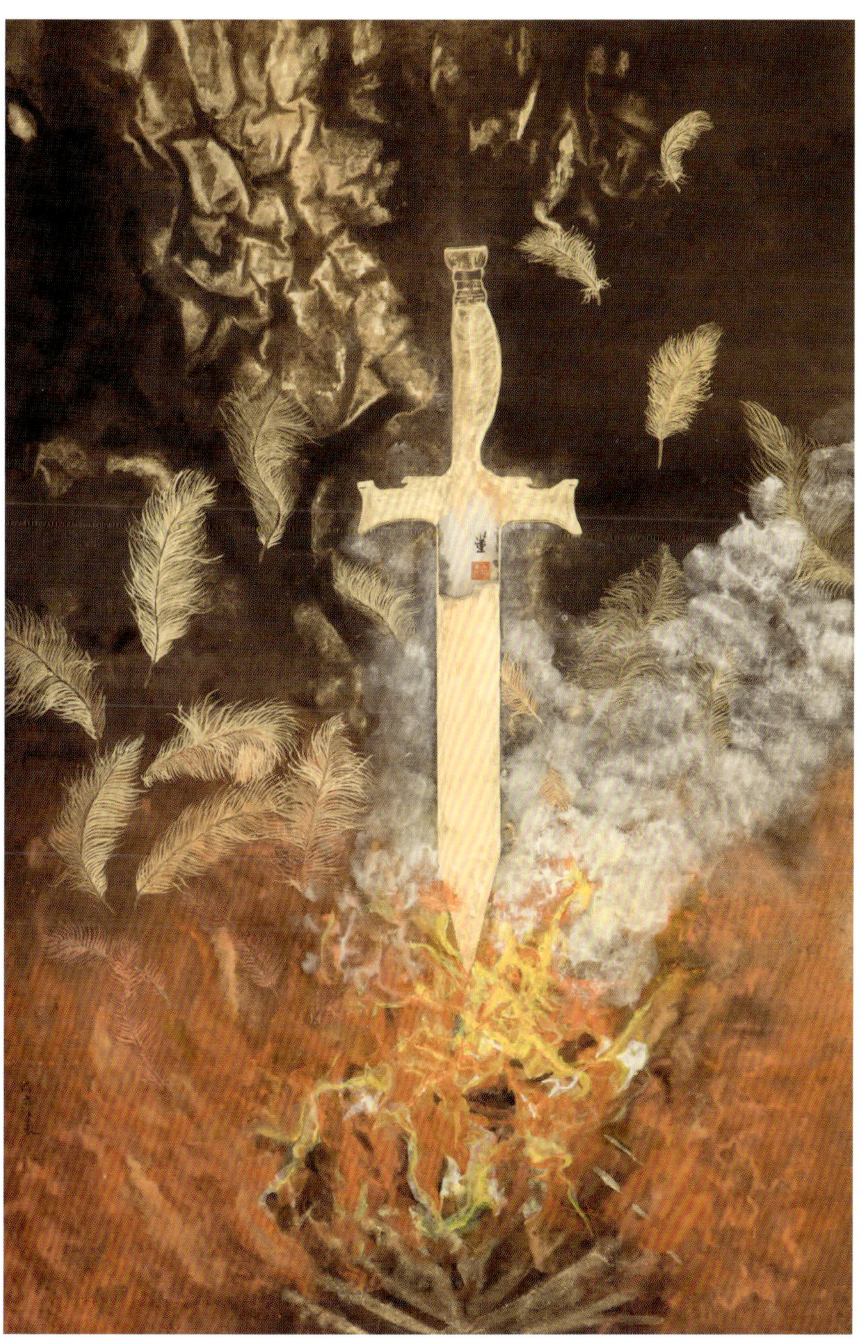

Liberation (2)
2019
Mixed Media on Rice Paper
109 cm x 69 cm

Reflection from Christina

The true meaning of freedom comes within
Beyond the bounds of time

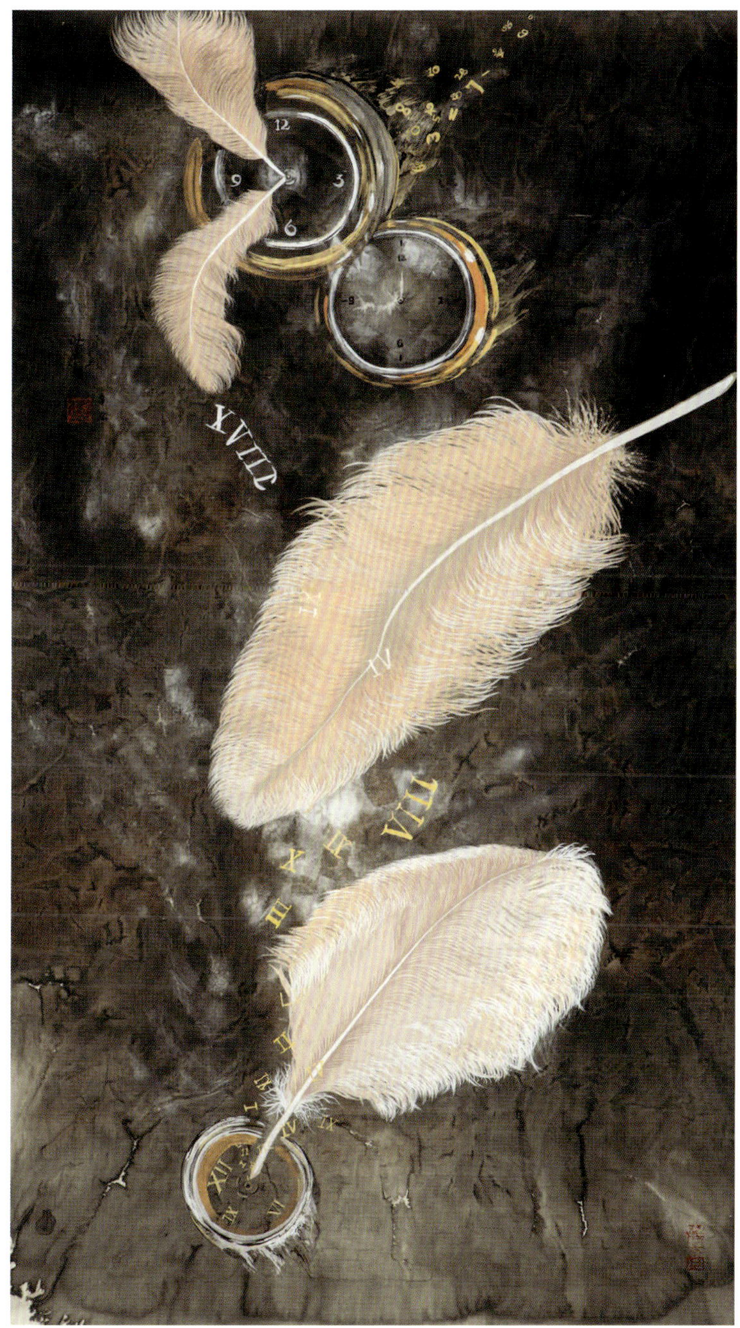

Infinity
2019
Ink and Colour on Rice Paper
125 cm x 70 cm

Reflection from Christina

In the dark is where you'll see my truest colours
Still, I can't help but be your shadow no matter where you go

Artworks: Rice Paper

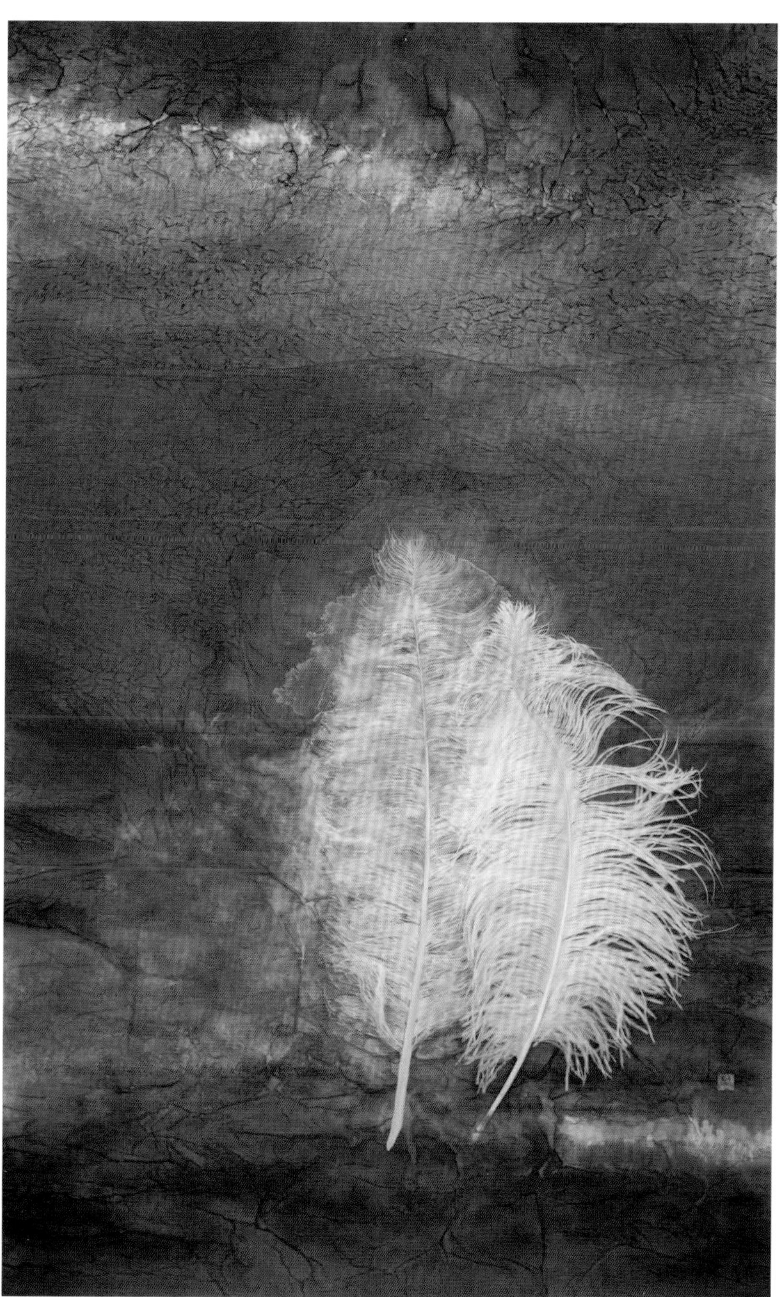

Be Your Shadow
2019
Ink, Colour and Feather on Paper
112 cm x 65 cm

RENDEZVOUS

Every speck of earthly dust weighs as it's preset.
A load on the mind can't come from nowhere to begin with.
Like where a raindrop lands, a flower re-blooms too.
We've come across each other; where no rendezvous is needed,
we're in love with one another.

He Jialin

[Translated by Allen Zhuang]

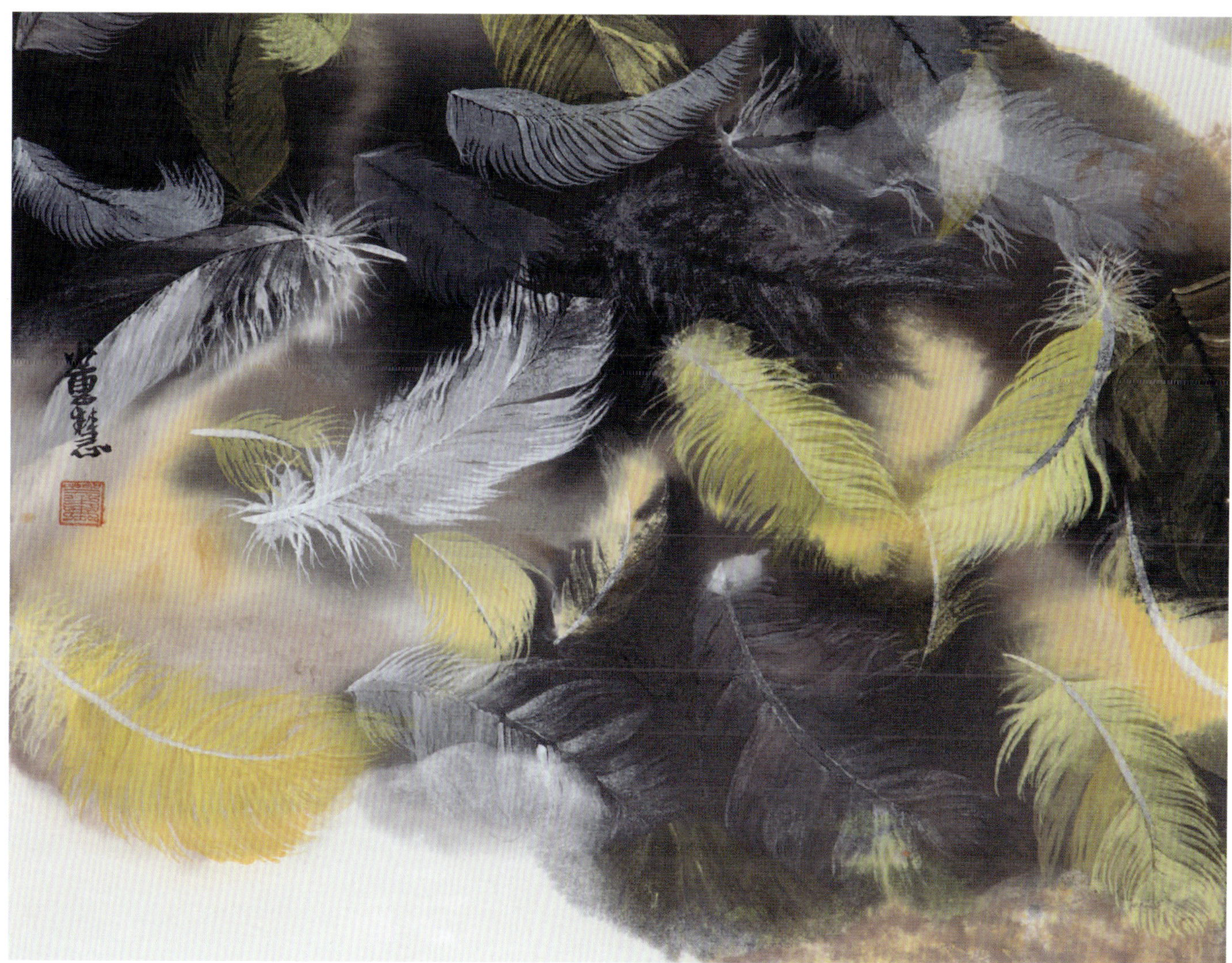

Courteously
2018
Ink and Colour on Rice Paper
33 cm x 42 cm

Edge Of Galaxy (1)
2018
Ink and Colour on Rice Paper
42 cm x 37 cm

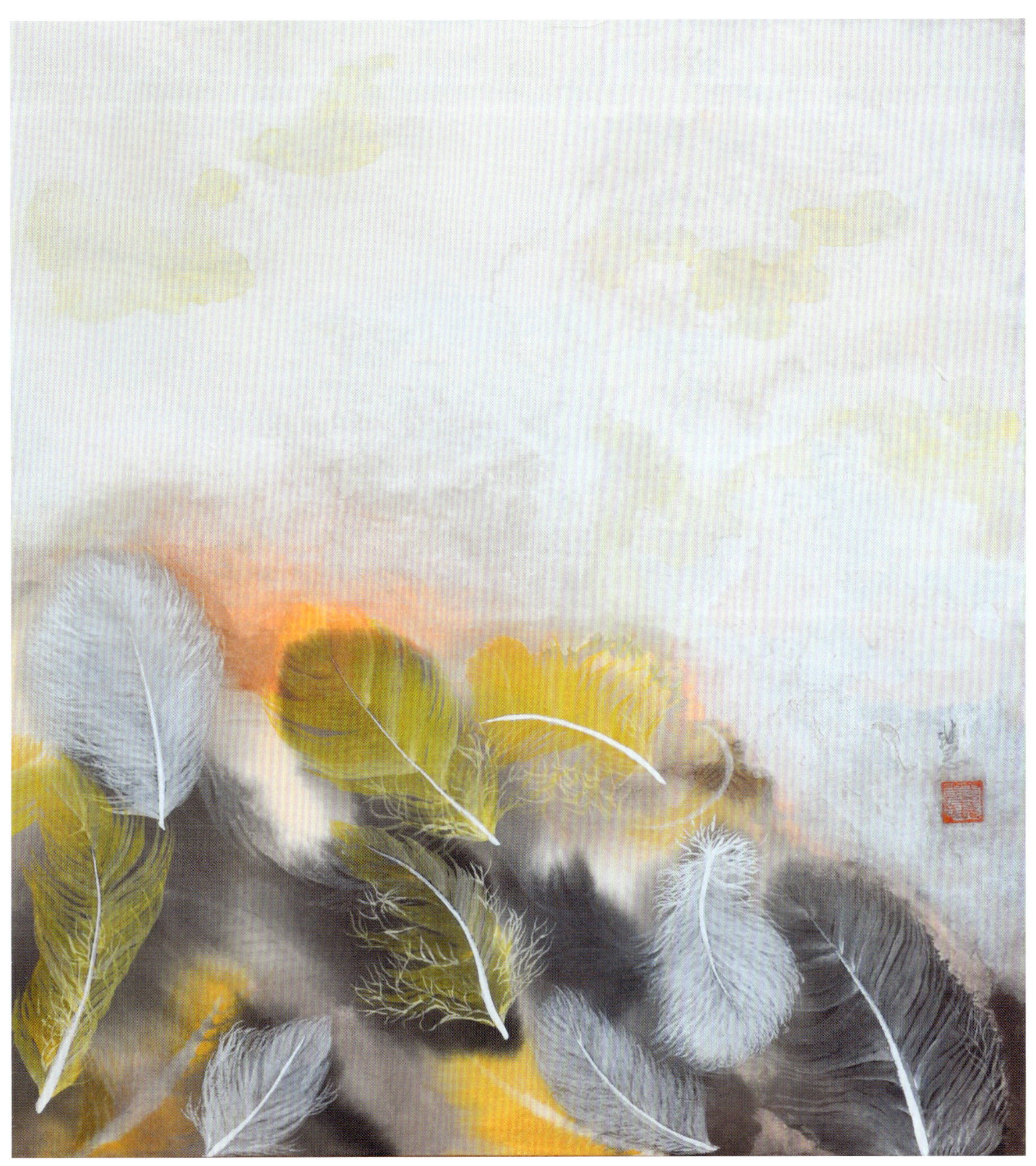

Edge Of Galaxy (2)
2018
Ink and Colour on Rice Paper
43 cm x 28 cm

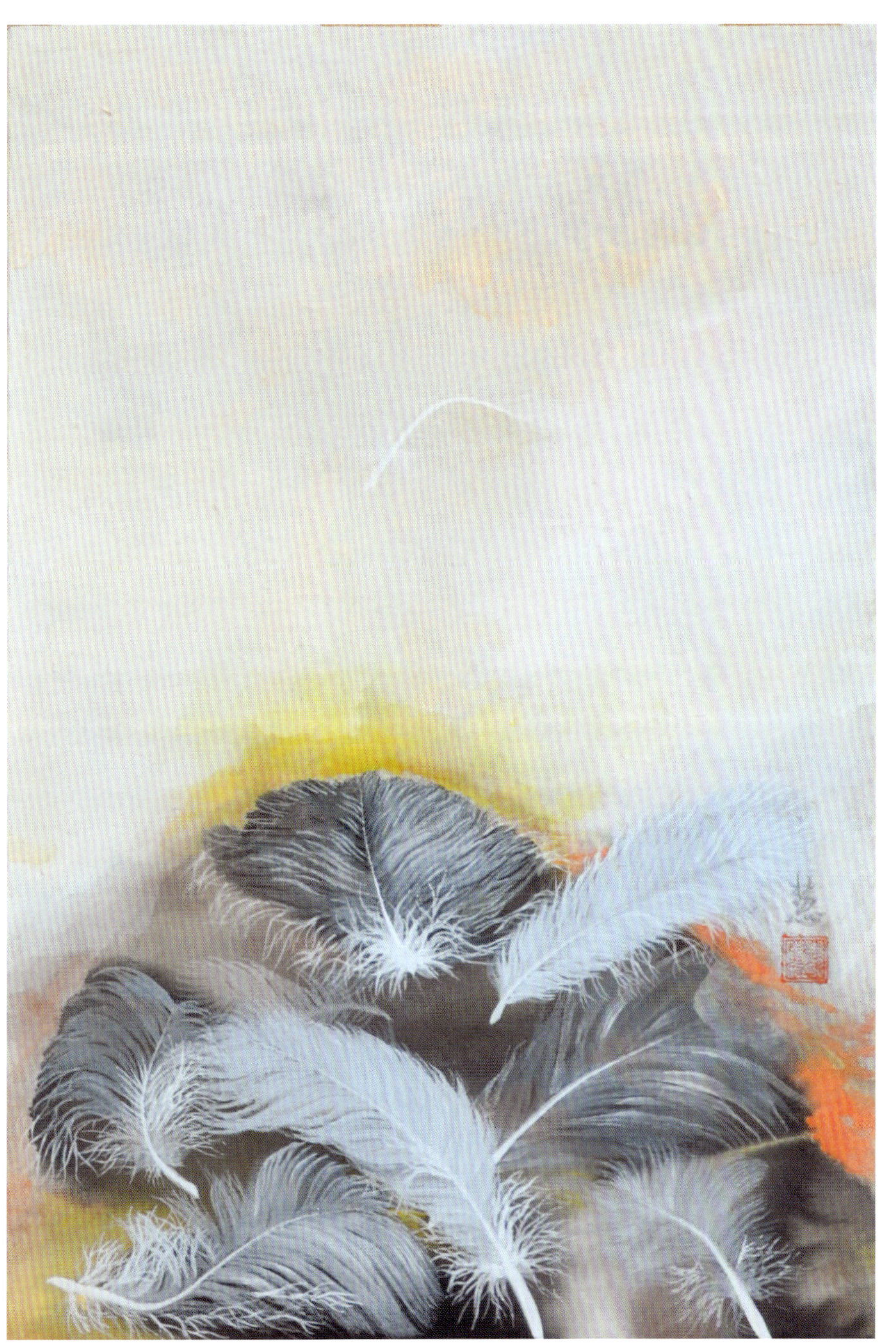

Reflection from Christina

Howling winds awaken me
Midnight blues are calling
Let the wind sweep everything away

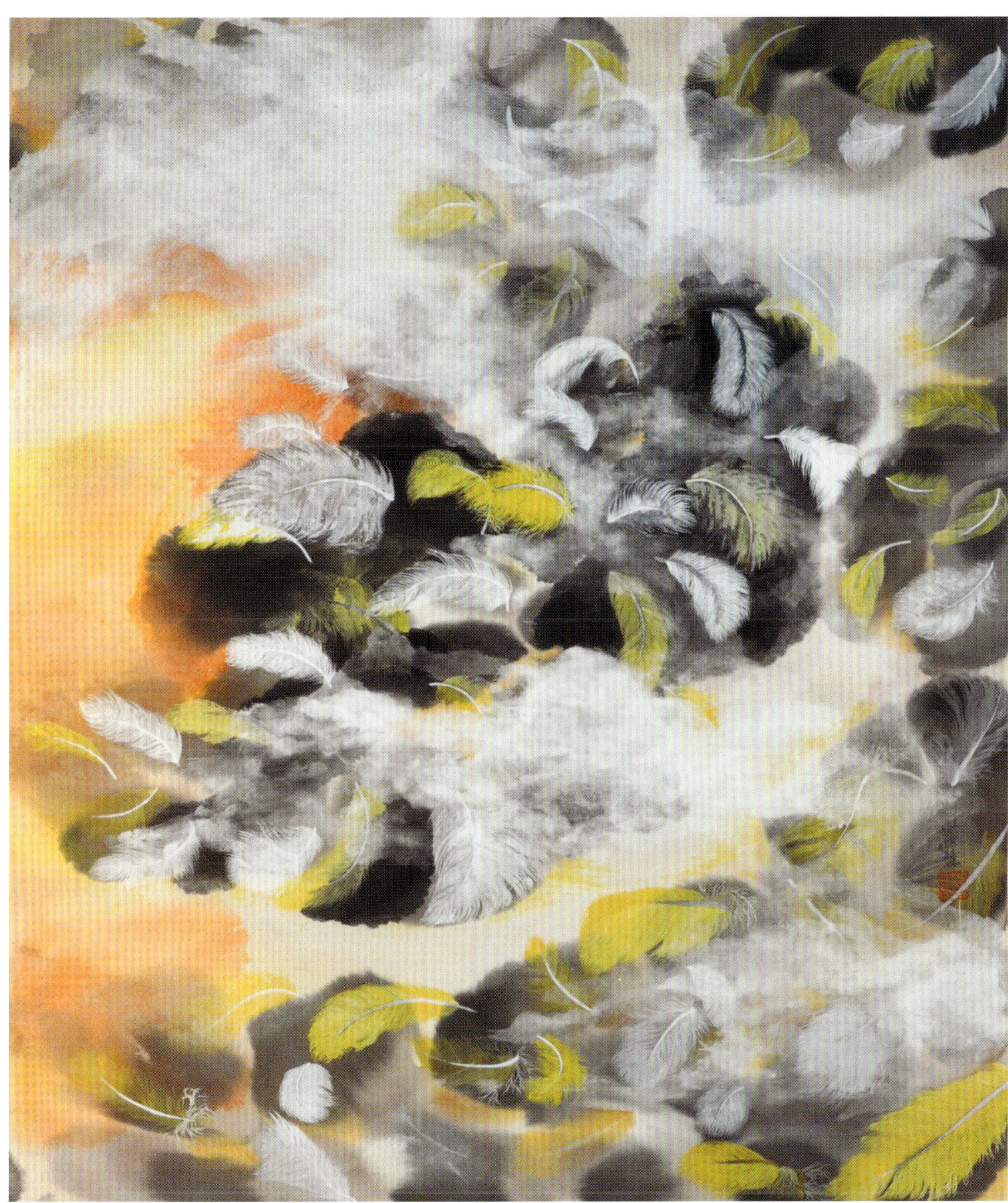

Follow the Wind
2018
Ink and Colour on Rice Paper
96 cm x 81 cm

THE COVENANT

O ye waves,
The oceanic language that ne'er fades!
With the softest, tenderest power,
You've subdued the shores,
Leaving upon their rocks,
Unpointed, smooth-edged memories.

Ah, the azure notes of music,
So simply pure yet so,
Unfathomable,
At the hard, rough feet of the shores,
They surge endlessly with lovesick infatuation.

Over the horizon comes,
A wavy band of blue feathers.
Time after time,
It's shattered by the billows.
And time after time again,
It's adorned with silvery brims and lifted aloft,
By the waves.

Impression (Yin Xiang)

(Translated by Allen Zhuang)

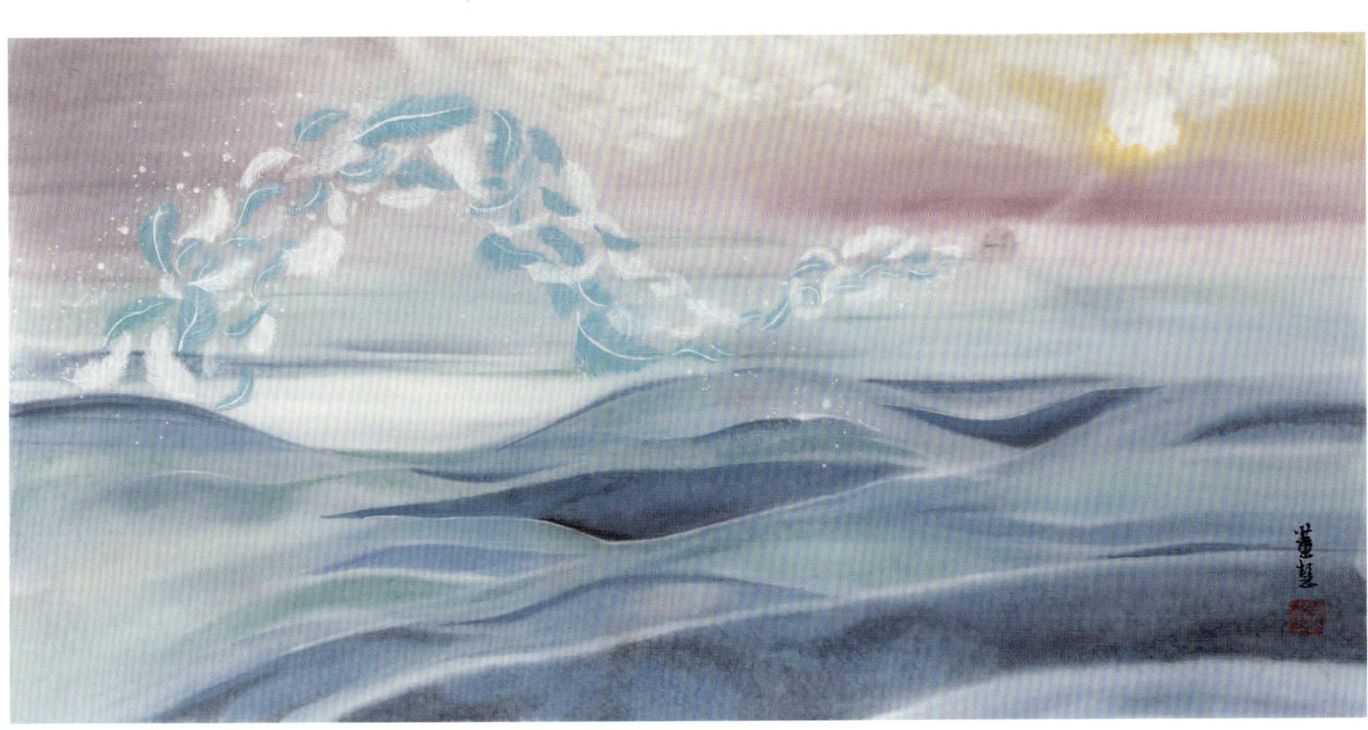

Over the Ocean
2018
Ink and Colour on Rice Paper
48 cm x 94 cm

Acquaintances
2018
Ink and Colour on Rice Paper
24 cm x 27 cm

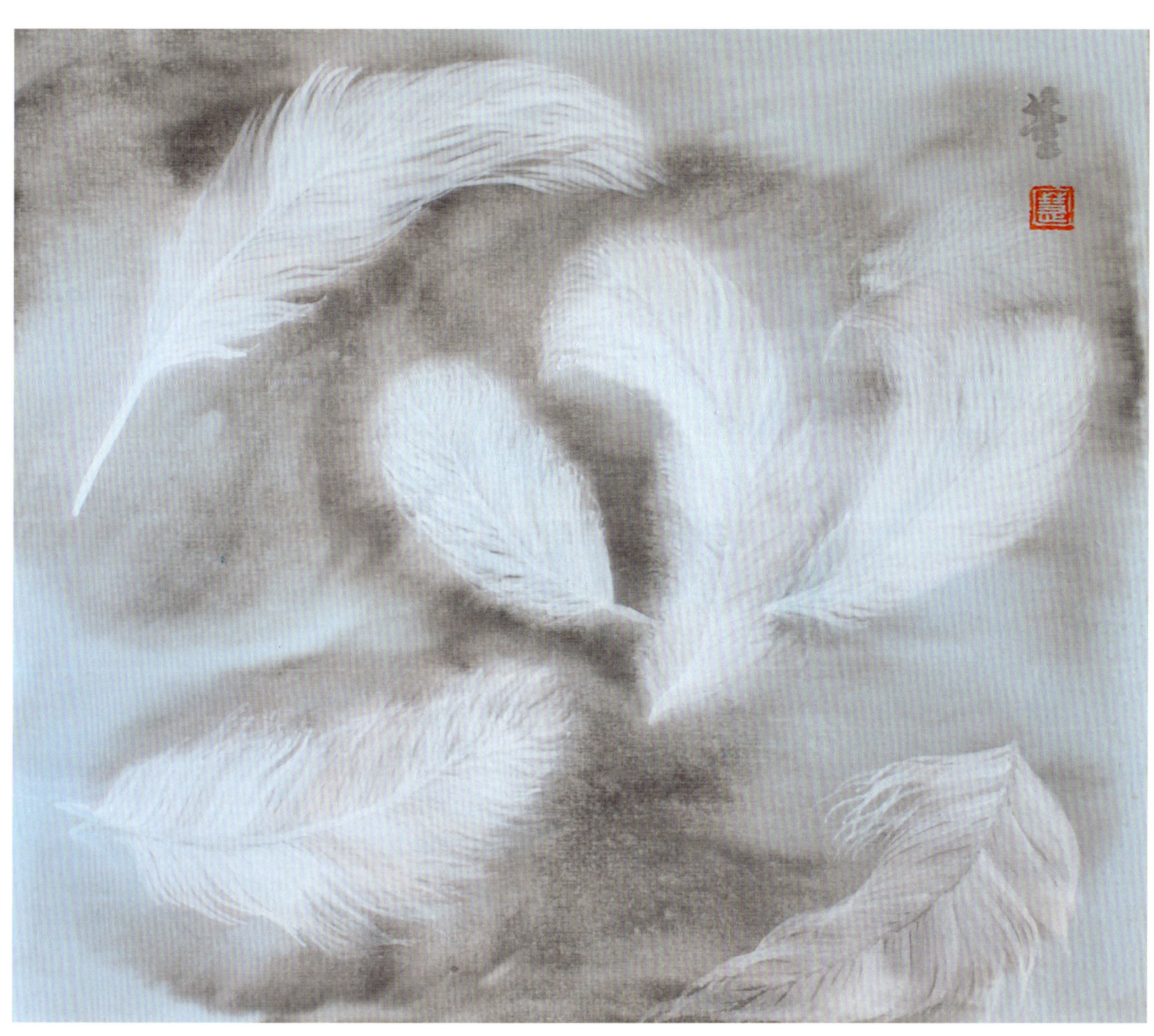

Love Nest
2018
Ink and Colour on Rice Paper
69 cm x 45 cm

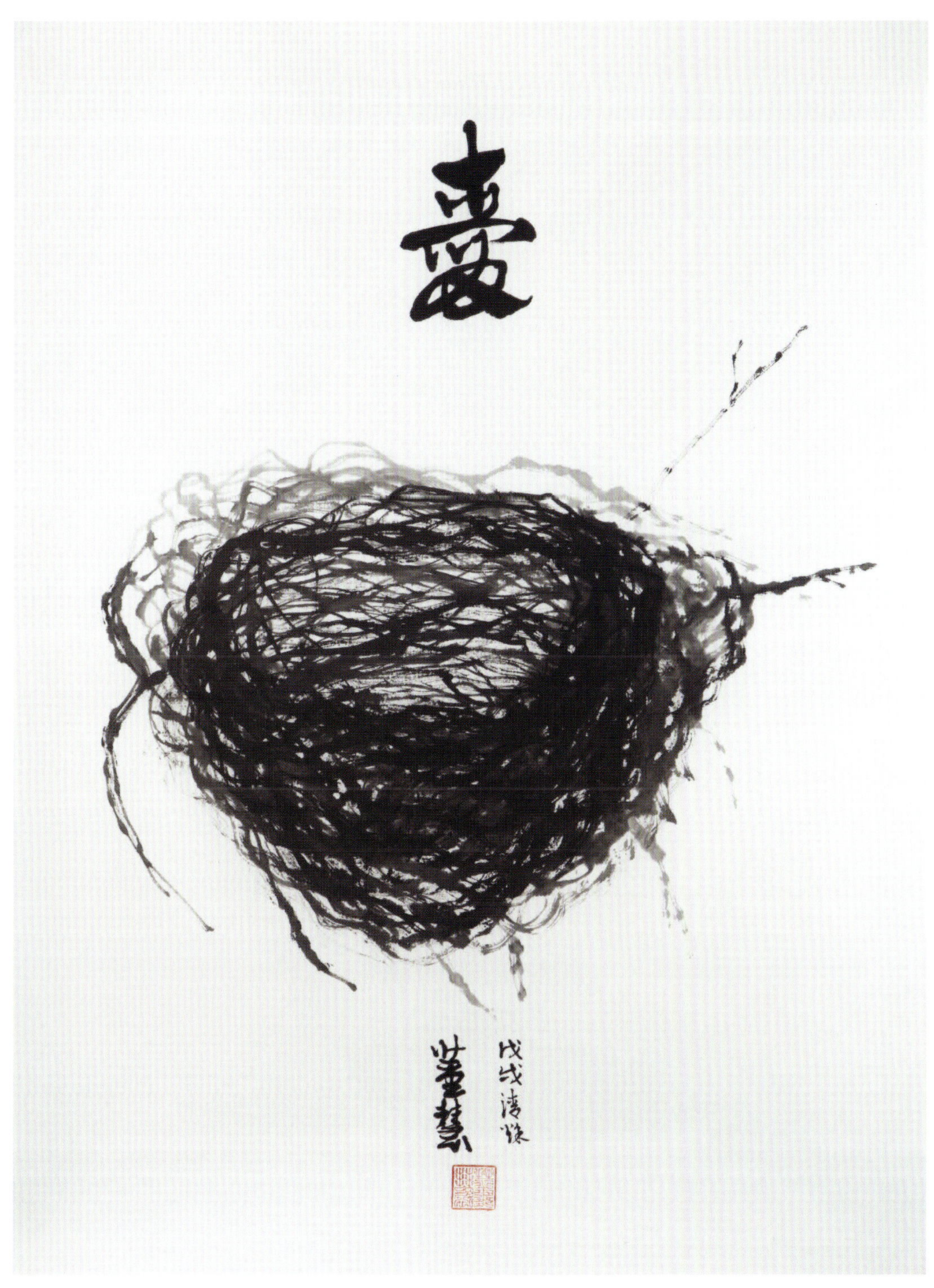

Reflection from Christina

Do not spoil what you have by desiring what you have not
Start by believing in yourself

Artworks: Rice Paper

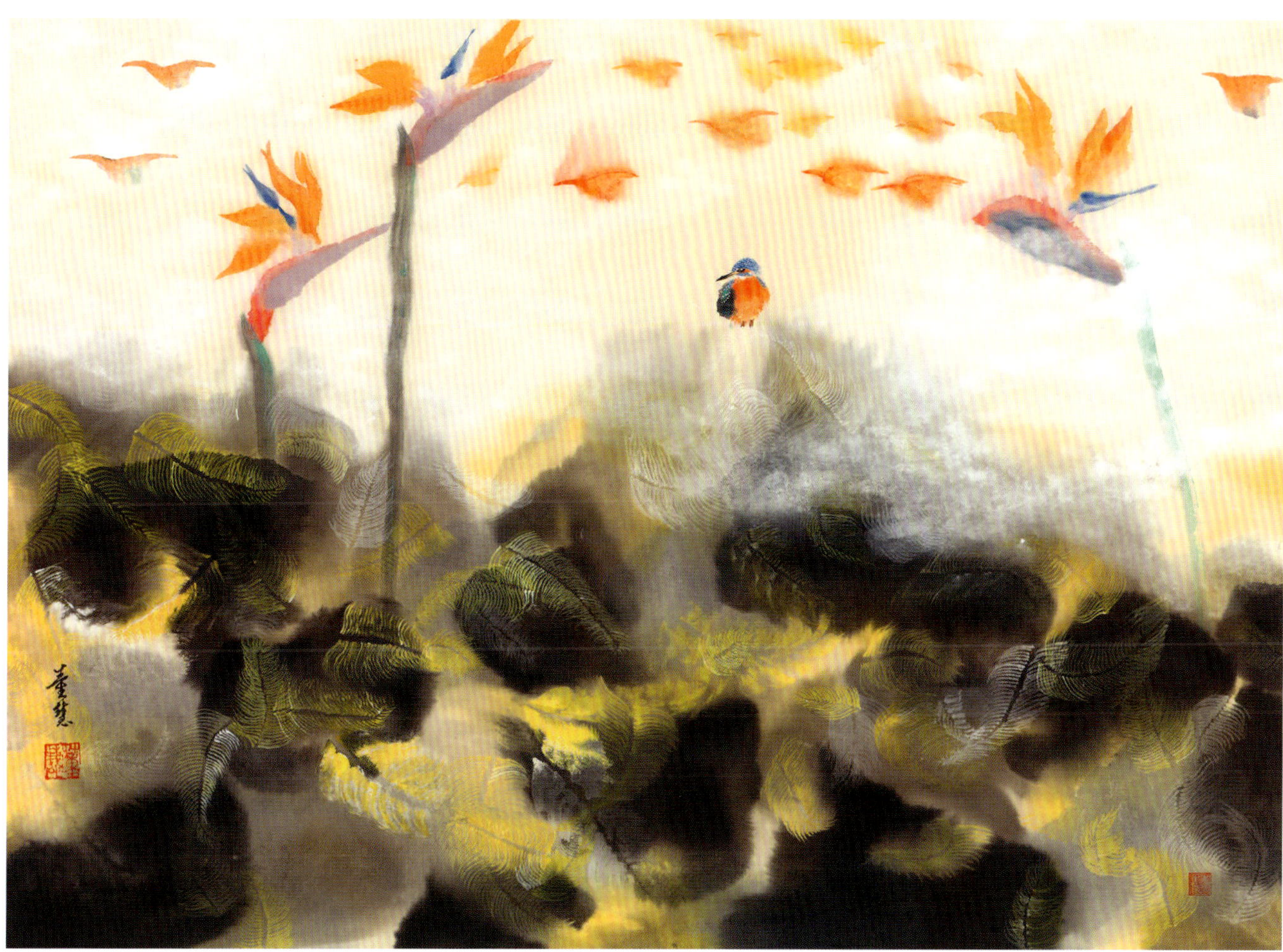

That's Me
2017
Ink and Colour on Rice Paper
63 cm x 83 cm

Reflection from Christina

The road might be lumpy-bumpy
As we follow the ones that came before us
But I know deep in my bones
That God is watching over me

Artworks: Rice Paper

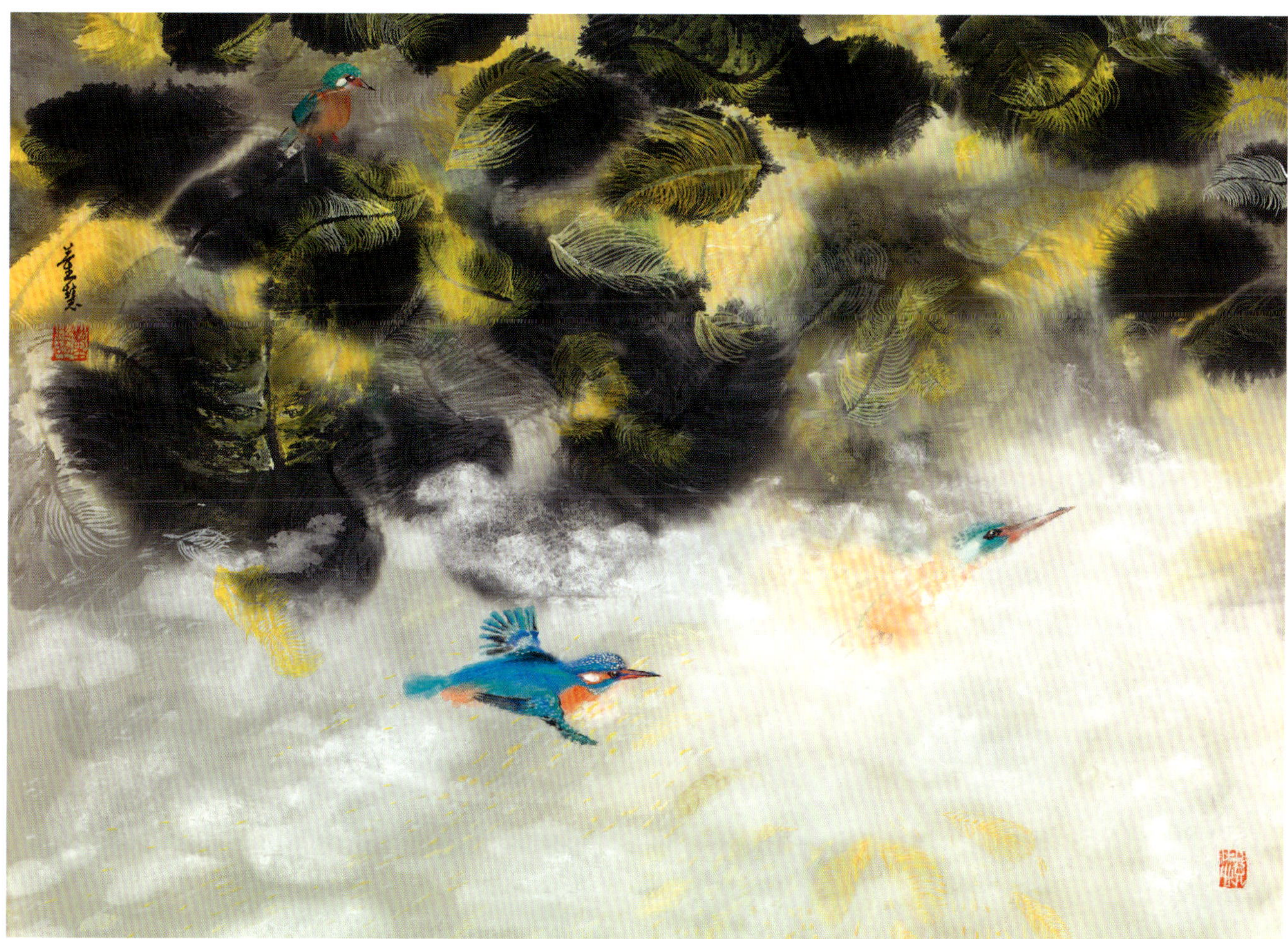

Beacon
2017
Ink and Colour on Rice Paper
63 cm x 83 cm

Still Loving
2013
Ink and Colour on Rice Paper
24 cm x 27 cm

See You Again
2013
Ink and Colour on Rice Paper
24 cm x 27 cm

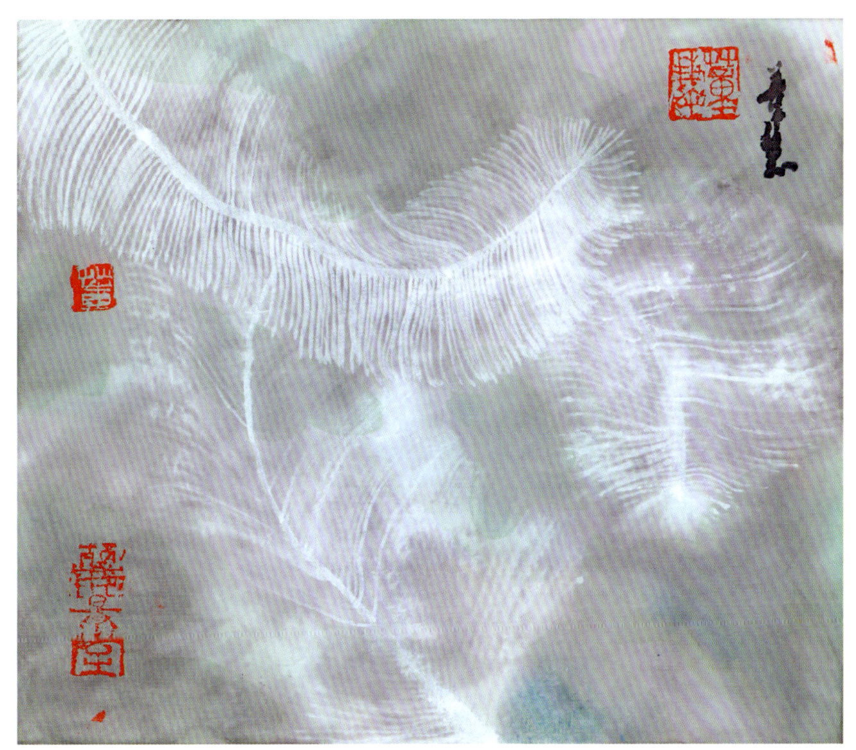

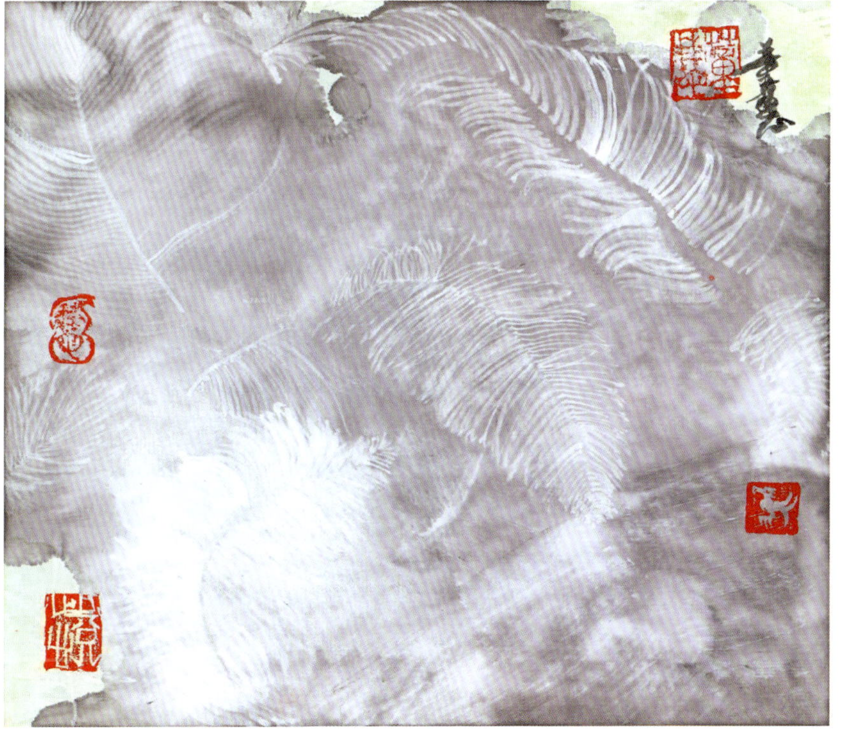

Artistic Path

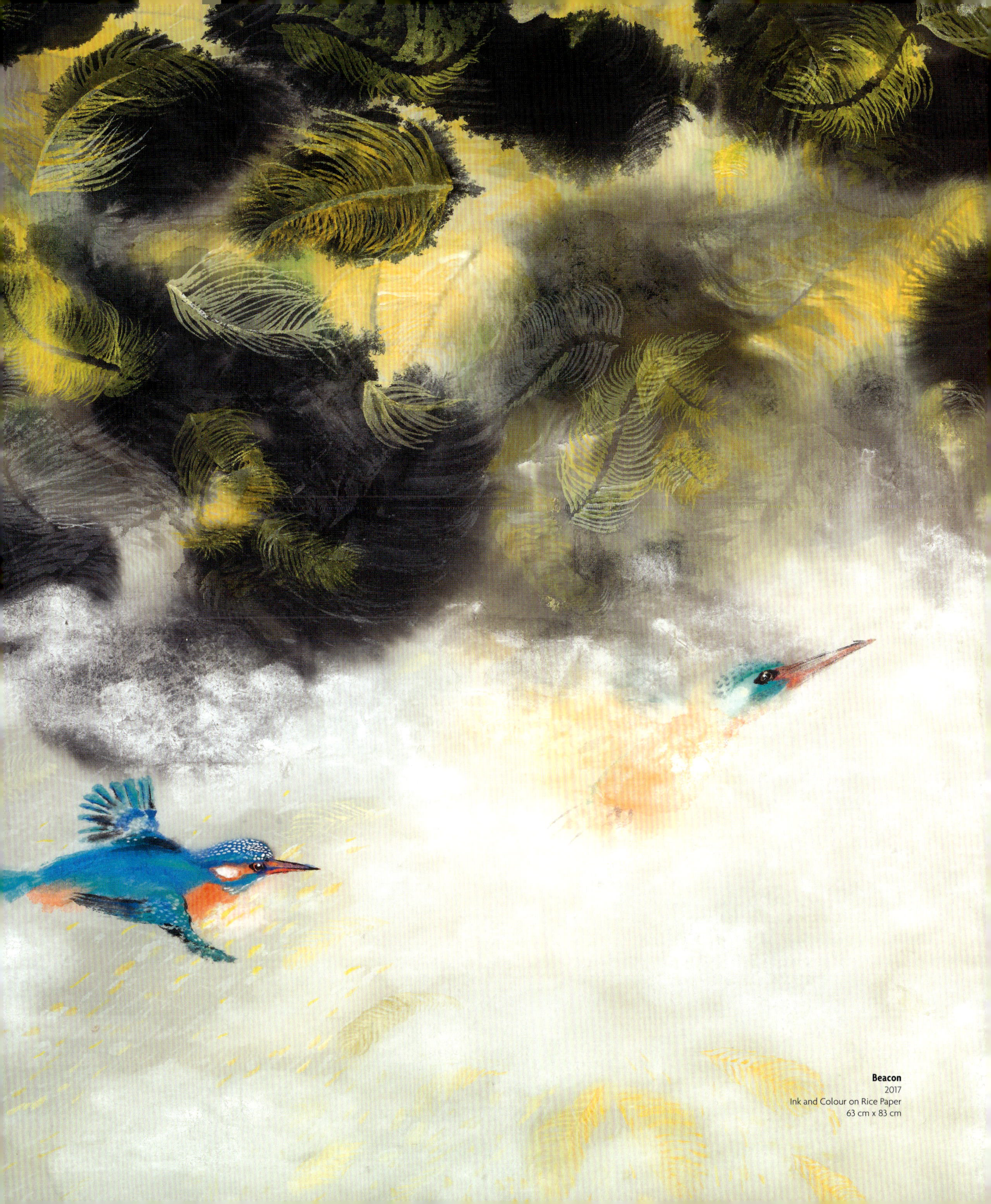

Beacon
2017
Ink and Colour on Rice Paper
63 cm x 83 cm

Artistic Path

Awards

April 2023
Artworks 'All I Have to Do is Dream', 'Propitious Portent' and 'Made in Heaven' were selected into the Golden Bauhinia Cup New Ink Paintings Competition 2023 presented by Hong Kong Art. Being one of the five first prize awardees, Christina Tung Wai's artworks were showcased at the award ceremony and exhibition space 'Hong Kong Art'.

April 2023
Artworks 'Blessing of the Night Sky' and 'Exploration' were awarded the Finalist Award at the 7th 'Open' International Juried Art Competition by TERAVARNA art gallery, Los Angeles, US.

March 2023
Artwork 'Frozen Echoes' was awarded the Silver Award at The 5th China International Abstract Art Exhibition.

June 2022
Artwork 'All I Have to Do is Dream' was awarded the Certificate of Excellence at Artist of the Month Competition by Circle Foundation for the Arts, France.

May 2022
Artwork 'Mobile Cabin Hospital – Reverence' was showcased at Fight the Pandemic exhibition by Tsi Ku Chai and was donated to frontline healthcare workers and units providing support to Hong Kong from mainland China.

May 2022
Artwork 'Fountain of Life' was awarded the Bronze Award at 'Bold Abstracts' 2022 International Juried Painting Competition by Camelback Gallery, US.

April 2022
Artwork 'How Did We Fall Apart' was awarded the Classification 4 Award at 'Abstract Art 2022' by Art Certificate, Spain.

February 2022
Artwork "All I Have to Do is Dream' was awarded the Finalist Award at the 'Open' 2022 International Juried Art Competition by Art Show International Gallery, US.

January 2022
Artwork 'Fountain of Life' was awarded the Crystal Award at Colourful Exhibition by Gallery Ring – Online Art.

January 2022
Artwork 'Woman Flower' was awarded the Bronze Award at 'Abstracts with Red' 2022 International Juried Painting Competition by Camelback Gallery, US.

December 2021
Artwork 'Woman Flower' was awarded the Award Winning Artist of Special Recognition Category for Excellence in Art at the 3rd Primary Colours Art Exhibition by Light Space & Time Online Art Gallery, US.

June–July 2020
Christina Tung Wai was the award winner in the shoe design collaboration between Hong Kong Art Gallery Association (HKAGA) and prestige Italian brand Salvatore Ferragamo.

The unique pair was showcased at Phillips' 20th Century & Contemporary Art, Famous Paintings, Design, Jewels and Watches auctions in JW Marriott Hotel, Hong Kong. The pair of hand–painted shoes was then collected by Salvatore Ferragamo.

April 2020
Artwork 'Dynasty' was featured in Art of Nature's Infinite Love – The Fight Against Novel Coronavirus online exhibition, paying tribute to frontline healthcare workers.

February 2020
Artwork 'Propitious Portent' was selected as one of the 500 ink masterpieces worldwide in 'Ink Global' 2020.

February 2020
Artwork 'Anti–coronavirus' was selected and featured in the 'Beijing International Art Biennale 'Fighting with Love' Anti–coronavirus Series (Hong Kong)'.

Solo Exhibitions

September 2024

Christina Tung Solo Exhibition 2024 – The 24th International Art Expo Beijing 2024

Beijing Exhibition Center, Beijing, China

May 2023

'Odyssey of Feather' | Awakening Desert – Hong Kong Outstanding Artists Exhibition

AsiaWorld–Expo, Hong Kong

October 2022

'Odyssey of Feather' – Fine Art Asia 2022

Hong Kong Convention and Exhibition Centre, Hong Kong

August 2022

'Odyssey of Feather'

Hong Kong City Hall, Hong Kong

April 2021

'Birds of a Feather'

Cheer Bell Gallery, Hong Kong

November 2018

'Inspirations'

Cheer Bell Gallery, Hong Kong

June 2018

'Inspirations'

Molbert art gallery, St Petersburg, Russia

May 2018

'Inspirations'

Russian Academy of Fine Arts Museum, St Petersburg, Russia

Joint and Other Exhibitions

October 2024

'Landscape Picturesque' - Exhibition by Artists in Hong Kong in Celebration of the 75th Anniversary of the Founding of the People's Republic of China

Hong Kong Central Library, Hong Kong

October 2024

Hong Kong Modern Ink Painting Society - Ink Asia 2024

Hong Kong Convention and Exhibition Centre, Hong Kong

September 2024

Celebration of the 75th Anniversary of the Founding of the People's Republic of China and Guangzhou–Hong Kong–Macao–Taiwan · Overseas Chinese Calligraphy and Painting Travelling Exhibition

Hong Kong City Hall, Hong Kong

August 2024

Celebration of the 75th Anniversary of the Founding of the People's Republic of China and Guangzhou–Hong Kong–Macao–Taiwan · Overseas Chinese Calligraphy and Painting Travelling Exhibition

Overseas Chinese History Museum of China, Beijing, China

May 2024

'Envisioning New Journey in the New Era International Painting and Calligraphy Gathering Exhibition'

Hong Kong Central Library, Hong Kong

January 2024

Contemporary Innovative Ink Painting Association 2023

Hong Kong City Hall, Hong Kong

January 2024

'2023 Joint Exhibition of the Shine Art Association'

Hong Kong Central Library, Hong Kong

November 2023
Affordable Art Fair Singapore 2023
F1 Pit Building, Singapore

November 2023
Make It Work HK Charity Art Auction 2023
(hosted by The French Chamber Foundation)
Christie's Hong Kong, Hong Kong

September 2023
'Whispers of Feathers & Blossoms' Clara Hung, Christina Tung Wai, Ho Kai Lam and Yin Xiang Multi-Art Exhibition 2023
Hong Kong City Hall, Hong Kong

August 2023
Golden Bauhinia Cup New Ink Paintings Competition 2023
Hong Kong Art, Hong Kong

July 2023
Hong Kong · Shanghai · Macao · Taiwan Ink Art Exchange Exhibition 2023 and Hong Kong Modern Ink Painting Society Annual Exhibition
Hong Kong Central Library, Hong Kong

July 2023
Hong Kong Research of Chinese Fine Arts Chinese Painting and Calligraphy Exhibition
Hong Kong City Hall, Hong Kong

June 2023
'Spring and Autumn, Continuity and Progress' The 30th Anniversary of the Hong Kong Xiamen Friendship Association and the 26th Anniversary of Hong Kong's Return to the Motherland Calligraphy and Painting Exhibition
Hong Kong Central Library, Hong Kong

December 2022
Chinese Painting Group Exhibition
Hong Kong City Hall, Hong Kong

October 2022
'Attainments' – Artwork Exhibition for 20th Anniversary of The 4–D Art Club
Hong Kong City Hall, Hong Kong

October 2022
Contemporary Innovative Ink Painting Association Annual Exhibition 2022
Hong Kong City Hall, Hong Kong

August 2022
Forging Ahead on a New Journey and Working Together for a New Chapter: An Art Exhibition Celebrating the 25th Anniversary of Hong Kong's Return to the Motherland and Greeting the 20th National Congress of the Communist Party of China
Hong Kong City Hall, Hong Kong

July 2022
Celebrating the 25th Anniversary of Establishment of HKSAR – Group Exhibition
Hong Kong City Hall, Hong Kong

July 2022
Group Exhibition of Hong Kong New Ink
Hong Kong Art Space, Hong Kong

June 2022
Celebrating the 25th Anniversary of Establishment of HKSAR – Group Exhibition
Hong Kong Central Library, Hong Kong

May 2022
'Fight the Pandemic' Exhibition
Tsi Ku Chai, Hong Kong

May 2022
Year of the Tiger – Joint Teacher–Student Exhibition of Xiling School
Tsi Ku Chai, Hong Kong

May 2022
Ink Global 2021 – Continuation
Wan Fung Art Gallery, Hong Kong

December 2021–January 2022
Ink Global 2021
Hong Kong Central Library, Hong Kong

October 2021
Shanghai · Hong Kong · Macao · Taiwan Painting Exhibition 2021 and Hong Kong Modern Ink Painting Society Annual Exhibition
Jockey Club Creative Arts Centre, Hong Kong

October 2021
Contemporary Innovative Ink Painting Association Annual Exhibition 2021
Hong Kong City Hall, Hong Kong

October–November 2021
'Art on Screen' – La broderie × Cheer Bell Gallery Collaboration
La broderie, Hong Kong

September 2021
Jeonnam International Sumuk Biennale 2021
Jindo Folk Cultural Center, South Korea

August 2021
Affordable Art Fair Hong Kong 2021
Hong Kong Convention and Exhibition Centre, Hong Kong

August 2021
Chinese Painting and Calligraphy Exhibition
Hong Kong City Hall, Hong Kong

May 2021
HKAGA Fundraiser 2021 · Art Basel Hong Kong
Hong Kong Convention and Exhibition Centre, Hong Kong

May 2021
France–Chine Art–Expo 'Metamorphosis'
Online Exhibition

February 2021
The Hong Kong Artists Association Exhibition 2021
Online Exhibition

November 2020
'Let's bond again' Joint Exhibition
Cheer Bell Gallery, Hong Kong

November 2020
The 10th Contemporary Innovative Ink Painting Association Annual Exhibition 2020
Hong Kong Central Library, Hong Kong

November 2020
Exhibition of Paintings from Shanghai, Hong Kong, Macao and Taiwan
Liu Haisu Art Museum, Shanghai, China

November 2020
The 4th International Exhibition of Abstract Art
Online Exhibition

October 2020
The 1st Joint Exhibition of Overseas Chinese Artists
Online Exhibition

October 2020
'Hua Shuo' – One Work, One Story Joint Art Exhibition
Gao Jianfu Memorial Hall, Guangdong, China

September 2020
France–Chine Art–Expo
Online Exhibition

April 2020
Art of Nature 'Infinite Love – The Fight Against Novel Coronavirus'
Online Exhibition

March 2020
Ink vs. Parfum
La Place Art et Parfum, Paris, France

February 2020
Beijing International Art Biennale 'Fighting with Love' Anti–coronavirus Series
Online Exhibition

February 2020
Salon du Dessin et de la Peinture à l'Eau 2020
Grand Palais, Paris, France

January 2020
Great Bay Area (Zhong Shan) Art Show
Ya Hao Square, Zhongshan, China

December 2019
Contemporary Innovative Ink Painting Association Annual Exhibition 2019
Hong Kong City Hall, Hong Kong

November 2019
Joint Exhibition of Christina Tung and Eric Lai
Marina South Clubhouse, Hong Kong

November 2019
'EVOCATION – CREATING AN IMAGE BY THE 4–D ART CLUB'
Hong Kong City Hall, Hong Kong

October 2019
HONG KONG ARTISTS ASSOCIATION ART CREATION – ZHUHAI EXHIBITION
Guyuan Museum of Art, Zhuhai, China

September 2019
'CONTEMPORARY INK ARTISTS SUMMIT PROGRAM' EXHIBITION
Shanghai Institute of Visual Art, Shanghai, China

September 2019
THE 11TH THAILAND–MALAYSIA INTERNATIONAL WOMEN ARTISTS ART EXHIBITION 2019
Universiti Sains Malaysia, Penang, Malaysia

July–August 2019
'JOURNEY THROUGH THE MOUNTAIN RIDGES' – GALLERY COLLECTION EXHIBITION
Cheer Bell Gallery, Hong Kong

June 2019
'MO SHANG WEN BO'
Lukka Packing (Dongguan) Industrial Park, Dongguan, China

May 2019
'MO SHANG WEN BO'
Lijia Creativity Cultural Industrial Park, Shenzhen, China

May 2019
'MOMENTS OF PASSION GROUP EXHIBITION' BY SHINE ART ASSOCIATION
Hong Kong Central Library, Hong Kong

May 2019
AFFORDABLE ART FAIR HONG KONG 2019
Hong Kong Convention and Exhibition Centre, Hong Kong

January 2019
'UNCONFINED SPACE'
Cheer Bell Gallery, Hong Kong

November 2018
CONTEMPORARY INNOVATIVE INK PAINTING ASSOCIATION ANNUAL EXHIBITION 2018
Hong Kong City Hall, Hong Kong

October 2018
ART TAIPEI 2018
Taipei World Trade Centre, Taipei, Taiwan, Province of China

January 2018
ARTWORK SHOWCASE
Hong Kong Cultural Centre, Hong Kong

November 2017
'SPLASHING COLOURS FROM OUR HEARTS' JOINT EXHIBITION BY THE 4–D ART CLUB
Hong Kong City Hall, Hong Kong

September 2017
JOINT EXHIBITION OF FEMALE ARTISTS FROM SHENZHEN, HONG KONG AND MACAU BY SHENZHEN FEMALE ARTIST ASSOCIATION
Shenzhen Civic Centre Exhibition Hall, Shenzhen, China

January 2017
JOINT EXHIBITION BY SHINE ART ASSOCIATION
Hong Kong Central Library, Hong Kong

September 2015
THE 2015 INCHEON GLOBAL CITIES ARTS EXCHANGE GRAND FESTIVAL BY INCHEON METROPOLITAN CITY ARTS ASSOCIATION
Incheon Culture and Arts Center, South Korea

June 2015
JOINT PAINTING AND CALLIGRAPHY EXHIBITION ORGANISED BY CHINA AND THE WORLD CULTURE OF HONG KONG
Hong Kong City Hall, Hong Kong

May 2015
'CHINESE CONTEMPORARY "SHUI MO" PAINTING JOINT EXHIBITION'
Cheer Bell Gallery, Hong Kong

December 2014
JOINT EXHIBITION BY SHINE ART ASSOCIATION
Hong Kong Central Library, Hong Kong

October 2013
JOINT TEACHER–STUDENT EXHIBITION OF COLOUR INK PAINTINGS WITH LAM TIAN XING
Hong Kong City Hall, Hong Kong

October 2013

1st Hong Kong Fu Tien Joint Calligraphy and Painting Exhibition – 'Mangrove Hong Kong'

Yachang Art Gallery, Shenzhen, China

January 2013

'Flower in Fog' by Shine Art Association

Hong Kong Central Library, Hong Kong

January 2011

Ceramics Showcase, Janet Tso's Solo Ceramics Exhibition

Hong Kong Visual Arts Centre, Hong Kong

PUBLICATIONS

April 2021

Selected in 'Chinese She Art'

(First large–scale Beijing publication in both Chinese and English, presenting works from Chinese female artists that represent the height of contemporary ideas as well as those that are more experimental with great potential; ISBN–13:978–988–70315–3–6)

March 2021

'Birds of a Feather' Art Album

(Second art album of Christina Tung Wai published in Hong Kong; ISBN–13: 978–988–14980–1–3)

November 2020

Selected in 'Chinese Contemporary Art Document (2018–2020)'

(An academic art book series published annually in Beijing since 2006. The 2018–2020 is a collection spanning three years in the making, presenting contemporary artworks from Chinese artists and creators; ISBN–13: 978–7–5356–9590–1)

May 2018

'Inspirations · Christina Tung' Art Album

(First art album of Christina Tung Wai published in Hong Kong; ISBN–13: 978–988–78773–6–3)

Art Critics

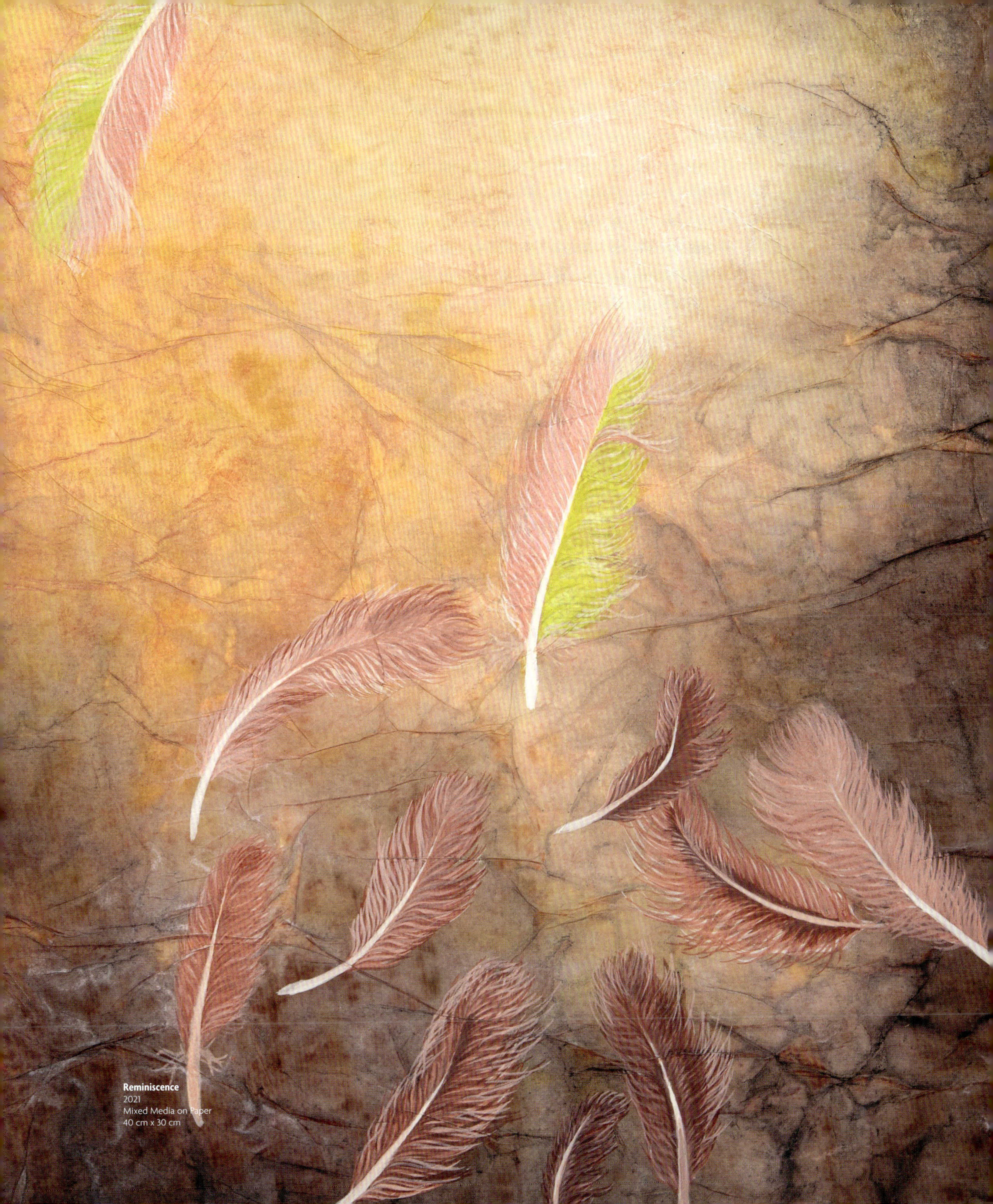

Reminiscence
2021
Mixed Media on Paper
40 cm x 30 cm

Comment on Christina Tung Wai's Art

Shao Qi

Editor in Chief of Chinese She Art by CCARTD
August 2021

The aesthetic characteristics of women's art are determined by the aesthetic motivation and spiritual characteristics of women artists themselves. Their spiritual openness and the uniqueness in aesthetic perspectives will then determine the spiritual value of women's art in terms of its aesthetics. The paintings by the famous artist Christina Tung Wai make an outstanding representative of such art. Her artistic creation fully shows the elegance and delicacy, sophistication and sentiments, as well as the rich and profound inner world of a female artist. What is more commendable is that she has elevated the beauty of women's art to a philosophical level. She showed us the secret thoughts deep in the heart of a female artist.

Christina Tung Wai's art creations are as beautiful as blooming flowers in summer, and crystal-clear streams in fall. They are exceptionally natural and splendid. Sapphire blue and maple leaf red overflowing in the paintings, as well as the rich ink textures, are particularly enchanting for viewers to surely indulge in. Without a doubt, there are profound sensational messages in all this gorgeousness. Those fluttering feathers, or falling leaves, give people a sense of solemnity. They make people feel the depth of time and space. Gorgeous and solemn, graceful and profound. These are the artistic characteristics and aesthetic uniqueness of artist Christina Tung Wai.

Christina Tung Wai's artistic creations are of contemporary ink painting style. While there are traces of traditional ink-wash inheritance, there are also experimental explorations with characteristics of the times. Her visual language and expression methods have strong cultural consciousness, contemporariness and openness. In Christina Tung Wai's art, we witness the aesthetic dimensions of Hong Kong women's art and the aesthetic diversity of Chinese women's art.

Shao Qi, founder of CCARTD, the largest database of Chinese Contemporary Art and Chinese Contemporary Art Document, and an independent curator. Since the 1990s, he has been engaged in art curation, art brokerage, art media and art publishing. He is currently the international art residency director and Editor in Chief of multiple publications, such as *Chinese Contemporary Art Documents*, *Chinese Women's Art*, *Chinese She Art* and *Contemporary Art Studio*.

Art Critic

Dr Yu Kaiyue

Hangzhou, China
July 2022

As a female artist, Christina Tung Wai interprets the depth of life from her unique perspective. Feathers are light but tough, soft with hardness, complex and yet simple, dense in structure but light in weight, can be still and in motion. The contradictions presented in Christina's works transcend time and space, giving people spiritual comfort and bringing them back to the present moment. Christina uses feathers as a carrier to engage with the audience and creates resonation with them, drawing them to reflect on and revisit life itself. In doing so, she brings the audience to her very own utopia. Her artworks drive the audience to pay attention to things around them and live life from a brand-new perspective, which is in turn a way of awakening one's consciousness. Christina elevates feathers to a philosophical height, in the way that she gives value to feathers that have no inherent life, showing her understanding and longing for life. This is a paradigm of 'achieving without the purpose to achieve'. Just as Laozi said, 'As it never claims itself to be great, it is thus able to accomplish its greatness.' This is the central philosophical idea of Christina's Feather series.

Dr Yu Kaiyue is a female from Shaoxing, Zhejiang Province. She studied respectively at the School of Humanities, Zhejiang University, the School of Chinese Painting and Calligraphy, China Academy of Art, and the School of Art and Archaeology, Zhejiang University. She is now a member of the China Calligraphers Association.

Christina Tung Wai: Transforming Feathers into Music

Dr Zhang Mengyang

Academy of Arts & Design, Tsinghua University
September 2023

Emmanuel Levinas pointed out that the infinity of 'other' precedes the oneness of 'self', because the infinite nature of 'other' grows beyond the enclosed domain of self-centredness continuously.[1] In Christina Tung Wai's recent works, she uses feathers as a symbolism of 'self' and the constantly changing form of 'inner other' to show people its endless possibilities, resulting in a visual construct of a highly personal and unique world.

Christina Tung Wai's creation with feathers as a theme began ten years ago. She was 'fascinated by the lightness and freedom of feathers' and her early cultivation in the field of bird-and-flower painting has laid the foundation for the Feather series. In her recent works, Christina has found a more personalised painting language and extended this thematic series into different media and styles. The series 'A Wintry Ballet' is a representation of one of the directions, where the artist paints on leather with ink. By simply using three shades of colour – black, white and grey – she created spaciousness and a sense of drama. The dark background highlights the purity of the feathers, and the combination of feathers in different poses appears as agile ballerinas. Christina said the inspiration of the series 'A Wintry Ballet' came from the frustration of not being able to venture out and see ballet performances during the pandemic. This is in line with Gilles Deleuze's notion of 'colour is a form of haptic sensation'.[2] The shaping of the background space strengthens the close-up effect of the feathers, making the personification more resonant with the audience. Presenting the series in a set of four adds to the continuity, bridging the three-dimensional space and the four-dimensional spacetime, mind and emotions. 'A Wintry Ballet' was the first work by Christina that I saw in person at an exhibition. Although the set of four is comparatively smaller in size, they are able to capture the audience's gaze particularly despite being among many more paintings. Apart from the raw emotions that filled the artworks during their productions, the well-balanced spatiality and the artist's mastery of the artwork also set this series apart.

The work 'Love of My Life' symbolises another possibility of feather paintings. In this artwork, two pieces

1. Lai, C. (2014) *Responding to the other: revisiting Levinas*. Taipei: Bookman Press.
2. Deleuze, G. and Felix, G. (1987) *A thousand plateaus: capitalism and schizophrenia*. Minneapolis: University of Minnesota Press.

of feathers, painted in dark brown colour, overlook the vase expanse of clouds. The feathers are no longer light and small, but rather they exude a sense of grandeur, soaring in the air like sacred objects. The soft blending of colours together with the bright colouring in the composition suggests characteristics found in the Lingnan School of painting. Christina has studied Chinese art for many years, learning from masters such as Lam Tian Xing, Liu Kuo-sung and Lam Wu Fui. Having absorbed the essence of traditional paintings while being influenced by contemporary ink art at the same time, Christina has forged her own path. The dark brown feathers in this painting are not purely from Christina's own imagination. Their prototype comes from the tail feathers of pheasants. Pheasants have long held a sacred position, being hailed as 'auspicious birds', and their feathers are often used as decorations in religious rites and processions. Pheasant feathers are commonly used in conjunction with musical instruments, with feathers used for dancing and woodwind instruments for playing music. As the poem goes, 'feather and musical instrument, one on left and one on right they complement each other' – feathers and musical instruments have been important symbols of senses of sight and sound since ancient times. The name of the artwork, 'Love of My Life', gives a humanistic sublimation to the grand picture, with feathers becoming an ode to love. This kind of synesthesia, achieved by transforming feathers into musical instruments, is also reflected in another work by Christina: 'Over the Ocean'. Similarly, this artwork is one that celebrates love. Christina added on elements of romanticism and surrealism to this piece: feathers transformed into the bridge of magpies (as in Qixi Festival), winding their way beyond the horizon; the pastel purple sky and blue ocean add a feminine touch to the work itself. Though love and affection are the themes of these two paintings, they do not involve any figurative depiction of persons. Instead, Christina reshapes feathers into various rhetorical devices through de-subjectification, underpinning feathers as a signifier and redrawing the boundaries of the signified.

From the contemporaneity of 'A Wintry Ballet', to the traditional aesthetics of 'Love of My Life', and to the feminist qualities in 'Over the Ocean', although Christina has been focusing on depicting feathers for many years, she did not mechanically portray repetitive themes, nor deliberately standardise the representational forms of feathers. Rather, she has constantly explored the many possibilities, shifting between personification and objectification, self and others. In her recent works, not only is the artist painting her beloved feathers, but also depicting her reflections and evaluations of the times and life from her personal experience.

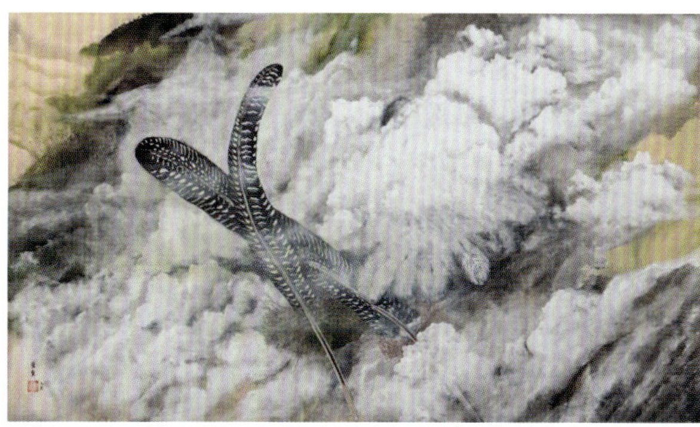

Love of My Life
2022
Mixed Media on Rice Paper
96.5 cm x 188 cm

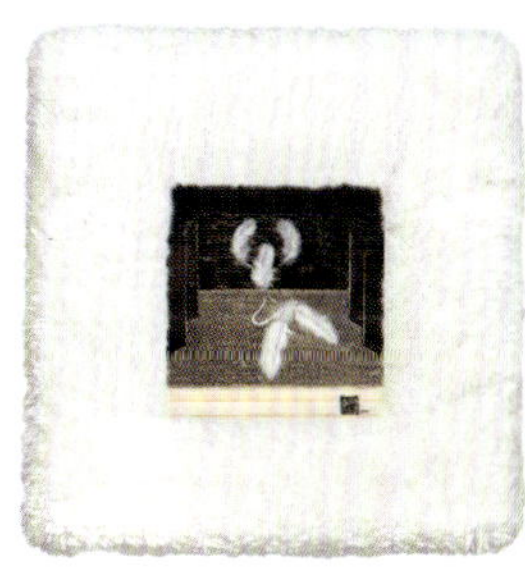

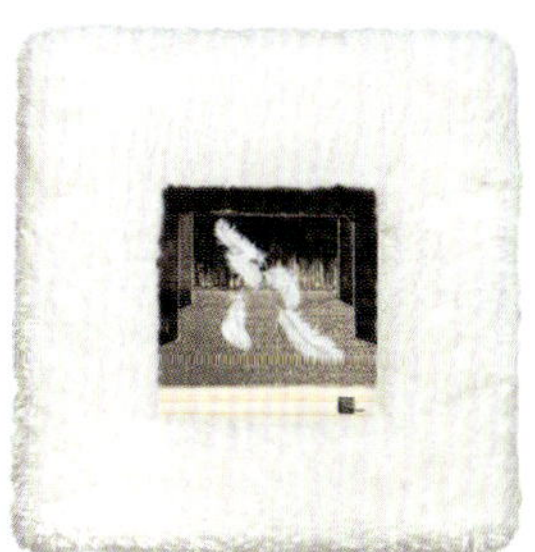

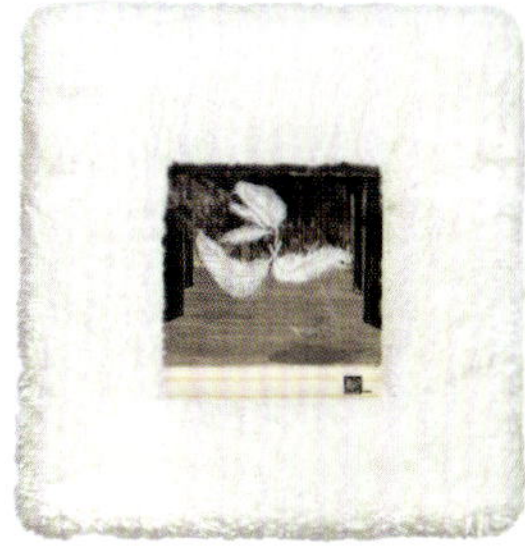

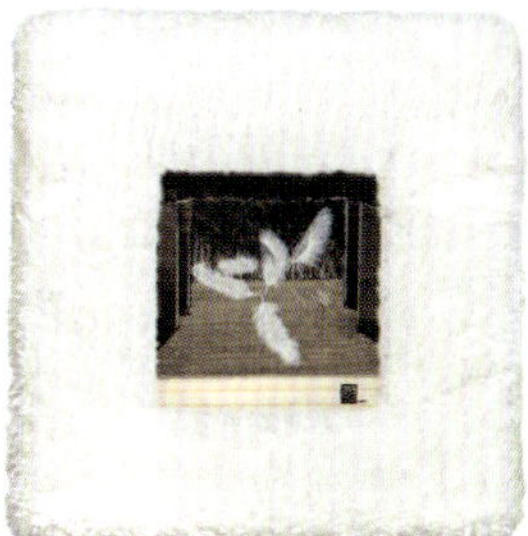

A Wintry Ballet (1) (2) (4) (3) (Clockwise)
2021
Ink and Acrylic on Cowhide Leather
31.5 cm x 31.5 cm each

Dr Zhang Mengyang holds a Doctor of Arts. He is an art historian, an artist and a curator. He is currently a member of the Association of Historian of American Art, the College Art Association, and the National Higher Art Education Association. He is the author of *African American Art during World War II*, *Art History for Children: The Story of Dali* and *Twelve Mandatory Courses at Central Saint Martins*.

Wings Touched by Angels - Christina Tung Wai and Her Feathers

Impression (Yin Xiang)

4 December 2023

Christina Tung Wai meticulously cultivates her feather works with unwavering passion, endowing them with a unique spiritual essence, and now, she has incredibly mastered the art of it. Seemingly, with a gentle breath, the feathers would rise and fly off to freedom…

A few years ago, a couple of female poets, myself included, were invited to visit an exhibition and workshop of hers at a prestigious store in Causeway Bay. If you did not witness Christina painting feathers on to leather pieces, you would be tempted to pick up the feathers whimsically as if they were real. Then you might just put the feather on the palm of your hand, let out a soft and gentle breath, and follow it as it drifts and seeks its next adventure.

Christina likes to collect all sorts of feathers, and occasionally she puts them into her paintings. In fact, it is quite difficult to distinguish between the real and painted feathers in her paintings. Every now and then, I went up to the paintings for a closer look. It is, as Cao Xueqin said in his novel *Dream of the Red Chamber*, 'When truth becomes fiction, then fiction may also be true.' [1] The feathers in Christina's paintings appear much more delicate, soft and elegant than the real feather.

There was this time I had this miraculous experience. Before heading to Christina's exhibition, I had a morning prayer session at the church where I waved three pairs of worship flags of feathers. Then I went on to read aloud chapter 6 of Isaiah – the six-winged seraph stood upon a throne: he used a pair to cover his face, another to cover his feet and the other for flight.

To my surprise, I found three massive wings made out of leather collage at the exhibition, no different from what I had just read about the six-winged seraph in chapter 6 of Isaiah that morning. A wonder as such will surely leave one exclaiming in astonishment – that the higher power, the creator of all beings, would actually talk to us directly? Encounters like this happen every now and then among our gatherings. Despite being a devout Buddhist, Christina remains awe-inspired time after time when God speaks.

Westerners hold a firm belief that wherever feathers appear, angels are near. The white and soft feather has always been considered a sign of an angel and a symbol of the truest and purest love.

1. Cao, X., Tao, Z. and Hu, J. (1992) *Dream of the red chamber*. Shenyang: Shenyang Publishing House.

Christina Tung Wai is a Hong Kong based contemporary ink feather artist, the founder of Cheer Bell Gallery and a curator. She is known for having feathers and Taoist philosophy as recurring subjects in her artworks as a representation of the revelations in her life and her longing for freedom. To Christina, the beauty of the feather lies in its lifelessness but that which bestows upon the bird a blissful life surfing the boundless sky. Enlivened with different forms under Christina's brushstroke, the feather is the epitome of softness and strength combined, a life philosophy of resilience: it is at once carefree at the whims of the winds, and at other times audacious, undaunted by limitations.

From a busy financial professional to a full-time painter now, Christina Tung Wai had her run of wild dream-chasing journeys. She seized every moment and every opportunity she had to apprentice herself to great masters of visual arts. She started her endeavour in art by studying ceramic art under Ms Janet Tso in 2010, and in 2011, Chinese ink art under contemporary ink colour Master Lam Tian Xing and Lingnan School ink painting Master Lam Wu Fui. Later in year 2018 and 2022, she began studying Chinese calligraphy under Chinese calligraphers Cheung Sing Kwo and Bai He, respectively. The year 2018 was also the one when she was selected to enrol in Shanghai Institute of Visual Arts' Contemporary Ink Artists Summit Program under the guidance of Master Liu Kuo-sung, Father of Modern Ink Painting, and Shi Mo, first-class artist in China. Christina goes to great lengths to contribute to the development of the local arts scene. She was once the host for an arts programme called 'Beauty of Arts' at a local streaming television platform 'Made in Hong Kong', where she interviewed numerous art masters.

In 2018, she made her debut and second solo exhibition at the Russian Academy of Fine Arts Museum and Molbert art gallery, respectively, in St Petersburg, Russia. She was then invited by the Consulate General of the Russian Federation in Hong Kong and Russian Club Hong Kong to hold her third solo exhibition in the same year. In November 2020, Christina was selected into the Chinese Contemporary Art Document. In 2021, her fourth solo exhibition was held at Cheer Bell Gallery. In 2022, her fifth and sixth solo exhibitions '*Odyssey of Feather*' were held at Hong Kong City Hall and Fine Art Asia, respectively. In 2023, her seventh solo exhibition '*Odyssey of Feather*' was held at the AsiaWorld-Expo, Hong Kong. Christina often takes part in various international and overseas joint expositions and exhibitions such as '*Salon du Dessin et de la Peinture à l'Eau*' 2020 of Paris, Art Taipei, Affordable Art Fair Hong Kong and '*Thailand-Malaysia International Women Artists Art Exhibition*'. Collectors of her works include financial institutions and collectors from all around the world.

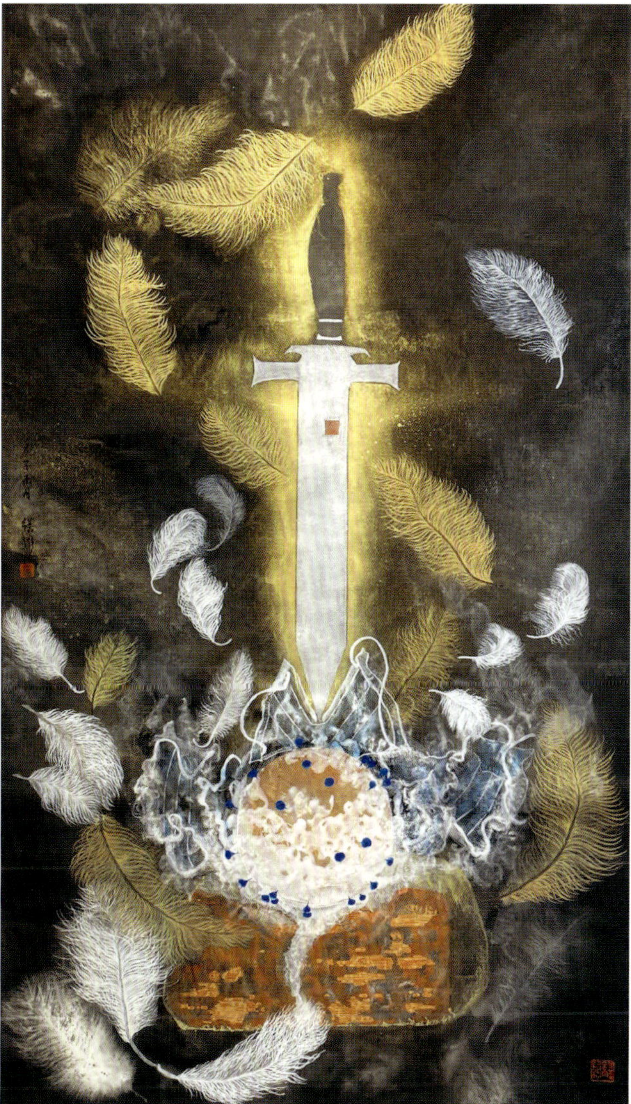

Anti-coronavirus
2020
Mixed Media on Rice Paper
120 cm x 69 cm

The year 2020 has been a significant one for Christina's art path. Her work 'Anti-coronavirus' was featured in '*Beijing International Art Biennale 'Fighting with Love' Anti-coronavirus Series (Hong Kong)*'. Moreover, her work 'Propitious Portent' was selected as 1 of the 500 ink masterpieces worldwide in '*Ink Global*'. Apart from that, she was the award winner of the shoe design collaboration between Hong Kong Art Gallery Association (HKAGA) and prestige Italian brand Salvatore Ferragamo. This unique pair of shoes, hand-painted by Christina, was showcased at '*Phillips' 20th Century & Contemporary Art,*

Famous Paintings, Design, Jewels and Watches' auctions in July 2020, and was collected by Salvatore Ferragamo then.

Under the tutelage of several masters, Christina was enriched with the vast knowledge of painting styles and techniques. Lam Tian Xing's works of colourful ink lotuses have profound influence on her. Admiring Lam's free and bold ink-splashing style, Christina has copied and imitated his works extensively. When she went on to explore Western ink later, she was able to achieve great precision in deploying and controlling colours easily. The resulting colour palette from countless experimentations has proved to mesmerise viewers incredibly again and again.

Being under Lam Wu Fui's tutelage laid a solid foundation of traditional Chinese ink work for Christina. Lam's strict and rigorous demands contributed to the culmination of Christina's first lithograph 'Noble Aspiration', created on site at the Russian Academy of Fine Arts Museum, St Petersburg, Russia, and later collected by the Consulate General of the Russian Federation in Hong Kong.

Studying calligraphy under calligrapher Cheung Shing Kwo has refined Christina's portrayal of feathers as well as their representation of Taoist philosophy of softness and strength. The duality conveys the dynamic appeals of feathers: the bony structure of wings, the flexible strength and the elegant demeanour of feathers. The juxtaposition of male strength and female gentleness, and their mutual nourishment and blend, embodies Christina's view and beliefs on life and marriage.

The guidance of Liu Kuo-sung at the SIVA took to the next level Christina's horizons and visions besides

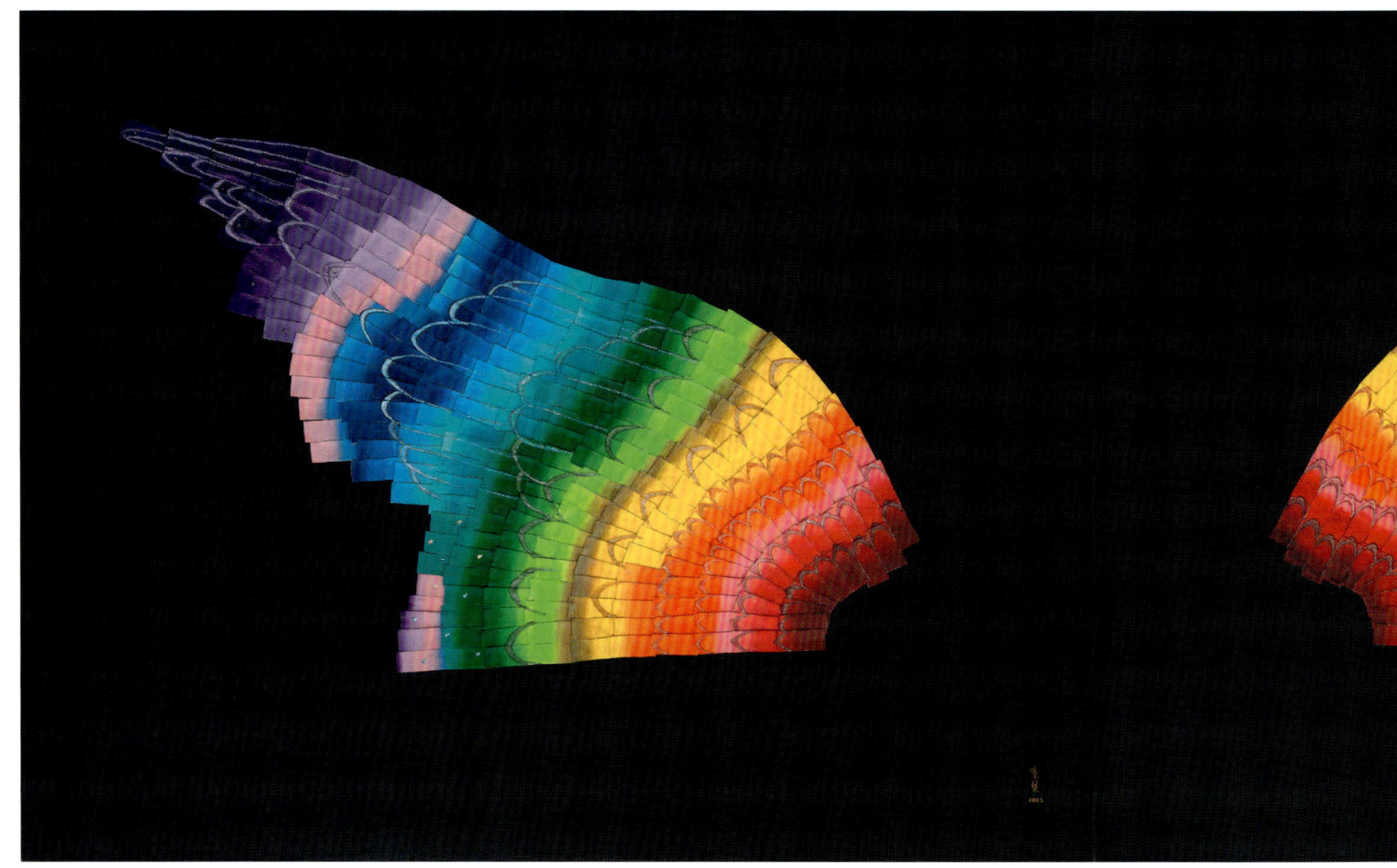

Blessing of the Night Sky
2022
Acrylic on Cowhide Leather
Set of two: 123 cm x 306 cm

the conception, composition, means of expressions, and spiritual virtue in her works. It just goes to show the best way to learn is learning from the best! Graduating from the 'Contemporary Ink Artists Summit Program' as a more sophisticated artist, Christina and her graceful feather art is truly a class of her own.

Like wings kissed by an angel, the massive wings in Christina's work 'Blessing of the Night Sky' have become a popular Instagrammable spot in the '*Hong Kong·Shanghai·Macao·Taiwan Ink Art Exchange Exhibition 2023 and Hong Kong Modern Ink Painting Society Annual Exhibition*', receiving notable media coverage from China News Service.

I thought of a poem by He Jialin that echoes Christina's feather arts vividly:

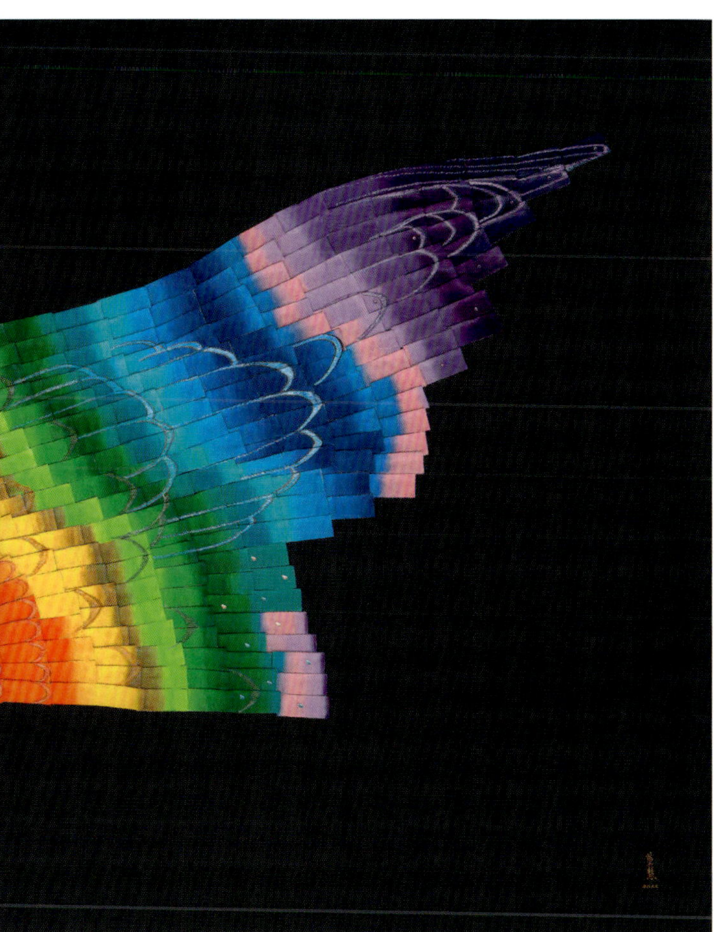

BREATH OF THE UNIVERSE –
A FEATHER'S TALE

Underneath a feather,
A flock of twittering birdies nests.
The single feather
measures time and space.
It is more like a gift from Heaven.
In an unknowing moment,
You came across it.
That feather, grows larger and larger,
Look afar beyond the birdies you will see,
There lies a band of dream chasers
beneath the feather

To measure time and space with a feather... is indeed a masterstroke. Jialin is very humble and dares not take all the credit. Rather, she said it was a sign from God.

In the year 2024, the three of us intend to publish a compilation album of poetry and paintings, titled 'Breath of the Universe – A Feather's Tale'.

May we be dream-chasers together, like feathers soaring in the sky, up in heaven, down on earth...

Yang Mengru, currently resident in Hong Kong, whose pen name was Mengru, started writing in 1986. She is the author of several collections of poems and has had works included in various genres such as literature history, poetry history as well as textbooks for universities, primary and middle schools. In 2017, eighteen years after she stopped writing, she entered the second chapter of her artistic life of writing and painting under a new pseudonym of Impression (Yin Xiang).

GALLERY

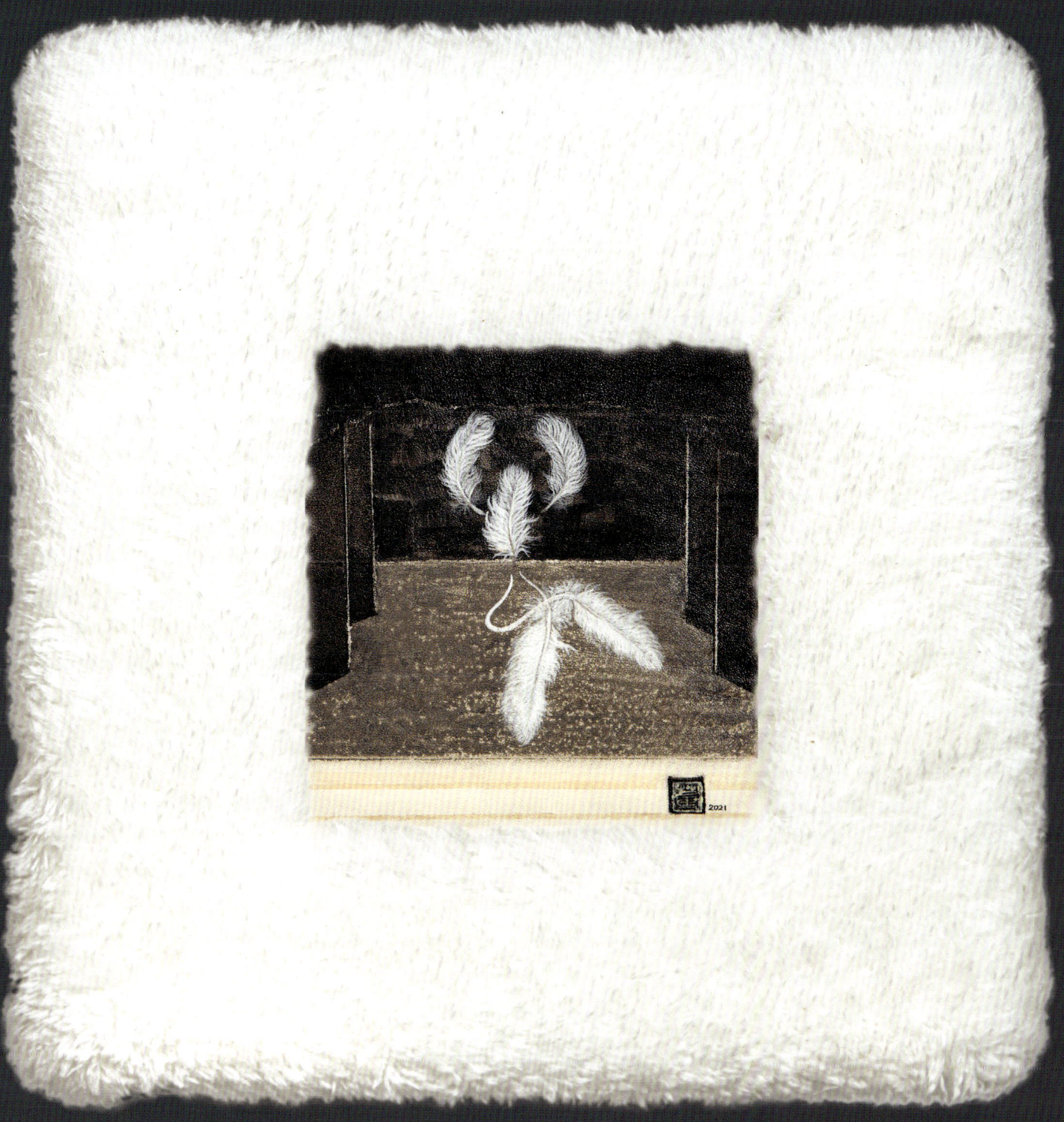

A Wintry Ballet (1)
2021
Ink and Acrylic on Cowhide Leather
31.5 cm x 31.5 cm

GALLERY

CHRISTINA TUNG WAI WITH HER MENTORS

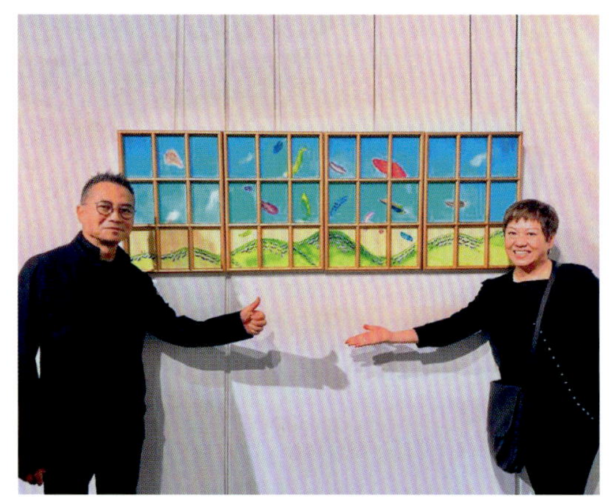

Photo of Christina Tung Wai (right) with renowned ink colour Master Lam Tianxing, chairman of The Hong Kong Artists Association (left), Christina Tung Wai's work 'Playing Around' (middle)

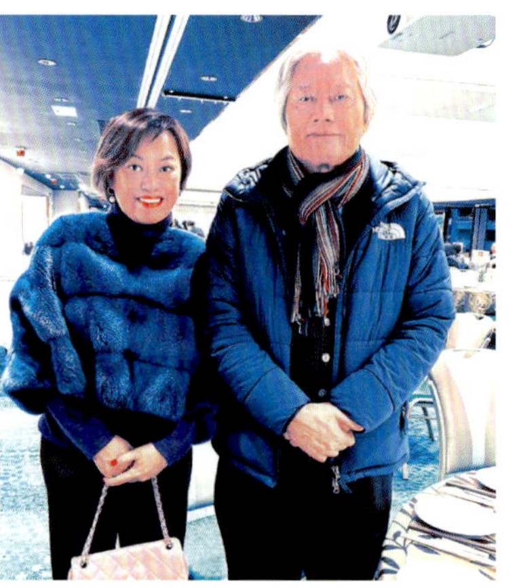

Photo of Christina Tung Wai (left) with Lingnan School ink painting Master Lam Wu Fui (right)

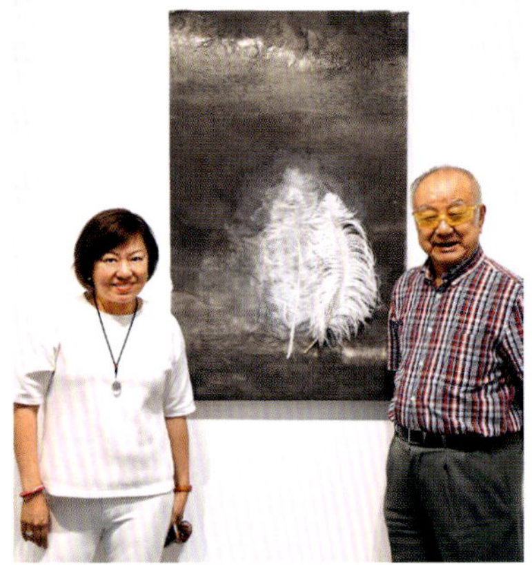

Photo of Christina Tung Wai (left) with Master Liu Kuo-sung, Father of Modern Ink Painting (right), Christina Tung Wai's work 'Be Your Shadow' (middle)

2022 | BEHIND-THE-SCENES HIGHLIGHTS OF CHRISTINA TUNG WAI'S ARTWORK CREATION

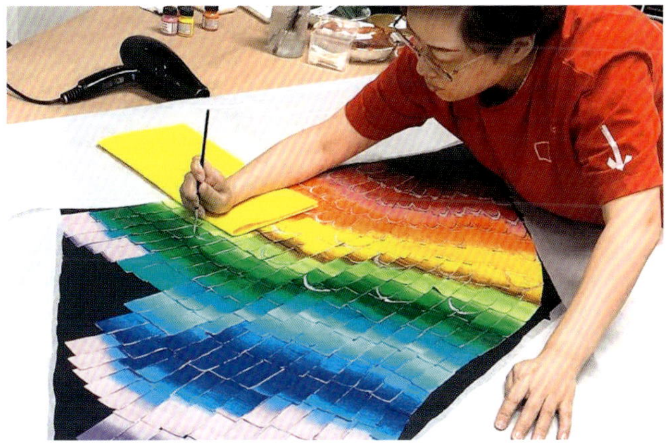

Christina Tung Wai creating her work
'Blessing of the Night Sky'

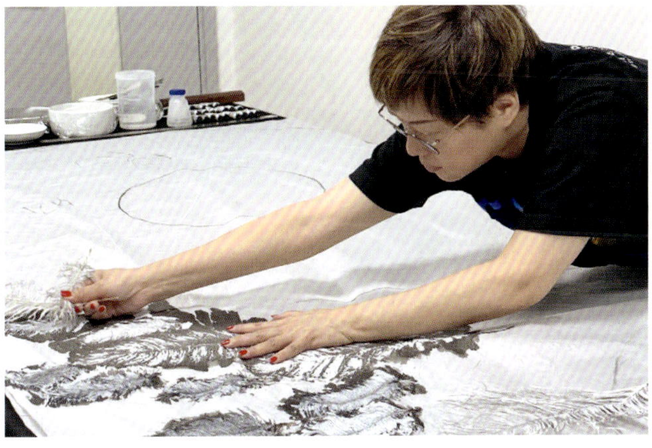

Christina Tung Wai creating her work
'Paving New Paths'

GALLERY

CHRISTINA TUNG WAI SOLO EXHIBITIONS HIGHLIGHTS

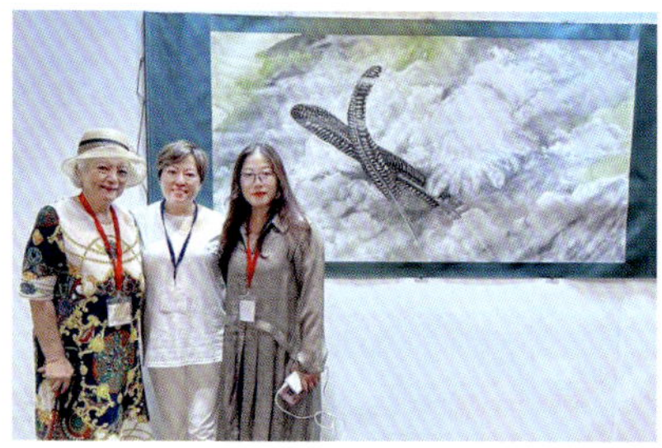

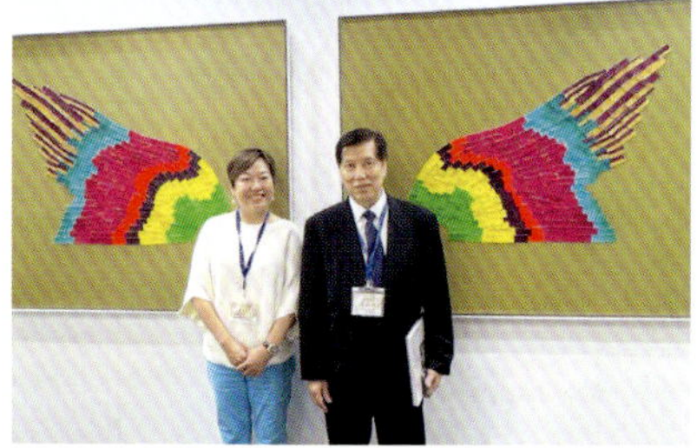

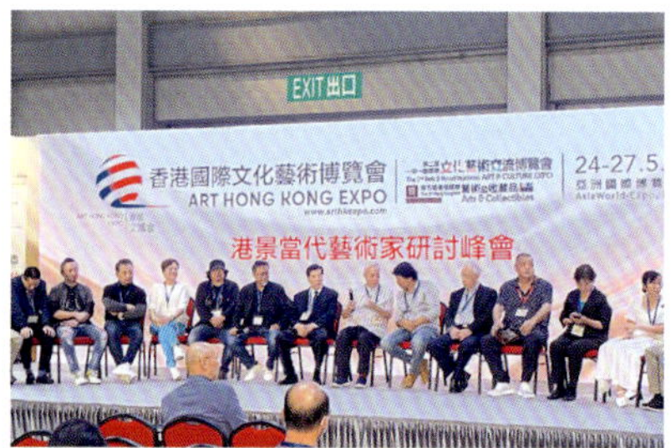

May 2023
'ODYSSEY OF FEATHER' AT AWAKENING DESERT – HONG KONG OUTSTANDING ARTISTS EXHIBITION
AsiaWorld-Expo, Hong Kong

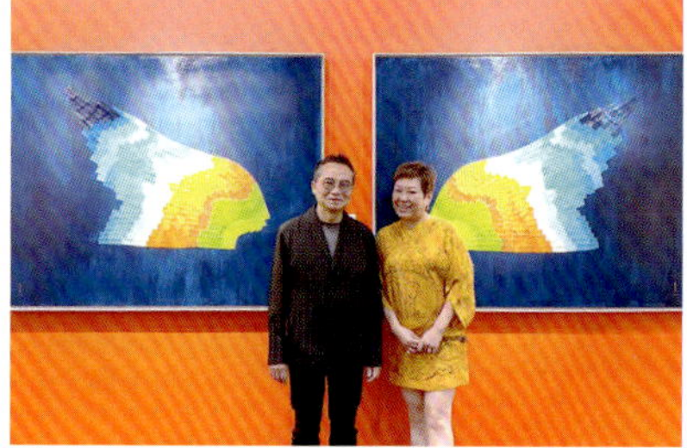

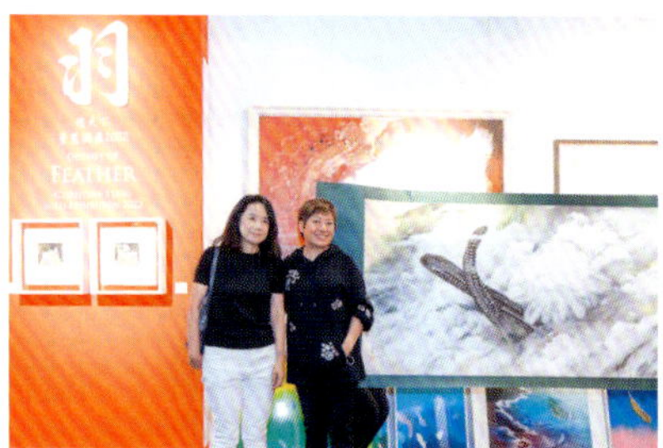

Oct 2022
'ODYSSEY OF FEATHER' AT FINE ART ASIA 2022
Hong Kong Convention and Exhibition Centre, Hong Kong

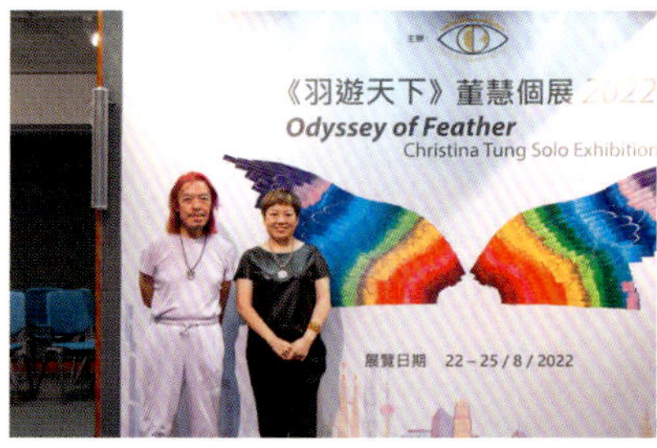

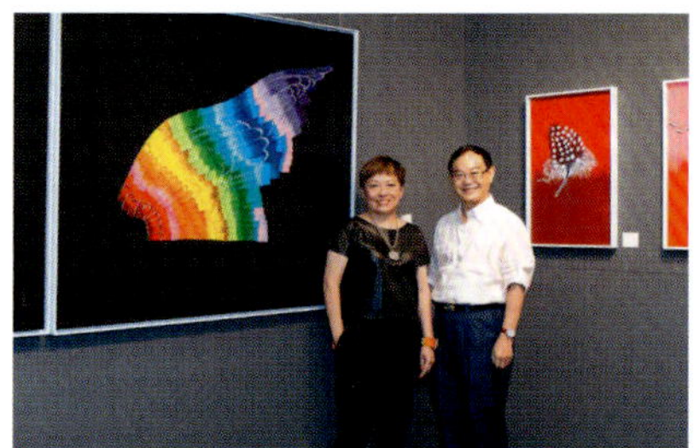

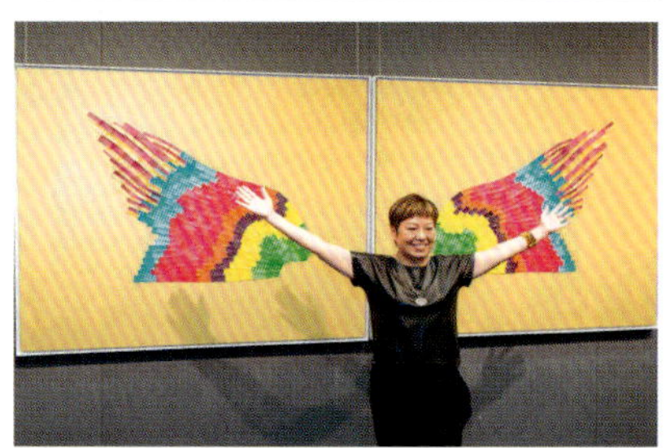

Aug 2022
'ODYSSEY OF FEATHER'
Hong Kong City Hall, Hong Kong

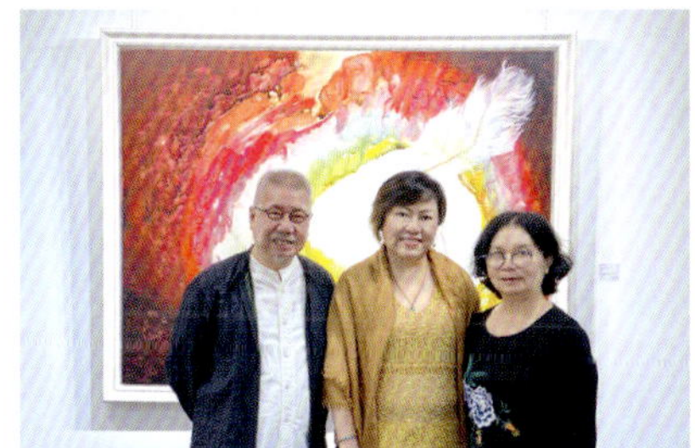

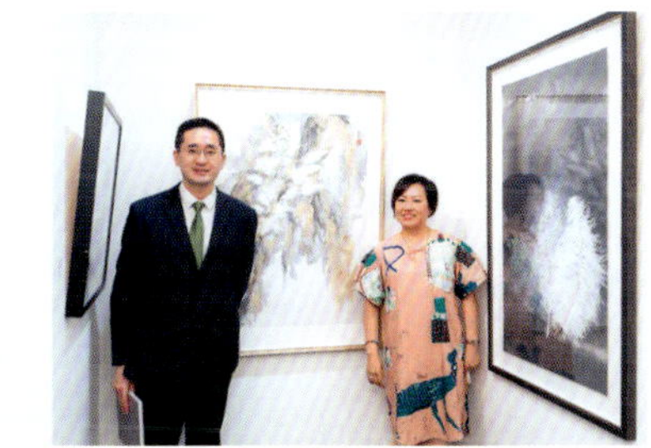

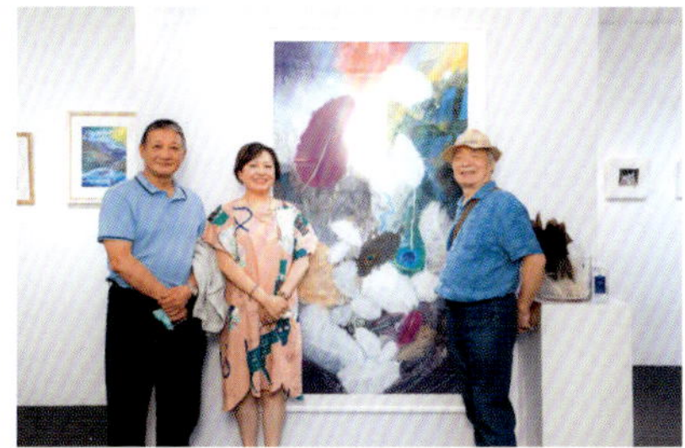

Apr 2021
'BIRDS OF A FEATHER'
Cheer Bell Gallery, Hong Kong

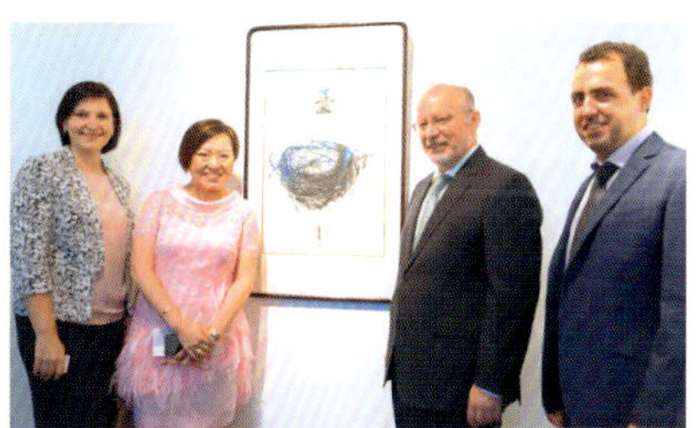

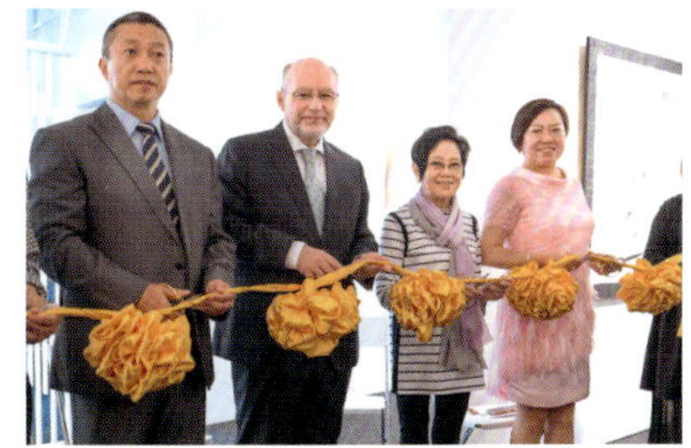

Nov 2018
'INSPIRATIONS'
Cheer Bell Gallery, Hong Kong

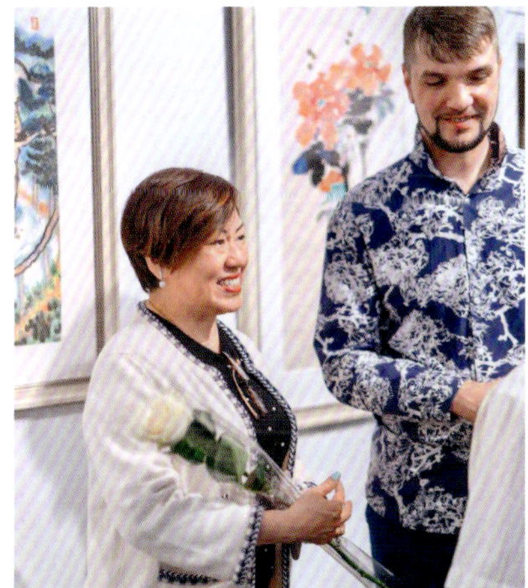

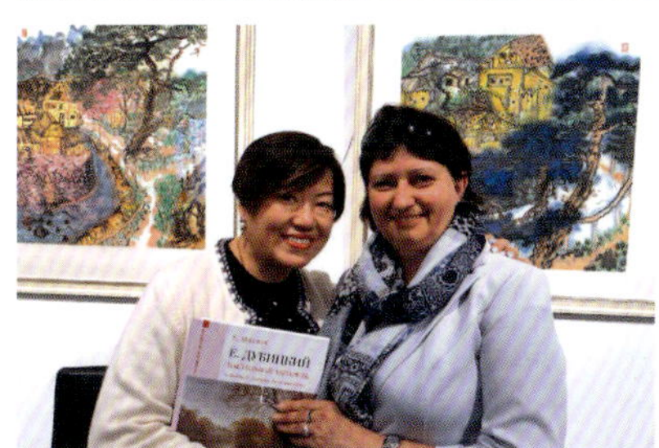

Jun 2018
'INSPIRATIONS'
Molbert art gallery, St Petersburg, Russia

Gallery

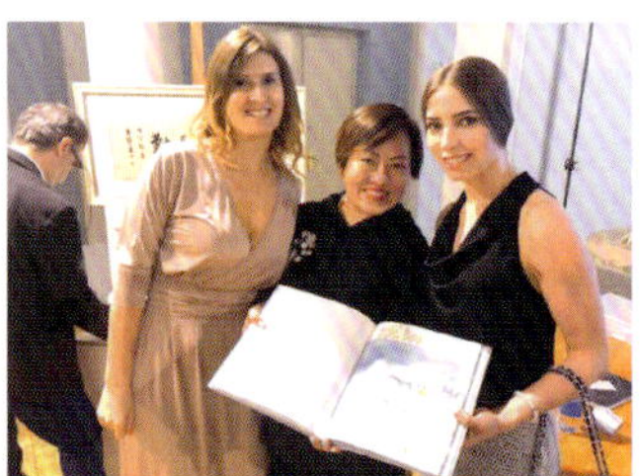

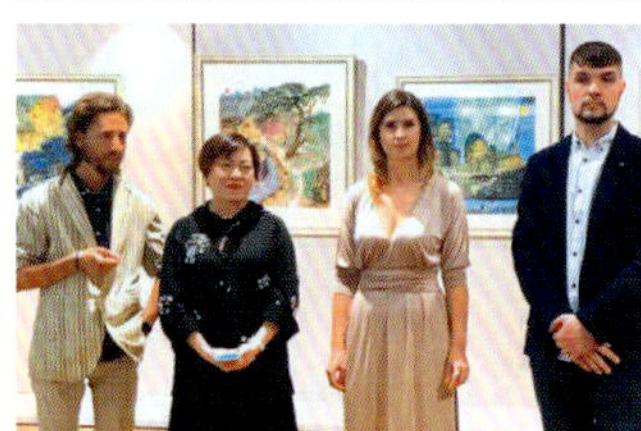

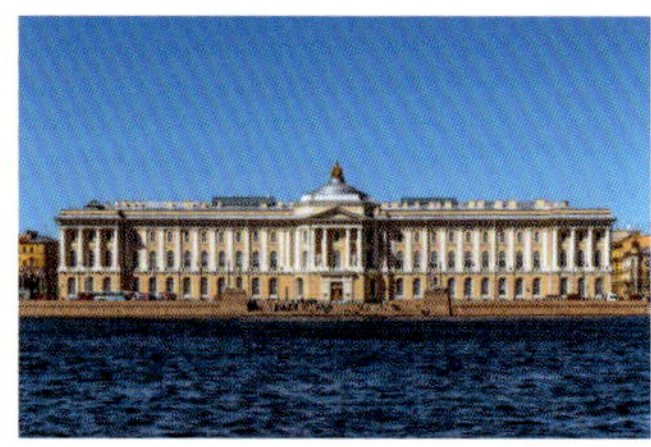

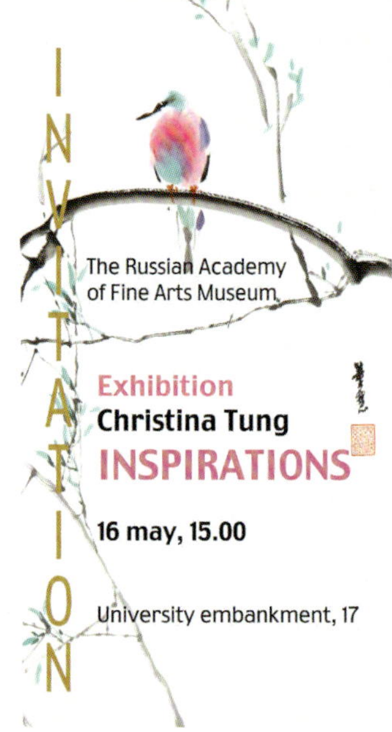

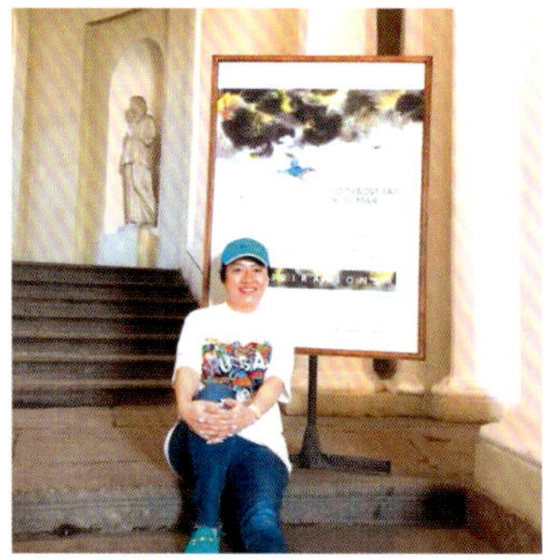

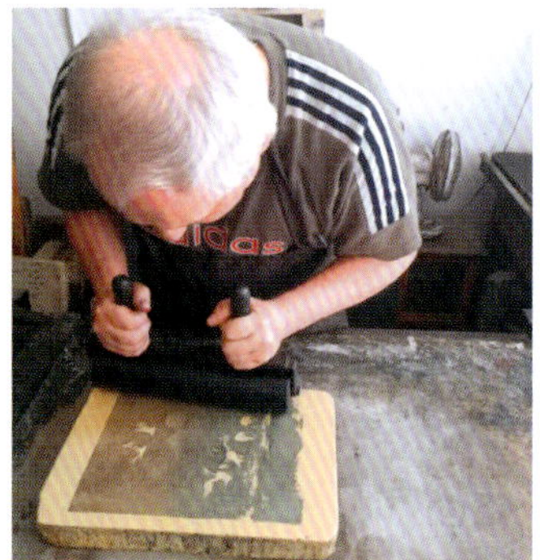

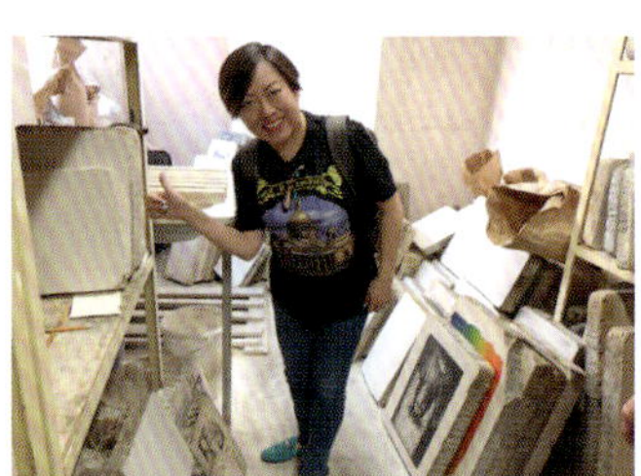

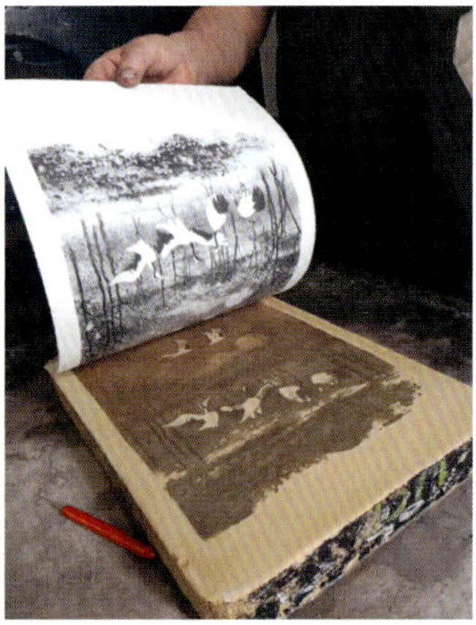

May 2018
'INSPIRATIONS'
Russian Academy of Fine Arts Museum, St Petersburg, Russia

Process of Christina making lithographs at St Petersburg, Russia
The lithograph work 'Noble Aspiration' by Christina then became a collection of the Consulate General of the Russian Federation in Hong Kong in November 2018.

Photo of the Russian Academy of Fine Arts Museum, St Petersburg, Russia

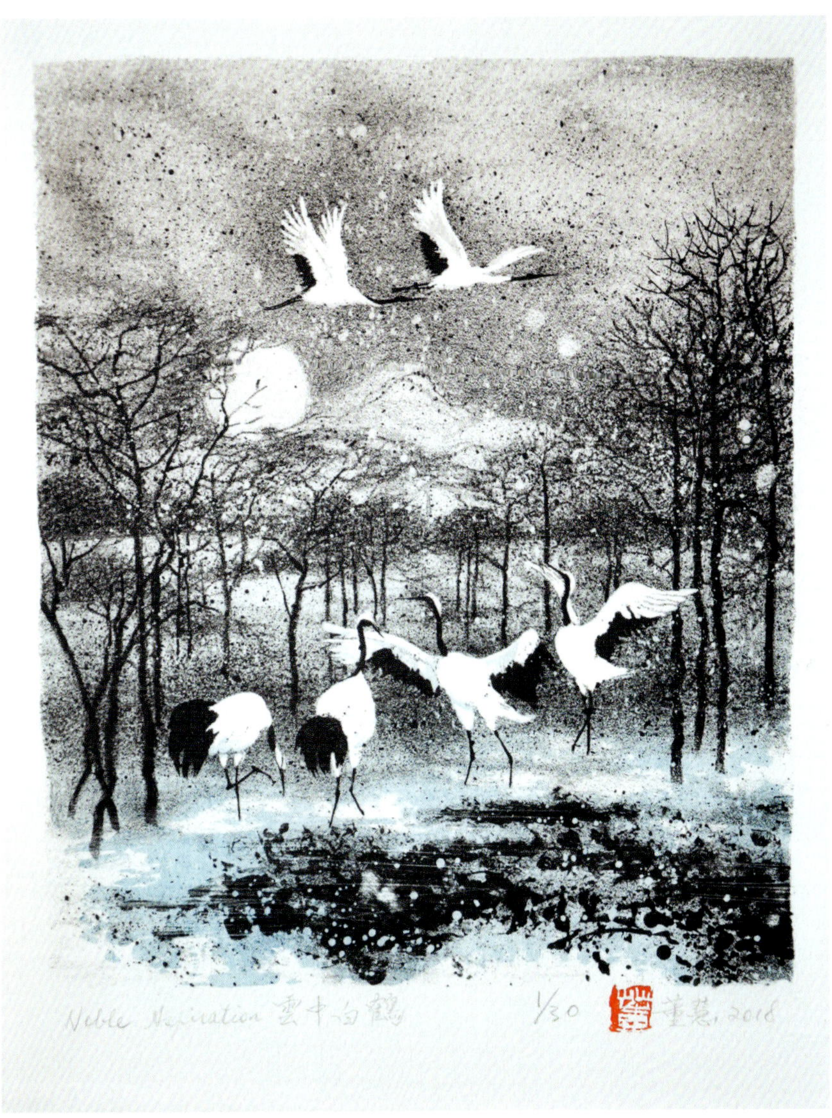

Noble Aspiration
2018
Colour Lithograph
39.5 cm x 26.5 cm

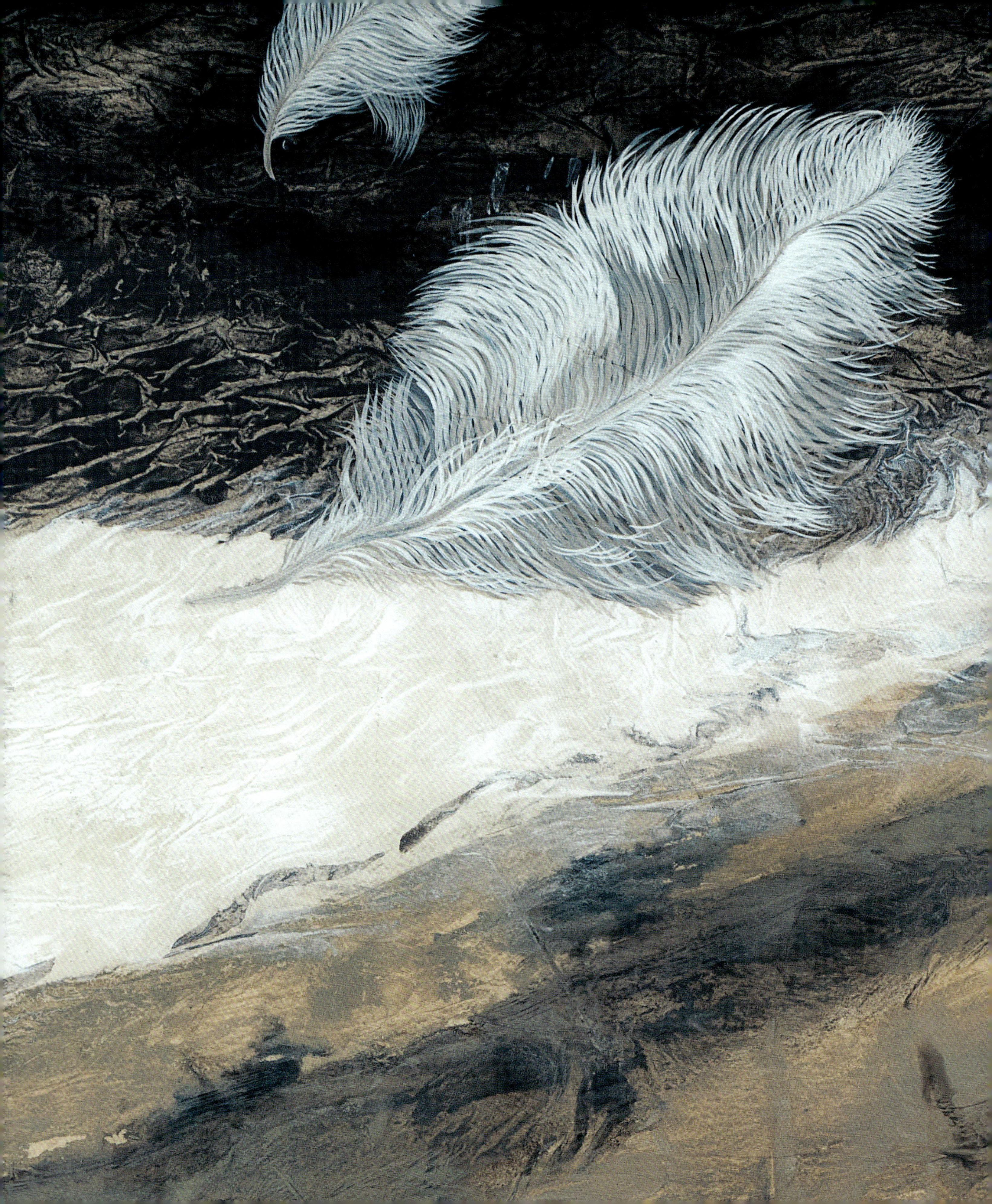

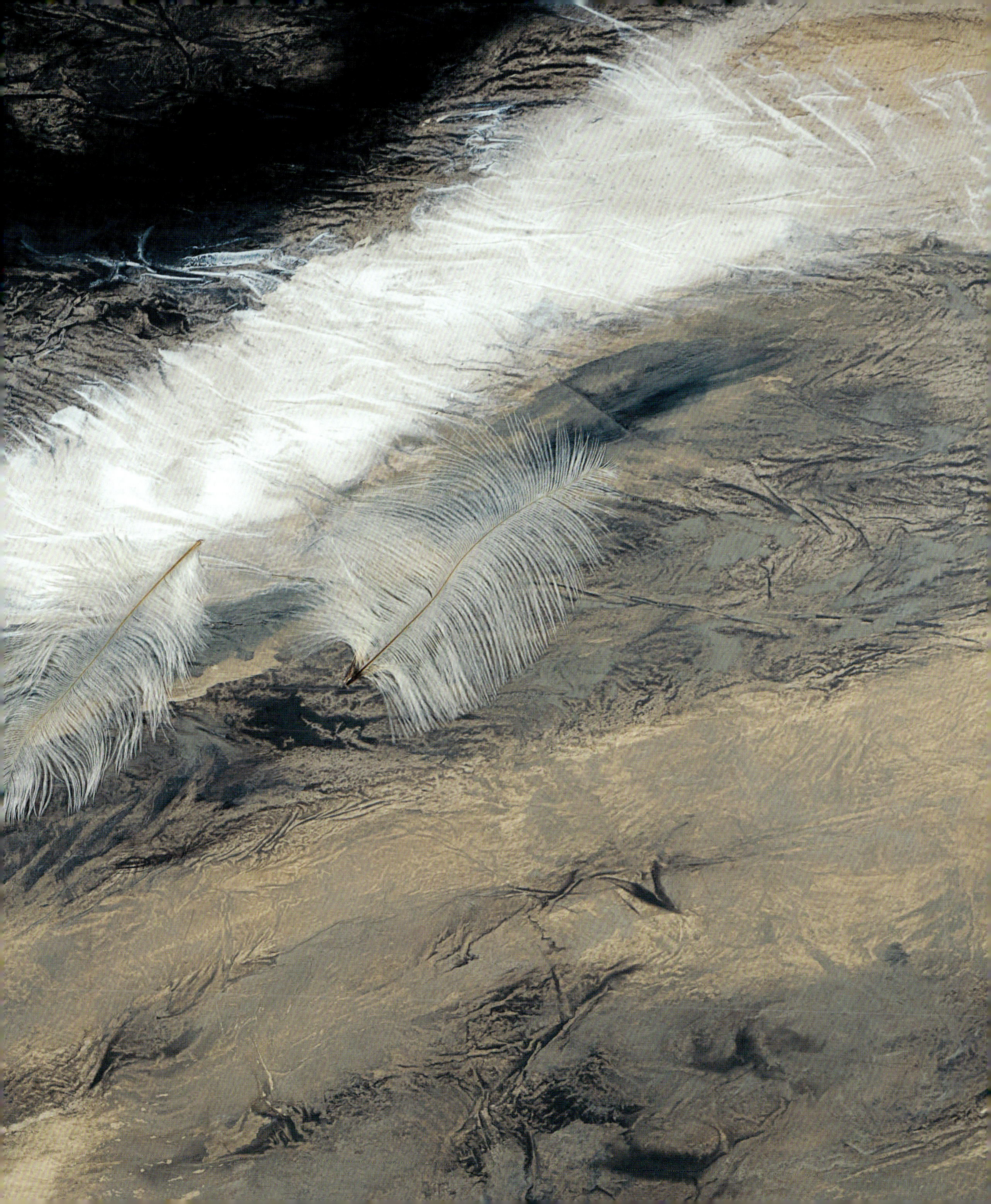

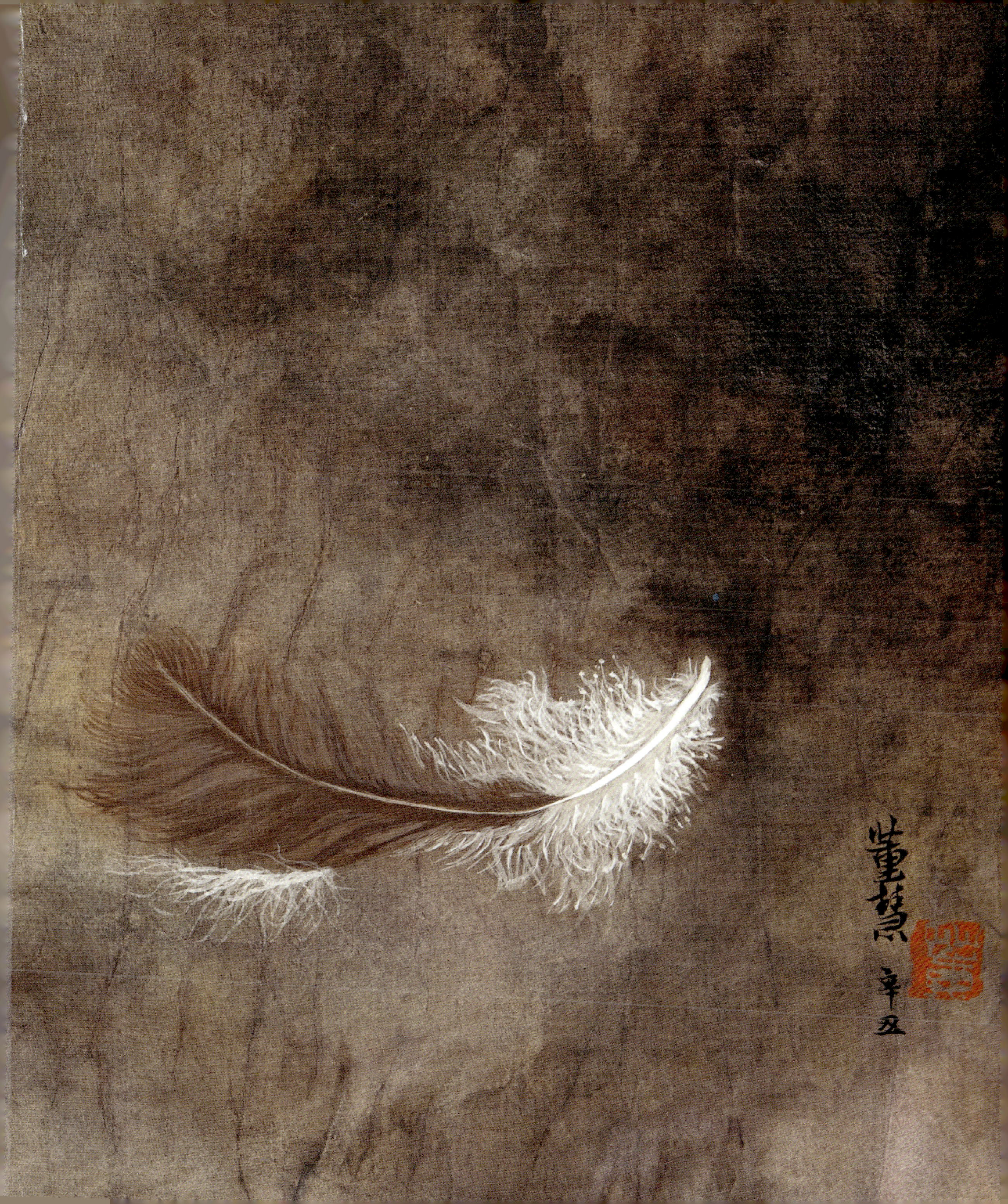
董慧
辛丑